Streams of Shattered Consciousness

Streams of Shattered Consciousness

A Chronicle of the First 50 Days of the
Israel - Hamas War

David-Seth Kirshner

To order additional copies of this book, contact:
Xlibris
844-714-8691
www.Xlibris.com
Orders@Xlibris.com
857238

Book Intro

On October 6, 1973, Yom Kippur Day, sitting on the hard wooden pews at a small synagogue in Pottstown, Pennsylvania, my mother, Barbara W. Kirshner, 9 months pregnant and 2 weeks past her due date was very uncomfortable. Word started to trickle into the hallowed services that Israel was under a surprise attack from Syria and Egypt. The nation state of the Jewish people's very existence was on the line, again. This was the fourth time in 25 years that Israel was in grave peril. The Jewish homeland was caught off guard on the holiest day of the calendar. What would happen?

Upon hearing this news, my mother was so upset, her water broke. A few hours later, on October 7th, around 2:25 AM, I was born.

Fast forward 49 years and 364 days to October 6th, 2023. I had just concluded a year of mourning for my mother, who at age 85, died suddenly and unexpectedly. She was my rock. Her death knocked the wind out of me. I spent the entire year in mourning. I did not attend any concerts, sporting events or movies, and I made it my obligation to attend a minyan, (a quorum of ten Jewish adults) to recite the *Kaddish* prayer daily. I did not miss one day.

Saying this prayer day-after-day adjusted my travel and personal schedule. This obligation was a set of handcuffs in a sense, that dictated where and when I went about my rituals, routines and habits.

As we reached the 6th of October, I was ready to exhale. How coincidental that my year of mourning would conclude the day before my 50th birthday. I was excited. I dreaded turning 40, but I was eager for 50. My wife and I planned a fun getaway to California golf country. It was supposed to be a relaxing and rejuvenating reset. I could not wait!

I woke early on Saturday morning, October 7th expecting to see an early flurry of Facebook birthday wishes and texts from family wishing me a great milestone bicentenary. Instead, I received a text from my dear friend Debbie telling me she was in Israel on vacation, and she was locked in a shelter and warned not to move from her space and to stay silent. Debbie texted me that bombs and missiles were landing all over the country, even in Tel Aviv where she was holed up, and that dozens of terrorists had infiltrated the country and were killing Israelis at will.

I instantly jumped to the Times of Israel website and then turned on the news. It was much worse than Debbie indicated. Little did she or we know how bad it would really be.

Two days later, the tallies were just commencing. 1400 murdered. 252 held captive. More than 1800 wounded physically. 9 million injured emotionally. The entire nation has been traumatized. Never have so many Jews been killed or injured in one day since the Holocaust.

My birth, and my milestone 50th birthday - two important markers of life's journey - are decorated by existential threats to the State of Israel. My birth and this half century mark are intrinsically and inextricably connected to the State of Israel and Zionism.

What I had hoped to be a reset and time to slow down has been just the opposite. Since October 7th, I have been running on all cylinders. I have had little appetite for food, I have been unable to sleep through the night and my anxiety is every which way but loose.

On the first day of this conflict, I decided to channel my energies into a short article. It was a response to the moment. I was not sure what I was saying. It felt like rambling. Who could make sense so quickly of the non-sensible?! I felt an imperative to share my thoughts with our congregation and greater community. It felt like a stream of consciousness loaded with anxiety.

The next day, my urge to be tethered to our community and to channel my thoughts were even stronger. I wrote again. The same happened the next day and the next.

In short time, I found that I needed to write my emotions and feelings, as disparate and discombobulated as they might be. It was cathartic for me. It released the pressure valve. I also learned that my congregation and followers on social media were appreciative of the streams of digestible thoughts I was penning.

I am not sure when, but eventually the Streams became bigger than me. The three to four hours I spent writing were the most restorative part of my day. I did not look at the news or read any breaking headlines during that sacrosanct time. I just typed my emotions and feelings and frustrations and worries and hopes and dreams. Ideas I could not say, thoughts I would not say, somehow felt safe and judgment free in this platform.

After about 35 Streams, I decided it was time to do turn this from a blog into a book. For a few years I had wanted to publish something. Streams is as organic, raw and honest a work that

I could have never imagined. Most decidedly, I could not have dreamt I would start and complete it in 50 days. I struggled whether the ideas and stories were the bones of a book to be reconstructed or if it made sense to share the thoughts that correspond to the days of the war, and the arc of my feelings and emotions in real time. I chose the latter.

All the proceeds from this book will go directly to Temple Emanu-El's Emergency Israel fund. These monies are targeted mostly for traumatic triage and PTSD for soldiers and citizens. The fund also supports Magen David Adom, United Hatzalah and other first responder organizations. Each purchase of the book in hard copy, eBook or audio form helps Israel in a direct manner. Thank you for partnering on this *Mitzvah*.

This work is far from complete. The war is not over after 50 days. But it is where I will pause for now.

I hope that within each page, you can appreciate the rich Jewish history in Israel, the deep connections to the land and its spirit and the unprecedented moral conundrums and ethical dilemmas this small country has had to face for 75 years of its existence.

Thank you for picking up this book. May God bless you. May God bless the State of Israel and the Jewish people.

Acknowledgments

Vladmir Lenin once said, *"There are decades where nothing happens; and there are weeks where decades happen."*

The last eight weeks have been tantamount to five decades in my life. The frenetic pace of running multiple missions to Europe, Israel, teaching on the history of the conflict and the current war for the congregation, along with special meetings with elected officials and clergy have made me burn the midnight oils. Nothing could have been accomplished were it not for the supportive, loyal and caring family, friends and social orbit I am blessed to be surrounded by daily. I want to acknowledge the impact they have individually and collectively and the multiple ways they have contributed to my life, in no special order.

I was blessed to be born into an affectionate household with two healthy parents who loved each other very much. I never went to bed hungry or cold. I also never questioned my parents' love for me or support of my passions and endeavors. As I grew older, I realized how fortunate and unique that made me. My parents have left this world, but I feel their presence daily. I know how proud they are of me. I hope they know how proud I am to have been born to Barbara W. and Phillip Kirshner, of blessed memory. I think of them and miss them every day.

To my brothers, Gabriel (*z'l*) Elliott and Larry. We did not choose to be brothers. We were born into our relationship. But I chose to call you my dearest friends and confidants. There is no one else I would have chosen to be my brothers. How lucky am I? I love you.

My father would regularly say, "You marry a person *and* a family." He was right. Marshall and Charlett Frumin were the family I was fortunate to marry into when Dori and I joined hands and hearts almost 25 years ago. You would be hard pressed to find kinder, more generous and more supportive souls than C & M, as we affectionately call them. For almost half of my life, they have been my second set of parents. I am honored to call them such. Thank you for your generosity, encouragement and unconditional love. I love you both.

Kim and Ben, you are both the epitome of goodness and sweetness. I love you and appreciate your soft hearts and admire your warmth and loving kindness.

I come from a tight knit family. My aunts and uncles, cousins - second and third – were all part of my life from the early days until now. Spoiling my nieces and nephews and marveling at their maturation is a sport for me. In the Kirshner house we longed for happy occasions which were an excuse for family to gather. The Frumin family comes from the same fabric. We are lucky to enjoy a shared ethic and to do so with family we love and adore.

Jewish tradition teaches, "*Hevruta oh Meetuta* – Give me my friends or give me death." My colleagues and friends have been my greatest gift and source of light. You are each a special treasure.

17 years ago this January, I agreed to become the rabbi of Temple Emanu-El in Closter, New Jersey. That was the best professional choice I have ever made. I have always said that if I won the

lottery, I might resign from my job, but I would immediately join the Temple as a proud member. That is because I adore our congregation and never want to be anywhere but amongst the amazing souls that make up our Temple community. For almost two decades, you have opened your homes and hearts to our family and included us in lifecycle events, shared your challenges and confided in me. Together, we have danced, laughed and cried. Dori and I consider it the highest honor to raise our children with your children and to have our values in sync with your values. These principles and values stem from the very top. The leadership of the Temple since the beginning of my tenure has always had my back and cheered for my success. I will forever be grateful and appreciative for your patience, guidance, support and unwavering love.

Our Temple staff is more like a family. We have succeeded in creating an environment where we look forward to coming to work. Special shout outs to the incomparable Julia Vazquez, Tiffany Garavito, Rachael Candoni and Tracy Anser for their amazing work ethic and goodness. Mario Salazar, you demonstrate commitment and a steadfast sense of duty with each sunrise.

Israel Singer and I have shared the bema for a long time. It has been an honor to be lifted by your voice.

Becky Skoff, you are a ray of sunshine and thoughtfulness. Having you on our team has been the greatest addition to our lineup. Thank you for all you do, always!

Chareen Kramer, you have been my right and left hands, my brain and my compass for the last decade. It would be impossible to characterize your love of Judaism and commitment to our community in just a few words. Anytime I succeed professionally or am in the right place at the right time with the right notes in hand, it is because you made it happen for me. Thank you for all you have done and do for me every single day. You are the very best!

I was first captured with Rabbi Jeremy Ruberg when I saw him dote over his father on a flight to Israel. Little did I know that a few years later, you would be like a sibling to me as well as my work colleague and partner. Your energy is unparalleled. Your compassion is unmatched.

Rabbi Gabe Cohen is soft spoken, sincere and hard working. Since you have joined our team, you have fit like a hand and glove. I am continually captured by your curiosity to learn more and your desire to grow personally and professionally.

It is a blessing to call you both colleagues. It is an honor to call you both friends.

Aaron, Josh and Marty, my B&H crew - you are more than colleagues and friends. You are brothers. Your ability to stoke my mind, stir my soul and tickle my funny bone is the balm that helps me through my toughest days. Your friendship is a cherished gift. I am forever grateful for each of you and all of you.

Whenever I need sound counsel or judgment free advice, Dovid Weizman is my man. Three decades ago, we were placed in the same graduate housing. You were 36 and I was 20 and we shared very little in common. The randomness of that housing assignment led us to becoming best of friends. I will forever be grateful to the powers that forged that connection and the friendship that has been a north star for most of my life.

Rabbi Joe Potasnik has been my rabbi. There is no one funnier or who has greater social skills than he. I have learned so much from

Joe. Most of all, I have learned how to be a trusted and reliable friend. Thank you!

In middle and high school, I had an English teacher who I will call Mrs. "N." She did not think much of me. She had no hesitation telling me and my parents that she was not sure I would amount to much in life, based on my scores in her class. Teachers should never sum up a child's potential based on test scores in 7th or 9th grade. SATs do not compute emotional quotient or intellectual abilities. Thanks Mrs. "N" for **NOT** believing in me. I have been fueled most of my life by trying to prove you wrong. I hope I did.

Special thanks to the Times of Israel for graciously hosting my blogs. I have been proud to write regularly for the Israel news site. Hosting, uploading and editing my daily writings and musings is greatly appreciated.

Early in our tenure at Temple Emanu-El, someone remarked how between me and Dori, we hold three jobs. Dori, who runs MATAN. I, as the rabbi of Temple Emanu-El and lastly, raising our kids and opening our home to our community is equal to a full-time commitment in any person's world. For 17 years we were only able to make it happen and keep all three jobs strong because of the support we have had at home. Rouchel "Sherry" Branche Henry and Juliette Scott have - and will always be - part of our family. Your ability to love our children, nourish our bodies and keep our household running is incredible. We appreciate all you do for us every day. We will forever be grateful for your spirit and support.

Dori, "The prettiest girl at JTS." You have made all my dreams come true. Not every day has been rainbows and sunshine, but most have. You are my cheerleader and my soulmate. You are my best friend. You are my greatest editor, my most biased critic and the best audience for my jokes. Thank you for believing in me. Thank you for saying yes. Thank you for continuing to work on us and for us. I love you forever and always. *L'olam Vaed.*

Eve Miryam and Elias Gabriel, the two strides in my step, the twinkle in my eyes, the sparkle in my smile. You are the reason and purpose behind everything I want to be and aspire towards. Thank you for tolerating my dad jokes and anticipating my rat face. I love you more than any ink could turn to words. More than any pages could contain. More than any string and spine could bind in a book. Of all the titles I have held in life, and any accomplishments I have achieved, nothing gives me more pride and satisfaction than being called your father.

Lastly, I want to thank God for the innumerable gifts I have been blessed with in this life. I never take them for granted. I know the source of all my blessings and of each new day is in Your mighty hand. I pray that I will live a life worthy of all that has been bestowed on my head. My cup runneth over.

David-Seth Kirshner
November 2023 - Kislev 5784
Jerusalem, Israel & Closter, New Jersey

To my parents, Barbara and S. Phillip Kirshner,
of blessed memory,
who planted a seed of Zionism deep in my soul
&
To Dori Frumin Kirshner,
My wife, my best friend, the love of my life.
Most importantly, my partner in planting
that same seed of Zionism in the two gifts
of life we have been blessed to call ours.

1

October 7, 2023

Eventually, Israel will regulate its breathing and start to metabolize the indigestible.

Questions will fester about failures and security breakdowns and hubris, protest movements and radical Knesset members all that precipitated the darkest day in 75 years.

These are all important questions, and they should and will be dealt with. But not now.

What I want to call to the floor now, is what we do from the Diaspora to offer support in the days and weeks ahead.

Israel will exact a crushing blow to Hamas. Like Japan's Emperor said after the airmen returned from the bombing sorties over Pearl Harbor with exuberance and pride, "Do not gloat. I am afraid we have woken a sleeping giant."

Israel will pummel Hamas to a place where the glee they celebrate today will be a foggy memory. Hamas will rue the day they woke this sleeping giant.

Israel MUST respond with unprecedented and sweeping force. That will and must happen because:

A) Israel must warn those other terror groups like Hezbollah and ISIS and Iran through our response, what their fate will be should they naively question Israel's resolve.

B) We will not allow these barbarians to hold Israeli civilians and soldiers hostage a minute longer than needed. We will not have a reprise of Gilad Shalit and releasing thousands of murderers for dozens of Israelis after five agonizing years. We will have to painstakingly enter Gaza and sweep every nook and cranny, cupboard and tunnel, until we find each one of them and bring them home. That will be messy. It will be long. It will result in more Israeli deaths and an even higher number of Palestinian deaths. But it must be done, and it will be devastating to the Hamas infrastructure and civilians of Gaza.

C) Israel must in word, but more so in deed, comfort the citizens of Israel by proving to them with their response to this moment, 'Never Again' on our watch. Never Again will we let you be victim to our failures. Never Again will we cause you to sleep softly again. The security of every Israeli is, and must always be, paramount.

If Israel does not annihilate, once and for all, the enemy on its border, who would ever consider living in the Gaza envelope, or anywhere in Israel for that matter. This will force the Israeli response to be fierce.

Any person or group that harbors, supports, celebrates, – and dare I say – is silent on condemnation about these barbaric terrorists and these acts, are a cancer on society and must be radiated out of commission for eternity without excuse or apology.

This operation will take time. I worry about that. Here is why:

After the shock settles, and world outrage dissipates, the international community will be quick to condemn Israel's disproportionate response. I predict that propaganda pictures will be circulated of innocent Gaza women and children dying at the hands of Israel. The world will scream at the power and cruelty of Israel and its war machine.

Some leaders will ask Israel to show restraint. Others will demand a 'proportionate' response. More will condemn Israel in International arenas like the UN and ICC. Some of those same entities are silent today. A few are even celebrating.

We must stop this preposterous spin and outrage, in all its venues, before it begins.

What happened in Israel today has eerie echoes of the Holocaust. Men, women, children, and the elderly, killed indiscriminately for the crime of being Jewish.

In many ways, October 7, 2023, is worse than October 7, 1973, since the targets were primarily civilians. No Israeli was off limits. No age was a barrier. No background mattered. Women and children were ruthlessly murdered, and their bodies strewn on the streets. Babies in car seats were riddled with bullets at a red light. Senior citizens barbarically executed in cars with their lifeless bodies held up by a seatbelt. Entire families brutalized in their homes. Wounded hostages tortured and paraded about in Gaza like trophies.

And the world will surely ask us to show restraint?! To be proportionate?! In short time, they will condemn Israel!

We must be armed and ready at the offensive for any print media source, cable news network, social media site or water cooler pundit who will try and turn the tables and reverse the narrative. We must be vigilant.

Some have said this is Israel's 9/11 moment. During those dark days in America, President Bush said, "You are either with us or against us."

So too, there can be no ambiguity in this moment. There are no middle of the road groups here. There is no place for fence sitting. There are evil doers and peace pursuers. It is black and white.

Make no mistake. This is not about occupation. It is not an invitation to discuss land for peace or normalization talks with neighbors. Do not get baited into that argument. This is about the undeterred focus of Hamas to annihilate the Jewish state and its citizenry. It is nothing less than old fashioned antisemitism masquerading as anti-Zionism.

Israel and lovers of Zion will never be the same after this fateful day. But our resolve is unwavering. Our support is unshakeable. Our bond has never been tighter.

Tomorrow, Israel will awaken to the reality that is its worst nightmare. They will begin their day by once again, tilling fresh soil to bury the dead, and send teenagers to the danger zone. As they do, know that our collective hearts are now and always in the East.

2

October 8th 2023

The numbers on our side are more than we can bear. Each person represents a family, grieving parents, siblings, community, friends, significant others, coworkers and neighborhood pals. The ruthlessness of their death adds to our collective trauma.

My heart physically hurts. Like it was punched. Hard.

I can't stop thinking that this is indeed an attack on Israel and an attack on Jews. Of course. But it is also an attack on Western civilians and civilizations.

Mexican, British, German, French, and American citizens are among the dead and those being held captive. It is an assault on all of us.

Hamas didn't check who was a Jew. They killed Bedouins. They have killed Catholics. They are a non-discriminatory terror organization.

For the past 24 hours I have been contemplating and strongly believe that this moment calls for a full-on physical and aerial war-based assault on Tehran, its infrastructure and its leadership. From the Supreme Leader to every member of the IRGC.

This evil is a cancer. We must remove the source of the cancer. The funding of the cancer. The condoning of the cancer. The weapons supplier of the cancer. Let it be known to the world that if they support, harbor or fund terrorism, we the people that love peace and support our ability to live in freedom, will radiate you.

For years we dreaded a nuclear capable Iran. Iran nourished and supported these evil doers who have wreaked a carnage that is as brutal as a nuclear reality. I worry that as Israel radiates Hamas, Iran will find and fund the next batch of assailants. It will not cease. We must rid the world of the evil doers of Iran.

I do not write this lightly or suggest this from the comfy position of my armchair. I am fully aware of what a coordinated Western attack spearheaded by Israel and the USA will look like and cost. Still, we cannot afford to be blind to this sponsor and supporter of terror one day longer.

It is time to bring the chemotherapy to the mullahs and the Supreme Leaders and Khomeini and his disciples. It is time to rid this world of this malignancy for good and to warn future cells what will happen to them should they follow with funding and support.

Stay strong. Hug those you love that you can. Am Yisrael Chai.

3

October 9, 2023

My mind is racing. It won't settle down. So many feelings all bubble to the surface. Anger. Pain. Frustration. Revenge. Hatred. Disgust. Sadness. Numbness. Sorrow.

I wrestle with which emotion to honor and is it right of me to feel some of these feelings. Of course, it is. But it brushes against the grain.

Even those of us who spend most of our time learning in and about Israel are totally lost. We have no clairvoyance in this moment. Nothing is particularly clearer or more obvious to us now. It is all a fog.

It hurts worse than breaking a limb. Worse than a cut that is flesh deep.

I don't know when the pain will abate.

Many of you reading this are sharing similar emotions, feelings and confusion. Know that those not-OK feelings *are* OK. And these abnormal responses *are* very normal.

Some very disparate thoughts rise to the front of my mind. Here are some more in no order. I'm sorry for the randomness of these thoughts.

First:
There have mainly been 2 identities of Israel. 1948-1967 and then 1967- 2000.

The first 19 years we were seen and treated like victims. We were felt sorry for. The aftermath of the Holocaust reverberated for many with pangs of guilt and inaction. We were given Israel as if tissues for our tears to comfort the world's silence and inaction.

In the aftermath of the Six Day War, we were seen as solvent. Strong. God's physical miracles. We had created an army, and we would no longer merit world pity. We would determine our own future from now, forward.

Over the past 55 years two generations have lived symbiotically and simultaneously: one who remembers our weakness and powerlessness and makes no excuse for our rise to power and greatness, and a second that does not know first-hand of that history. That has only known of strength, power and might.

That divide crossed generations and manifested itself at Shabbat and Holiday tables when grandparents and grandchildren would share history and backgrounds. They were worlds apart with no appreciation or at least understanding, one for the other. One generation nostalgic and trying to explain what it was having coal delivered and another generation trying to describe how Uber-eats works. There was a huge chasm between these two generations living at the same time.

As my dear and wise friend, Rabbi Aaron Brusso brought forward, October 7, has bridged that divide into a shared victimhood and collective narrative between these disparate generations. The elderly are saying, "It is happening again." The youth are saying, "This is what they were describing to us for years. We feel it now." For the first time, these generations are on the same page.

Second thought:
The degrees of separation here are and will be close.

My kids attend(ed) a Jewish day School. It is loaded with children of Israelis and kids who have Israeli relatives.

These kids, like my own, spend vacations, winter, and summer in Israel. For kids in America visiting family in Israel is primarily about connecting with grandparents and cousins. That has always been a hallmark of the Israel-Diaspora visits.

Two of the most notable victim populations are the innocent teens and children, the cousins, and the helpless Savtas and Sabas..... the grandparents.

Kids my kids go to school with and kids your kids go to school with and know from synagogue and soccer will know and be related to victims. Some will be first degree and others fourth degree relations, but the rings of the pain will radiate to America and the Diaspora in little time.

Thought Three:
I have seen a few posts on social media and in print journalism jockeying to blame partisan figures for this tragedy. Some claimed it was Biden. Others Trump. Some Ben Gvir, and Bibi and others the likes of Meretz. Some point at left wing groups like INN (If Not Now) and T'ruah and others say it is the fault of Settlers.

This is NOT the time for such blame games.

If anyone thinks Hamas did this now for any other reason than Jew hatred, you are naive and wrong.

This attack was well orchestrated. It was brazen and far from haphazard. It was assembled over a long time. Like 9/11 It surely was being devised over multiple Knessets and US presidents. No one person or party is to blame.

To engage in partisan divide and pushing shame on one side versus the other or one organization against another, is petty and useless. I assure you, the barbaric terrorists did not care which political affiliation one voted for or which organizational group another subscribed towards when they shot, raped and abducted people.

Partisanship divides. This is not the time for those fruitless games of blame and finger pointing. Its satisfaction is short lived, if at all and it takes our focus off the wrong targets.

Last painful thought.

My daughter, who spent last year in Israel and basically every summer since she was 5 years young, has friends that are not accounted for. It is not known if they are alive and hiding, hospitalized, dead, or held captive.

She said to me and my wife, "I know they are dead."

I replied, "Honey. You must have hope and believe."

She said, "I can't have hope. It hurts too much when that hope is destroyed."

Those comments leveled me.

On one hand, she is right. On the other hand, the watchwords of Israel are *HaTikvah* - The Hope. It declares in song; we can never abandon our hope. But we also can't be naive and foolish.

That is the paradox of this moment for her, for me and for all of us.

I apologize for these streams of anxious consciousness. For me, expressing them is mildly cathartic.

Keep praying and for now, let's not abandon our hope.

4

October 10, 2023

My 'rabbi' on most things Israel, Yossi Klein HaLevi, wrote a reminder in the <u>Atlantic</u> this week about the tragedy masterminded by Samir Kunta against the Haran family. In 1979, in the town of Nahariya, a gruesome brutalization of innocent civilians took place. Israel considered instituting the death penalty for Kunta because his crimes were so heinous, and his acts were so depraved and inhumane.

Yossi's retelling was a reminder to all about Israel's vulnerability and fragility and the eerie reminder of helplessness we felt, not long ago.

Haran's only crime was being Jewish and living in Israel. Kunta was not seeking a partition of land. He did not aspire for two states for two peoples. He wanted all of Israel to be Jew-free.

Ironically, Samir Kunta was exchanged to Hezbollah, very much alive and nourished, along with four other bloody-handed terrorists for the cadavers of Eldad Regev and Ehud Goldwasser. These two soldiers were abducted from sovereign Israel in 2006 and died soon in their captivity.

Fast forward 23 years.

In 2002, shortly after the towers fell in Manhattan, WSJ reporter on assignment, Daniel Pearl was captured in Karachi, Pakistan. There he was tortured and video-taped saying, I am a Jew. He was then gruesomely decapitated for the world to see.

We were reminded that simply being Jewish is a crime for many in the Middle Eastern world.

Pearl was not Israeli. He was not working for Israel. But his identity as a Jew and, de facto, a Zionist, were intrinsically connected.

Fast forward again, this time 21 years.

Hamas terrorists behead and butcher and brutalize innocents for the crime of being Jewish.

Judaism and Zionism are strands of the same DNA. For some it is more pronounced while for others it is less prominent. But we cannot divide them or separate their identities. They are rooted together.

The death of more than 1,200 (that seems to be the latest number) was not only because they lived in Israel, but also because they are Jewish. There is no separation for our enemies. There was no division for the Nazis. No division for the Cossacks and Isabelle and Ferdinand didn't care one iota which stream we were from. It has always been about Judaism. Not Israel. And our enemies don't care which group we affiliate with or who we voted for; I assure you.

It is ironic that we spend inordinate amounts of time and energy fighting over streams and denominations and differences and interpretations. From how we pray to who can join our prayer, to how we interpret Gods will and then judicial reform, elected government leaders and more. What a seemingly silly act of bickering and backbiting that divides us.

Then an evil and indiscriminate act happens against some that affect all of us, for the crime of simply existing. For breathing. For living. All because some haters think our DNA makes us felons.

Ironically, that venom espoused towards us is more unifying than any concoction ever mixed. Ironically, it is the antidote to all denominations, differences and flavors.

Fire shapes us. The hotter the heat, the more we bend towards one another. The more intensity of the flame, the clearer we can see.

What a sad and painful paradox.

The Haran family died for being Jewish. Daniel Pearl died for being Jewish. More than 1,200 people died for being Jewish or for living in a Jewish state. The thing that unites us is the very vice we have been trying to break for generations.

5

October 11, 2023

I wish I could say that reality is getting easier. In fact, it is quite harder. The names surfacing are attached to pictures which are connected to families which are tied to histories fastened to characteristics and tethered to funny and meaningful anecdotes. Each name is a rich, sweet and beautiful tapestry that was senselessly ripped away from the world.

My daughter's friend, who she has been anxiously awaiting word from, has now been identified as one of the dead. The finality was a gut punch to her. All of us, really. I guess there actually was a sliver of hope that we held on to. Hope flickers as if we are lighting a candle in the wind.

A few disparate thoughts on this evening that is still an endless and unmitigated nightmare.

The distance from the United States to Israel never felt closer. At the same time, I have never felt so physically far away from my homeland and my people.

Strangers and those who offer check-ins and support have buoyed my spirit and restored my hope in humanity. At the same time, never have I been more disappointed in some leaders of colleges, organizations and companies as well as a handful of people in my social circles who have been radio silent.

The Jewish world as we know it will never be the same. Every synagogue, Jewish Day School and the alphabet soup of the Jewish organizational world will change its foci, its budgets and its operations for decades to come. No Jewish Federation will go back to business as usual. Like America after 9/11, our Jewish DNA has been irrevocably altered by this tragedy.

One manifestation of this change will be future conversations on land and peace. Unequivocally, the two-state solution was beheaded this week. Not in my children's lifetime will a sovereign Palestinian State be established bordering Israel. I am OK with that, today.

There is more than one reason why October 7th achieved Hamas' goal and ruined peace-loving people's dreams: Yes, it was proven and verified that we cannot ever have a hostile neighbor in arms reach to Ben Gurion Airport or Tel Aviv. Ever. But worse than that, the silence from much of the Islamic world, especially in the West Bank, is a clear condonation of these despicable acts.

Not all Middle Eastern countries fit into that bucket. The UAE expressed solidarity with Israel as did Bahrain and a few select other countries. But far too many, from Tehran to Tunis, were dancing and celebrating this heinous loss of life.

Further to this point, Hamas proved that leaving Gaza in 2005 was not an opportunity seized but a terrorist enclave established. It was declared by the actions of Hamas this week and the celebration of others in the Middle East, that statehood sits a distant second to ambitions to annihilate Israel. In fact, I doubt statehood is even – or ever was – on the top of the agenda.

On Sunday, October 8th Mahmoud Abbas, the head of the "moderate" Palestinian Authority claimed that Palestinians should have the right to defend themselves and called on the UN to intervene to protect Palestinians in Gaza. This is the moderate we should negotiate with? These are the factions we should establish a state with? Discuss security concerns with? C'mon! That idea was set ablaze this Saturday.

Some have lamented the lost momentum of peace with Arab countries. Some called it the cessation of the Abraham Accords. I read one blog that exclaimed how close we (Israel) were to brokering peace with Saudi Arabia.

Yeah. I am sad about that too. But, if Saudi Arabia is not on the side of condemning Hamas, we do not need normalization with them. We survived 75 years without peace with Saudi, we can survive 75 more. We cannot, however, survive another day of terrorists and those sworn to our destruction as our neighbors.

I was the loudest cheerleader of the Abraham Accords. I rejoiced at the new horizons opening for all that extended an olive branch and new opportunities. But what good are the Abraham Accords and peace with countries once hostile to us, if our very existence hangs in the balance.

Last disparate thought for now:

When 9/11 happened and many Americans targeted Islamic people living in America, from taxi drivers to fellow employees, I joined the marchers and chorus that said, "Stop. No. We will not tolerate this hatred towards others."

When a white nationalist opened fire on a Sikh church in Wisconsin, I joined the marchers and chorus that said, "Stop. No. We will not tolerate this violence towards others."

When Covid broke and many Americans bullied, taunted and abused Asian Americans, I joined the marchers and chorus that said, "Stop. No. We will not tolerate this behavior towards others."

When a white police officer held his knee on the neck of a black man for long enough to kill him, giving fuel to critical conversations of race in our country, I joined the marchers and chorus that said, "No. Stop. Black Lives Matter. We will not tolerate this behavior towards others."

As tragedy has now befallen my people, I have taken attendance at who is part of the marchers and the chorus. I am hurt by the absence of some. I am heartened by the attendance of many.

For those who are sitting this march out or who have squelched the megaphone or are equivocating and offering 'what-aboutisms' and 'both-side' conversations, I have two things to share:

a) History will delineate you not as freedom seekers or peace lovers. Rather, as people that see Jewish blood as less-than or cheaper-than other groups. When one of the largest chapters of BLM claims to be on the Palestinian side only, and proudly posts pictures of terrorists entering Israel to murder seniors and rape teenage girls, you are ironically saying that Jewish lives do NOT matter.

b) When faced with a moment that I hope never happens again, but most likely will, whether another terrorist attack in America by radical Muslims, white nationalist shooting against a minority group, any attack against Black people or Asian Americans, I assure you I will

STILL stand up and join the marchers and the chorus and chant even louder, "Stop. No. We will not tolerate this behavior towards others."

My advocacy is not to curry favor or earn chits. My marching and chanting are because of my moral compass and values. The reason I am often surrounded in those moments by fellow Jews is because we share those values, and our compasses are aligned. It is core to our Canon and part of our genes.

For all of those that are not of my faith but still share my coordinates and values, thank you. We are warmed by having you stand close. For those that are absent and silent in this moment for the Jewish and Israeli people, I am heartbroken that your values and ours were never really in sync, all along. What a painful awakening!

May peace be upon us soon. God, please protect the soldiers and citizens of Israel that are protecting their country and Jews worldwide.

6

October 12, 2023

Elizabeth Kubler Ross' stages of grief are hitting in micro and macro circles. Walking around and seeing the sun shine down on faces and people go about their business reminds me of when I rose from Shiva and walked to my local bagel shop. Everyone around me was fine. I was not. My hurt and pain were so profound I was sure all could see it. Like walking with a severe limp or a gushing wound. Except, our cuts are inside. Our bruising is internal. Our pronounced limps are in our hearts and minds, not visible to the naked or uninformed eye.

Our grief hits closely because this was an attack on Jews. It happened in Israel, but any Jew is a legitimate target for this group, wherever we are. It is in the Hamas charter. It is their core mission. We are saying, "There but for the grace of God, go I."

As Israeli boys and girls, men and women gear up for war in Gaza and deterring the enemy in the North, there is another front that you and I must gird up for. A war that is equally important today and especially tomorrow. That is the war against biased media.

I plan to mention any journalist on any channel that reports critically, unfairly or untruthfully. I will call out every network, and every anchor that crosses the line. This is an attack on their journalism, not their character.

I will begin with Richard Engel, from this morning's Today show, who showed a gruesome picture of a pile of rubble in Gaza where men pulled out a lifeless baby covered in soot. It was a painful sight.

What Richard Engel failed to do was show one picture of a baby, a toddler, a grandparent that was maimed, murdered or incinerated by monsters days before. This pile of rubble and the dead civilians in Gaza of any age, did not happen indiscriminately or in a vacuum. This was a direct response to the brutal massacre and kidnapping of sovereign citizens.

But here is the real kicker: No rationale Israeli is celebrating the death of that Gazan baby. Even in their rage. Even in their wrath. That is not what we seek. That is not a revenge that satisfies a soul.

Juxtapose that thought to the images we have seen of a five-year-old separated from parents and taunted, spit at and beaten. Contrast the lament of death with the candies shared in Khan Younis where babies' heads were paraded about. This is the moral difference that makes this more than a war with bullets. It is a war of ideology. A battle for the soul of humanity. It is a conflict of enduring morality. It puts so much more at stake than just territory and history.

Engle talked about the strict blockade on the Gaza strip that Israel imposed for years, limiting supplies like food, water and medicine to the people of Gaza. Richard ignored that Hamas – which governs Gaza – had the wherewithal to get RPGs and AK-47s, and grenades and tunneling equipment and elaborate explosives, all which are expensive and hard to acquire, during this *strict* blockade into Gaza.

For less nuanced readers, I am calling bullsh*t on Engels' reporting. There was no blockade, so to speak. There *was* an abuse of Hamas' humanitarian aid that was channeled for weapons and not welfare, for firing bullets instead of food or first aid. For rockets instead of roads and repairs. For indoctrination instead of education. For building terror instead of trust.

Simply put, the people of Gaza are hungry because of Hamas. Not Israel. The citizens of Gaza are homeless because of Hamas. Not Israel. The residents of Gaza are sick because of Hamas. Not Israel.

As time ticks forward and the world's attention span dwindles, we must fight the television, radio, printed papers, internet, social media and water-cooler pundits, wherever and whenever we see them raise their nasty head. We must combat lies, abuse, mistruths or unfounded claims of human rights violations with facts, figures, trusted sources, honesty and loud reminders of why we are here today.

It is a time that beckons all of us to embrace our Zionism. To run towards our Jewish identity, to proudly unbutton our shirts and show our Jewish star dangling from our necks. We need to put up lawn signs that unequivocally state that we stand with Israel. Our communities and shops should be littered with blue and white flags that declare our unwavering support. We should be sure to patronize those shops that bravely demonstrate their moral fortitude and stand with us, now.

While not apples to apples, we saw the power and potency of communities, merchants and common folk who stood – and continue to stand – with Ukraine. Like that war, there are clearly good guys and bad guys. Evil doers and peace seekers. Instigators and defenders. We know which side we are on. We need to enlist the world in our cause. Displaying communal pride will help do that.

I am appreciative for the full-throated support displayed by Secretary Blinken today on behalf of the United States. Saying those words in Israel, now, meant even more. That is what friends do. They come to be physically present when we are hurting. They bring love to let us know that during the hard journey ahead, they will be by our side.

Secretary Blinken did make one comment that I have been wrestling with. He said, "Hamas does not represent Palestinians."

Hmm.

I know he is right. I am friends with and have met countless Palestinians who are not in any way, shape or form part of Hamas and their charter. But have they declared that?! Today? Now?

When some political factions called for a Muslim ban in America, under the banner of patriotism, I used my voice to state, that political stripe does not represent me.

When Proud Boys and Oath Keepers marched waving a U.S. flag, I declared that their so-called patriotism does not represent me.

When the KKK espoused views of racism and hatred on behalf of Americans, it was made known that this was not my America and did not represent me.

When we use our voice to share that with which we agree and with what we object, we delineate which side we are on, and how history should judge us, accordingly.

This is why so many memes on social sites today are about silence and complicity.

I know that freedom to share ideas and feelings are a gift for those in this country that we cannot take for granted. It is not as easy in Gaza City or Jenin or Ramallah to speak out against Hamas. But if enough disagree with them and are willing to challenge them, they can grow in a force larger than the terror community Hamas has become. They need the courage second. But first they must WANT to stand and delineate which side they belong. Let us see and prove that demarcation. Then we can claim Hamas does not represent Palestinians. Until then, I am afraid the jury is still deliberating.

My last thought for today.

The roaches come out at night. In this dark hour, the roaches of the world are seizing on the momentum of fomenting hate and fear and spreading Jew hatred. They are a fierce minority and a loud but small sector of our world. Their roar makes us think they are lions when they are really cowardly mice.

The last thing we should do is be cavalier about threats nor should we ignore animosity or disregard acts of hatred. Especially now. At the same time, think of Mister Rogers, of blessed memory, who would say, "Look for the good people running to help."

There are indeed many more people that silently help and quietly offer support, and sympathetically stand next to us. The more of those good-hearted souls that rise to the surface, the brighter the light that will keep the roaches at bay.

God of mercy, look after the troops defending Israel, Her citizenry and Jews and good-hearted humanity, worldwide. We need your embrace and your comfort today and tomorrow.

7

October 13, 2023

The Shabbat has come and gone. With the sun setting, a new moon has waxed. It is called a bitter moon because of the deflation we experience after the holiday barrage. Today its bitterness has added meaning.

When we gathered in the synagogue, I shared with the congregation a few thoughts.

First, I felt like an *Onen*. This is a unique category of a person who has learned of a death of a relative but has not yet buried said person. Jewish law says that an *Onen* is free from any positive Jewish commandment or precept. They cannot eat a cheeseburger since that is a negative command. However, they are not required to put on *Tefillin*, *Tallit*, utter daily prayers, learn Torah or anything of the like. The main reason is we are supposed to be preoccupied with the needs of burying the dead. The second reason, less discussed, is we are in no head space to talk to God.

The latter is exactly how I feel. I have little to say to God right now.

I *did* crave being with my congregational family. Seeing faces and hugging bodies soothed me, even if just a little bit.

Sitting on the bema each week, I get a unique perch to see the goings-on of the congregation. Who comes in and who leaves, and when and with whom.

I noticed as people were filing into Friday night services, many familiar faces that had resigned from the synagogue over the past handful of years were in the crowd. They did not leave in any brouhaha or upset, just to save money and because they were not using the Temple's resources. Yet, this tragedy brought them back. To me, this underscored the need for community and the value it offers in times of peace and turmoil.

Next
I have been fixated on a <u>video</u> that has been circulating over the past days. It was taken on a random passer-by cell phone. It is of a Knesset Minister who *tried* to visit the wounded in an Israel hospital. Family members loudly rebuked her at the door and told her she is not welcome. Then a young doctor (assuming by his scrubs) screamed at her and told her, *"You and your government created this. We do not want you here. Leave! We will govern this land. Not you!"* His screams were accented with tears.

That moment to me was a first salvo of what will surely come. There will be a huge political reckoning. Not now.

Like a person being wheeled into the Emergency Room for a heart attack, this is **NOT** the moment for a lecture on poor eating habits. But that lesson will come in time.

For the past forty weeks, Israelis have been protesting the government. Most Israel's citizens were upset with the composite of the government and the agenda they were shoving down the throats of the country. Israelis would not stand for it. At least not without a fight.

A valuable lesson was learned. You can add or remove some laws, change doctrines, move coordinates, but never flirt with the soul of a nation.

While this grandstanding and swagger was happening by leadership, the most important job the Knesset were tasked with fell by the wayside, protecting its citizens. The bluster of Ben Gvir and obtuseness of Levin and naivety of Smotrich and haughtiness of Bibi are a memory now, that will come back to center for a proper reckoning in due time.

What that short video clip demonstrated to me was a burp. A prelude of what will undoubtedly be a vomiting out of the bile that was this Knesset. Like when we eat bad food, our bellies hurt with gastroenteritis. The miracle of the human body is our bodies know to evacuate the toxins.

After this war, the moral center of Israeli society will spit out these toxins and the people that caused us to take our eye of the ball. While it will add to the pain and messiness of this chapter, I am confident that a grassroots and purer form of leadership will rise from the despair to lead a post October 7th, Israel and the next generations.

This is what countries must do. I thought this would happen in America on January 7th, 2021. It started to and got stopped with a visit to Mar a Lago. It still might. We need to remove the bile that builds up and allow newer, cleaner, more wholesome and organic leaders to nourish our country.

What has flummoxed me though is, with Gaza in ruins and this just the very beginning, where is the vomit of the innocent people of Gaza? Where are the masses claiming to Hamas, *"You did this to us. You caused our homes to be in rubble. You made this suffering. You caused our children to die. No more!"* Where are their voices?

If we dare claim that they cannot use their voice for revolt against Hamas, how in the hell are they able to use it to call for help? To decry the humanitarian crisis? To beg for days of rage?

Could they not use that voice to say to Hamas, return the hostages so water and electricity can flow again? Stop this siege so we can live? I mean, who is the real oppressor here?

There comes a point where the red line is defined, and all can stand on the right or wrong side of morality. No ambiguity or equivocation can exist. This is such a time.

Any people that stand with Hamas are on the wrong moral and ethical side of history and humanity. One cannot claim to want to aid the civilians of Gaza and ignore the blockade and cruel conditions Hamas has inflicted on its people. You cannot blame Israel for strikes and ignore the atrocities Hamas has inflicted on its citizens. You cannot ask for humanitarian intervention of the innocents of Gaza and ignore the humanitarian catastrophe of the Israeli hostages in Gaza.

To blame Israel for the reality of Palestinians in Gaza is a cop-out at best and antisemitism at worst. To turn a blind eye to Hamas cruelty and attempt to fabricate Israel's role and responsibility for the turmoil is a cop out at best and antisemitism at worst. For the world to beg for intervention for Gaza today and ignore them yesterday and tomorrow is a cop-out at best and antisemitism at worst. The stench of the hypocrisy is overwhelming.

The people of Gaza have a voice to call for water, food, safe passage and to blame Israel for their fate. Why can they not band together and topple the true culprit who has created this painful life for them? Why are their amplifiers squelched for that message?

The coming days will have all soldiers cross the threshold. Some on the dusty battlefield of Gaza, others on the border with Lebanon, and those fighting bias media and hatred on social streams.

This moment calls for focused messaging that is succinct, impactful and collectively shared.

I have drafted three statements that all can and should say, EVERY Jewish organization should subscribe to, and every supporter should share:

- There is no equivocation or justification that can excuse the brutality and heinous murder of innocent civilians committed by Hamas.
- Israel has every right – indeed an obligation – to defend itself, its citizens and to ensure that this terror can never happen on its soil again.
- Hamas is responsible for the death and suffering of innocent civilians in Gaza. The Jewish people do not celebrate the plight of Gazans subject to the chokehold and terror of Hamas. The civilized world must hold Hamas responsible for this sad reality.

Further, when defending the plight of 1.2M Palestinians looking for safe refuge in Gaza, I would recommend the following responses:

1. Gaza shares a border with Egypt. Concerned citizens should demand Egypt let Gazans in. Or any other Arab country marching for Palestinians today could open their borders. It is no accident that they do not.

2. Iran funds terror in Gaza. Billions of dollars a year. Let them fund the safe passage of innocent civilians in Gaza.

3. When the Israeli army tells innocent people to evacuate, and Hamas tells them to stay and literally blocks their egress – which one is committing the war crimes?

4. To decry the humanitarian plight of Gazans and ignore the welfare and wellbeing of the untold number of hostages held by Hamas IN Gaza is hypocrisy and antisemitic.

We need to be unified not only in our outrage but in our response. Our fight is sadly, just beginning.

Last
The biblical plague of darkness that we learn about in the Passover story was so intense that the Midrash explains one could not see their spouse or neighbor, even if standing directly in front of them.

This moment has made me feel that I am living through another plague of darkness.

As we extend our hands to feel around, we can sense another human. Our fingers touch, our hands grasp one another, and we hold on tightly. In unspoken words, we are reminded, we are not alone.

A story to illustrate that touch amid darkness.

Marciel is our family and Temple landscaper. The name of his company is GB Landscapers, which stands for God Bless. Marciel and his family are devout Christians. He is a son, husband, father, brother and a special soul. We adore him and his family.

Since October 7th, Marciel has texted me daily to check on my family's emotional well-being and the physical safety of our family in Israel. On Friday, Marciel came to the Temple. I hugged him tightly. He dropped off a generous check to support Israel. I said he did not need to do that. He told me that he wanted to let us know we are not alone. It was the first time I cried throughout this nightmare.

The world is full of people like Marciel. Good souls. Kind people. Religious followers who can delineate good from bad, right from wrong, and love from hatred. His hand touched mine in the darkness and I was reminded we are not alone.

If you see Marciel or any of his trucks on the road, honk and wave and thank them for standing with Israel and for their warm touch during this cold time. It helps more than words could ever describe. Do the same for the thousands of "Marciels" that are out there.

May we all stay safe and healthy. We have a dark road ahead and thankfully, many hands that we can hold onto to help find our way. Shavua Tov.

8

October 14, 2023

It only took eight days for the keyboard commandos to come forward in full force, hiding under the shelter of a screen, a camouflaged name, and begin the process of infiltrating social feeds. They dig trenches by making up facts, figures and denying truths.

I vacillate between wanting to singlehandedly take them all on, one refuting text at a time, or ignoring their hatred and staying focused on the task at hand. I think also represents my macro emotions. Sometimes, I want to address those solely focused on the plight of Palestinians or their masquerading antisemitism, and other times I realize no matter how hard I swat, deny, refute, push back or whack the mole, they will keep popping up. That is true for after this conflict as well.

For some naive reason, I think if I could just get through the thick-headed folk, they would hear reason and sensibly support the good fight. They would then cross over to the winning team, they would fall in line and the whole world could sing Kumbaya.

Good news and bad news on that: The good news is the majority of America thinks Israel is right and justified in its response.

Overwhelmingly. We are not alone, and we should carry forward, as we will. The bad news is the haters will always be present, and they will always be loud. I suspect they will get louder.

I do seriously worry about the information war that has begun. Or shall I say, misinformation war. In the last 48 hours I have been told by nameless and cowardly anti-Israel supporters and read on the news from Hamas leadership hiding in Qatar that:

- Hamas did not kill any babies [FALSE]
- Hamas only targeted IDF soldiers [FALSE]
- Hamas does not have any hostages [FALSE]
- Israel bombed the safe passage route it instructed Gazans to flee on [DEBUNKED]
- Israel provoked this conflict [FALSE]
- Ukraine provided weapons to Hamas [DEBUNKED]
- Israel is using chemical warfare, including white phosphorous in its warfare [FALSE]
- Israel has not allowed water or electricity in Gaza for 18 years [FALSE]
- The Greek Orthodox Church of Saint Porphyrios was destroyed during Israel's bombing of Gaza. [FALSE]

The list goes on.

Some of these lies are shared by uninformed typewriter terrorists who sit at their computers and imbibe falsehoods and then spew them back out. Others just make data points up and puke them to the internet. These liars represent Hamas and live in a world of convenient lies and hide from painful truths.

Since November of 2020, I have regularly preached and written on the grave dangers of creating a post-truth world. I contend that Western civilization cannot function in a world that is devoid of truths or markets 'alternative facts.' Honesty is like oxygen. Take it away and eventually, we will be unable to breath.

The most dangerous part of lying and falsehoods peddled as the truth, is that when we enable or allow it and traffic it, it gives license to any other lie, fabrication or untruth any person utilizes.

Much like the hymnal I suggested we all sing from in addressing the justification of Israel's response, so too must we all be armed with facts. We need to throw truth bombs at the vicious keyboard commandos and typewriter terrorists.

Here are a few. Feel free to add to the list:

- Hamas is an offshoot of the Muslim Brotherhood and was born around 1987 during the first Intifada.
- Israel unilaterally withdrew from Gaza in 2005. Not a single Jew has lived in Gaza since that time.
- Hamas charter calls for the murder of every Jew world wise, and the eradication of the State of Israel.
- Hamas (as well as Hezbollah) are deemed terrorist organizations by The United States, The European Union, The United Kingdom, Japan, Australia and Japan as well many members of the United Nations.
- Hamas has never endorsed a two-state solution with Israel.
- Hamas leadership has declared that Iran has funded their terror for more than a 18 years in Gaza.
- Gaza was afforded the opportunity for self-rule and governance in 2005. 16 months later, Hamas took over by a coup d'état, of sorts and has ruled ruthlessly since.
- Despite a "blockade" Hamas was able to amass and launch more than 25,000 rockets in 18 years. They have built elaborate terror tunnels. They smuggled in hundreds of RPGs and thousands of machine guns, tons of explosives

and used sophisticated reconnaissance to seek out where children play in Israel.

- In that same time the schools, hospitals and infrastructure have suffered by stagnancy because Hamas used their resources and energies for terror.
- Hamas and Palestinian leadership including Khaled Meshaal, the estate of Ya'asir Arafat, and Mahmoud Abbas are sitting on Billions of dollars that were embezzled from taxpayers across the world who sent in foreign aid to the Palestinians. Some estimates have Meshaal's (head of Hamas) wealth at near $3B dollars. United Nations financial support has been absconded, to use for weaponry and not nation building. This is fraud and theft that has added to the suffering of the Palestinian people. It needs to be addressed in the world bank and sanctions need to be established and tightened.

I have always underscored the value of truth and aimed to be honest, even when it hurts. This is not a time to traffic and trade in untruths. Frankly, I can think of no time when telling lies should be the standard. Honesty will matter now more than ever, as will the integrity and honesty of those sharing the information.

Rant warning!

I swear if I hear the word "proportionality" again, I am going to lose my s**t!

The best answers to this term were provided from a well circulated meme and an even better circulated video of British journalist that touch on the same response. Both were along the lines of, Israel does not and will not rape women, murder babies and kidnap the elderly and infirm. There is no notion of proportionality against barbarism.

As of writing this Stream (VIII), Israel has yet to send in the ground forces waiting anxiously on its border. The reason given by the IDF and President Herzog as to the pause, is Israel is waiting for more Gazans to evacuate to the South. They are giving ample warning and have extended their timetable by 48 hours, so far, for citizens to evacuate.

Did Hamas give us any warning to vacate? Were we offered an evacuation route? Did we get sufficient time to reach a safe space? That would seem "proportional."

This notion of "proportionality" is ridiculous. It needs to stop being tossed around so loosely and recklessly.

Last
Armchair generals have the life! They can sip on a beer and tell the world how to win wars, fight the media and rebuild nations. If only it were that easy.

We are facing an enemy that aspires to die. "The Israelis are known to love life. We, on the other hand, sacrifice ourselves. We consider our dead to be martyrs. The thing any Palestinian desires the most is to be martyred for the sake of Allah, defending his land." Hamas spokesman Ali Baraka was quoted as saying in the WSJ. How does one win such a conflict against such a people?

The enemy wins if they kill Jewish people. They win when they die trying to kill Jews. Either way, Jews are killed or killers, which is a lose/lose for the good guys and a win/win for the bad guys.

The complexity of this incursion, coupled with the obvious challenges on the ground in the West Bank, East Jerusalem and the wounded morale and spirit of the Israeli people is not simple to navigate.

Israel is facing a multi front war. Hezbollah, also controlled and financed by Iran, has more than 120K rockets that are much more precise and sophisticated than Hamas. They are staging acts of aggression with Israel this week. A two front war will be harder for Israel to fight, win and recover from. Hezbollah is keeping their finger on the trigger to deter Israel from total annihilation of Hamas, which protects the Iranian investment, and which would leave Hezbollah as the most feared and more closely watched target of terror, afterwards.

None should be envious of the position of the IDF leadership or the Israeli government. There are many difficult choices ahead that address life, death, and impossible split-second decisions.

When a Hamas terrorist is holding a baby and shooting at you, does an IDF soldier shoot back? What if the Hamas terrorist is holding an Israeli hostage? What if they are firing rockets at a town and shooting out the rockets would endanger the hostages?

These scenarios are not farfetched and far from simple. The intricacy and complexity of the days and weeks ahead will be painstaking for any moral soul. Sadly, there is only one side with a moral soul that is engaged in this war. Let's pause before we become armchair generals in this conflict.

Please stay strong and healthy. Eat. Sleep. Hug those who need it.

God, bless our country and its people today and forever.

9

October 15, 2023

The sheer confusion for so many educated people about *if* and *how* they can take a stand on this issue, is mind blowing. We are not adding integers here. This is good versus bad, evil versus noble, kind versus cruel. And some need time to consider it? It is not hard.

To be fair, there is a lot of congestion and traffic at the intersection of Israel, progressive, terror, history and liberal. A first-time traveler can get easily honked at. Maybe even lost.

For example, LGBTQ+ advocates usually are categorized as liberal. Many Progressive Jews are fierce LGBTQ+ advocates. Many liberals are opposed to Israel's occupation of Gaza. Thus, many LGBTQ+ advocates are siding with Hamas and against Israel because it is where their traffic flows.

The ridiculousness of the above sentence is beyond description. Hamas believes that every gay, bisexual, transgender, queer and lesbian person should be tortured, mutilated, and then killed. Every. Single. One. Yet, they stupidly stand with Hamas because that is how their social commerce runs.

The kinder and more deferential side of me says that people in these liberal groups are myopic. They think in a linear fashion. Black and white. One side or another. And at the risk of writing in sweeping generalizations, the liberal side, at least for the past 25 years, has been sternly anti-Israel. Thus, when there are two sides against each other, and one is Israel and the other Palestinian, we know where too many of them land.

The more cynical side of me responds to these groups with screams of, 'Grow up! Wake up! It is not that complicated. If you claim to be smart, nuance does not need to be paralyzing."

I use one knife to spread cream cheese and another to slice brisket. So too, can we use different parts of our brains to deal with different realities and complexities. It is not that hard to call on varying degrees of sharpness.

But, for whatever reason, Twitter (not literally) has dumbed society down to a few characters. It has made us run away from semicolons. It pines for simplicity and either-or-isms. Israel has been a hard topic at times. Indeed, Israel *can* be complicated. Why should that keep us at bay?

Marriage is hard. It has not stopped me from loving. Religion is complicated. It has not inhibited my devotion. Support for America is involved. It has not suppressed my patriotism. Why do we think that the realities and complexities of the Middle East require us to disengage at best and to demonize Israel at worst?

One of the places where this simplicity is on full display is the American college campus. Higher educational institutions have long been places of liberal and independent thinking. That is great. But while one goes to college to gain Intellectual quotient,

(IQ), they should not be squandering emotional quotient (EQ) in the process. Some of these schools are demonstrating you need to do well on tests to get in, but you do not have to be wise. If only students could enroll in Common Sense, 101.

Since when is Hamas worth rallying for? Since when is killing innocent elderly people, raping women and beheading babies part of the liberal agenda? Since when do we support Hamas and persecute Israel on the very campuses that founded movements like Take Back the Night and were at the vanguard of racial equality?

And if kids are learning sophisticated concepts on the campus of Columbia, Penn, Harvard, Yale, Indiana, Emory, Syracuse, Miami, Tulane, Wisconsin, Georgetown, Michigan, and USC, to name a few, then they can surely learn to hold two truths.

It is true that Israel can and should do better in many ways for their shared future with the Palestinian people.

It is also true, that there is no justification for murder, rape and kidnapping the likes of what took place on October 7th.

One can be a proud liberal *and* support Israel. They are not exclusive of one another. We need to break this myth, now.

A few years back on the campus of University of California, Berkley, a social science experiment had someone wave an Israeli flag on campus. The student was ridiculed, yelled at, called terrible names, spit on and threatened, all in 90 minutes. Later, the same student waved an ISIS flag. Not a word was said.

A vocal population that is wildly uneducated is a dangerous combination.

One area that does not need to wait to be addressed is education. Zionist history and instruction are lacking in America and American Jewry, in particular. It is time to increase our knowledge which will organically lead to the deepening of connections. We are bigger and better than 140 characters, memes and sound bites.

Next

Now that we are 10 days into this nightmare, I am thinking about the Israeli needs of tomorrow. Beyond the field hospitals and warm socks for soldiers, the necessity for serious emotional and mental triage for the Israeli populace will be overwhelming. Whether one lived in the Gaza envelope, survived the attacks, had a relative killed or abducted, was a first responder and witnessed the carnage, or even if one lives 100 miles way, the ripple of emotional pain and suffering will be unparalleled. We have a responsibility to support and address this growing need for emotional care today and beyond.

Most of the organizations and institutions that will deal with this problem in the coming 24 months were conceived on October 8th, 2023, and after. They will be born through the generosity of communities like ours and others that rise to the moment and offer bricks, mortar, personnel, outlets, and resources.

This level of trauma will not be contained to the borders of Israel. Jews worldwide are dealing with shock and many painful awakenings that will need similar levels of mental and emotional support. Sadly, post COVID, the world was already suffering a serious shortage of qualified therapists, psychologists, psychiatrists, and counselors. This moment will increase the need exponentially and emphasize the shortage.

When we say the prayer for healing each Shabbat, we request a healing of body and soul. We cannot forget the need for the emotional care our collective people and communities will need immediately and after. This will be ongoing and will not get better, anytime soon.

Last
I heard that President Biden is going to Israel this week.

I think that is wonderful.
I also think it is terrible.

It is wonderful because the U.S. President standing **IN** *Israel is even more powerful than saying he stands* **WITH** Israel. Biden's presence will be an unmistakable statement to any country that is scratching its head, wondering if Israel is weak, compromised, or which country has Israel's back. In case the two aircraft carriers off the coast of Haifa were not enough to deter Hezbollah and Iran to not even contemplate engaging in this war, Biden's presence will make that even clearer. It also speaks to Saudi Arabia, Morocco, the UAE, Egypt, and Bahrain that peace with Israel – some recently established and some yet to be – is also reinforcing peace with America.

Love Biden or loathe him, he has been pitch-perfect in his full-throated and resolute support, to date. His team, including Secretary Blinken and Secretary Austin, have been masterful and reassuring. The Israeli people will be galvanized by his visit. American families who have been captured or killed will appreciate his presence and empathy. Moments like these prove that years of collaboration and investments offer dividends when we need them most.

I *hate* Biden's visit now because a U.S. President coming to Israel during a time of peace and quiet is paralyzing to the country. Entire cities shut down. Air spaces are closed. Security forces are quadrupled and thousands of security personnel scope out each inch of travel, rest and meeting space. The Israeli security forces are already spread thin. The country is already paralyzed in suffering and fear. This will pull at much needed resources and make a hard time, harder.

Further, the photo ops might turn into political theater.

Courting the Jewish vote has always been critical to an election. The Jewish demographic in 2024 will be no different. This is not a time for partisanship or to take advantage of Biden's strong, thoughtful, and supportive response to Israel's national tragedy. Closer to the election, Biden can use his successes in advertisements, debates and talking points. This is not the time.

His visit does not chip away at my gratitude for his leadership or my unwavering support for his candidacy.

Each night I go to bed, hoping that I will wake up to what was a terrible dream. It has yet to happen. Maybe tonight?!

Until then, stay safe.

God, look after the IDF and help them protect our homeland. May they know of our love and embrace, always.

10

October 16, 2023

In football parlance it is said, 'Offense wins games, defense wins Super Bowls.' The idea being that the better the defense, the better the chances of a team winning it all. But if one has no offense and is constantly on defense, the players get exhausted, and no points get on the scoreboard. That is not a feasible option for success.

Israel and Zionist supporters worldwide have been on defense since October 7th. The idea we must defend our right to exist is preposterous. The notion that some could look to disqualify our retaliation is outrageous. This defense spans far past the battlefield. It is in the world of media, especially.

A hospital in Gaza City was bombed today. Innocent people died. Before the smoke reached the sky, Hamas, and the Palestinian Authority condemned Israel for targeting civilians. Claims of 500 fatalities quickly circulated. Countries including Morocco, Canada, Saudi Arabia, Turkey, and dozens more, condemned Israel and claimed it was a gross human rights violation. Russia is demanding that Israel be called in front of the UN Security Council. Such morale outrage by these entities; a sense of unity and outrage that has been missing for 10 days. Hamas, who is blind to their hypocrisy, demands justice for their innocent victims.

The only thing is, about 90 minutes later, Israel was able to show verified footage of an errant Palestinian Islamic Jihad (PIJ) missile barrage that hit the hospital. So, PIJ were the actual murderers. Palestinian Jihad terrorists are responsible for killing the innocent and infirm. Even Al Jazeera reported that Hamas and PIJ were to blame for the attack on the hospital.

Did you catch the retraction by the NY Times? Did you hear Turkey or Canada or Morocco rescind its condemnation? Did you get a correction on your breaking news alert? Did you hear Abbas apologize for his accusation that Israel committed war crimes? Did Russia withdraw its actions to take Israel to the Security Council? Did the outrage get squelched?

I tuned up my hearing aids and still, nada!

The PR damage is done. We are on defense. Again.

The truth is that those headlines were written before the rockets were even fired. This is the second battlefield where the terrorists are waging war. They have enlisted a simple, unsophisticated, and willing bunch of people who will fall in line without seeing a shred of evidence or hearing a single fact or retract even if their claims are disproven. They will take on Israel, and by extension Jews, wherever they can. As one friend posted online, 'media sources are more hellbent on being first than being accurate.'

Meanwhile, this wrong reporting caused the Israeli Embassy in Amman to be stormed. It was the catalyst for Mahmoud Abbas to cancel his meeting with Biden and other relationships frayed.

My friend continued, 'Whenever ANY media outlet quotes HAMAS as a trusted source, it is journalistic malpractice.'

Why does Israel have to constantly be on defense? Hell, the title of its army even includes 'Defense.' What other army has that as its very definition? It is draining to our collective morale.

If only truth bombs were as effective against the enemy as their rockets are to us. If they kill Israelis, they score. If they kill their own, more points for them, in a public relations touchdown. How can they lose?

And how can Israel put points on the proverbial board when we spend a disproportionate amount of time debunking lies, repudiating false claims, and refuting shoddy reporting?

Can someone please teach me how to un-ring a bell?

I am starting to seriously worry that fighting an amoral enemy cannot be achieved by following the rules of morality and virtue.

The fantastic irony is that this war is freeing Palestinians from the stranglehold of Hamas. *Nudniks* who are oblivious to facts, reason and reality are trying to inhibit that progress which benefits the good people.

A handful of years ago, just over the Greenline in Israel's Westbank, there was a factory which employed Palestinians and Israelis. They were making Soda Stream drink machines. It was a beautiful harbinger of an Israel that could be. It demonstrated possibility and hope. The workers ate breakfast and lunch together, daily. The company built a mosque and a synagogue on its campus, so each person could pray. Coexistence was real and tangible. Most of the Palestinians were excited to be employed with a good wage and fed daily, as were the Israelis. The company grew and life was good.

Until Soda Stream became the target of BDS [boycott, divestment, and sanctions] claiming that by being 1.6 miles over the Greenline, it was in violation of law. They faced an aggressive boycott that was hurting revenue. These pot stirrers and mud slingers raised such hell, never speaking to a single employee at Soda Stream or ever visiting its property, that they forced the company to relocate. In doing so, it made the over 1200 Palestinian employees lose their jobs and their source of daily nutrition.

Were the BDS'ers interested in a viable and vibrant future for Palestinians or only to single out Israelis where and when they could, regardless of what was really gained and lost? It sure felt like the latter.

I am getting déjà vu, all over again!

It feels like demonizing Israel is the goal of the outside world. Where and how they accomplish that objective is dynamic.

Next
I saw a verified video posted online of a gaggle of people on the Penn campus today chanting that they want genocide for the Jews. You read that correctly. *"Israel - Israel you can't hide. We want Jewish genocide,"* they repeated.

These students marched bald-faced, waving Palestinian flags and in broad daylight. This is not Skokie in the 80s and the Ku Klux Klan! This is Philadelphia, Pennsylvania on one of the most prestigious Ivy League campuses in the country.

What if one crazy person decides to now kill a Jew? What if a Jewish kid is beaten on campus? What if a Hillel or Jewish fraternity or sorority is vandalized? Are these not hate crimes? Are the people not fomenting animosity? Should not all these people be brought up on charges for hate?

I am pretty sure if a group of white students marched through Dartmouth or Cornell asking for death to Black people or genocide to Asians, they would be brought up to the school leadership and summarily expelled. Free speech is not a license for hate speech.

Why will this NOT happen at Penn? Why the double standard?

In the past few days, when it comes to university contributions, we have heard the checkbooks of quite a few billionaire-philanthropists slam shut. It is about time. More should follow.

When Penn hosts anti-Israel activists and antisemitic speakers and falls on the sword of free speech, it is revealing its cowardice. Is that the educational and moral standard Penn wants for its student body? I did not see Penn inviting David Duke to its lecture halls. Or the Aryan Brotherhood to lead a campus rally? Does not the same free speech protect those abhorrent beings?

After October 7th, generous donors called out the lack of actions of school administrators, their tepid written responses to terror and their gross equivocations on rape, beheadings, and murder. It is about time the dollars stop flowing. It might finally hit these places where it hurts most.

For years, the deeds of these institutions said Jewish blood is different. Less than. But money of Jewish donors is sought after. Revered. Welcome. Encouraged.

It will be interesting to see how universities address these double standards and how, if at all, they try to earn the trust of Jewish leadership and students, again.

This one got me.

Wadea al Fayoumme was killed in Chicago this week. His only crime was being born Palestinian. He was an innocent and sweet six-year-old boy who had his entire life ahead of him.

I mourn his tragic and senseless death. His murderer should have every lever of the law adjusted against him to exact the most severe punishment for his heinous crime. There is no room for Islamophobia or Muslim hate.

Less than 24 hours after Wadea's death, more than 100 Jewish organizations, spear headed by the JCPA, signed on to a joint statement condemning the killer and lamenting the death of Wadea. Our collective condolences stand with the Al Fayoumme family.

Full Stop.

Why did it take only twenty-four hours for 100 plus Jewish groups to condemn one murder - as they should> Meanwhile, we are still waiting for dozens of nations and thousands of Muslim organizations to condemn the murder of 1400 Jewish souls? Where is their collective statement? Their outrage? Their unity against Hamas?

I am asking for a friend…. actually, 16.1 million friends.

Last
The flatfooted posture of Israel and its army last week is a serious source of embarrassment. Much time and energy will surely address how we were caught off guard. Creating unity in a time of crisis is exponentially harder than if unity existed beforehand. The war time unity government took almost 90 hours to be formed. Those were critical days wasted on political posturing and back-room deal making.

The United States - and any other Western civilized country – should be aware that a radical attack on a sovereign nation and its citizens can happen here, too. No one was prepared for 9/11. No one was ready for the attack on the USS Cole. Who brought guns to the Bataclan theater in Paris?

God forbid it were to happen in America while we have no Speaker of the House, I worry. We have no agreement on budgets and debt ceilings. Infighting and bickering will ensue. We will spend inordinate amounts of timing uniting under pressure and ONLY then, will we address the threats and response.

We must get our act together. Now. Too much is at stake. Not just for Israel but for America. To quote from the movie, The American President, *"This is a serious time that calls for serious people."*

Can we get serious? Please?! Before it is too late?!

I feel like Jerry Springer (obm) whenever I sign these blogs off. I stop myself from writing – "Take care of yourself – and each other." But maybe – just for right now – that works.

11

October 17, 2023

On the day they appointed Rabbi Elazar, they removed the guard
from the study hall and allowed anyone who wished to enter. When
Rabban Gamliel was in charge, he used to say: Anyone whose inside
does not match his outside may not enter this study hall!

Babylonian Talmud, Tractate *Berachot* 27b-28a

A clear Jewish precept, illustrated above, is that our actions, feelings, and words must agree with one another. We cannot say one thing and think something different. It is against the grain of our values and beliefs.

In the Middle East, this is a teaching that seemingly only applies to Jews.

A pair of high-ranking Arab diplomats told a leading news source today, on the condition of anonymity, that they and their countries were appalled with the images and gruesome savagery that came out from Israel last week committed by Hamas. They could not say it publicly because their nations had not condemned the killings or denounced Hamas. They also went so far to say that these sentiments were shared by most of their "rationale" Arab brethren.

In case your mind is exploding reading this – let me try and boil it down.

They are disgusted by Hamas. They cannot say it publicly but privately hope Hamas' demise comes to conclusion, soon. Again, they just cannot support Israel on the record.

SMH – That is text talk for **Shaking My Head** in total incredulity. On June 7, 1981, Israel bombed the nuclear reactor at Osirak, deep inside Iraq. It was a daring mission that eliminated a serious threat to the Middle East. It humiliated Saddam Hussein and shamed the nation of Iraq. Most of all, it deterred other nations from following suit.

As you might expect, the United Nations swiftly condemned Israel.

United Nations Security Council resolution 487, adopted *unanimously* on the 19th of June 1981, having noted representations from Iraq and the International Atomic Energy Agency (IAEA), the Council condemned the attack by Israel.

In September 1981, the IAEA Conference condemned the Israeli attack and voted to suspend all technical assistance to Israel. A draft resolution was introduced to expel Israel from the IAEA.

Countless Israeli delegates to the United Nations shared on various occasions that multitudes of officials of all ranks, privately told Yehuda Zvi Blum, Israel Ambassador to the UN at the time, 'Thank you for handling Iraq and their nuclear ambitions.'

The world sensed then, and were proven later, of the maniacal intentions of Saddam Hussein. Could you imagine what the invasion of Kuwait would have looked like, nine short years later, were Israel NOT to have taken that reactor out?

The Arab world also knew that Saddam was dangerous. They just didn't want to deal with him and most certainly could not go on the record thanking Israel for taking out their communal trash. At least not in public. But privately, they all did, as did other civilized countries.

Inside feelings and outward statements sure did not match!

A little more than a decade or so ago, Shimon Peres was invited to meet the King of Saudi Arabia in a convening of nations. The King was nervous about shaking a Jewish person's hand in public. The King worried it would cause himself shame.

Salman got word to Peres through messenger that when he meets Peres, he would not like to shake his hand. Though, if Peres extends his hand, he (King Salman) will shake it, even if it would cause the King embarrassment out of courtesy.

Peres, the brilliant gentle and statesman met the King and politely bowed in deference and respect, not creating a yucky public relations episode for King Salman.

Salman was taken with Peres' grace and ability to offer a sense of deserved nobility and rise above the moment. Salman invited Peres to a private meeting the next day. The King purportedly said to Peres that if Israel would remove the Iranian threat, King Salman would lobby to bring Israel into the Arab League.

What always captured me about this story – regardless of how exaggerated it might be - is that King Salman could not publicly shake a Jew's hand without explanation or reprisal. But privately, they could break bread and share ambitions.

Our Western political world is quite opposite. We say kind things and make bold assurances aloud and in private we are nasty, mean, promise-breaking and speak our mind.

How do we circle the square of two opposite ways of operating? How can we navigate in a society with leadership that does not have consonant words and deeds?

The same whispering Arab diplomats claimed that Israel's crushing response in Gaza to the Hamas attacks has led to the evaporation of goodwill that Jerusalem had briefly obtained from some of its Arab allies.

My not-so-rhetorical question is, how long should empathy last? What is the statute of limitations on good will and timing for revenge? Do killing babies last a week? Beheadings 10 days? Human immolation 17 days? Seriously? Is there an equation? An algorithm?

On a British news channel last night, a journalist was interviewing a fellow Gazan journalist about the situation in the Strip. The British journalist asked the Gazan woman, "What is a proper and proportionate response to the slaughter of 1400 people and abduction of 200 people?" Good for her for asking the question!

The Gazan woman hemmed, hawed, explained about years of persecution and extreme living conditions. The British journalist held this Gazan journalist's feet to the fire and kept asking her. She refused to answer. It was a simple and brilliant journalistic tactic. If only more journalists had her temerity.

What *is* the answer to that question? What *is* the timing window for retaliations? Can we quantify our payback? Is there an egg timer ticking on how long we can retaliate? Or when the world's sympathy runs out?

The concept that Israel is open to garner pity but forbidden from creating deterrence is ludicrous. We have no interest in being the world's *nebechs* (misfits). We have seen that movie before, and we know how it ends. As Micha Goodman said, we want the Middle East to fear Israel and the Western world to love Israel. It is a zero-sum equation.

I do not want to be pitied. I also do not want to be feared. But if I had to choose just one......well.... you know which one we *must* choose.

I want to make sure that what I say and what I do and how I feel are all harmonious so I can be true to myself and to those in my world. It will better allow me to put my head on a soft pillow at night. Alas, if I could only sleep through this nightmare!

Be safe.

12

October 17, 2023

There is a fantastic paradox brewing. As one congregant told me, "Rabbi, I am so worried about antisemitism. It is going to skyrocket. It already has."

He is right. Antisemitism always sleeps lightly. Moments like this will cause Jew hatred and Israel hatred – which is just another form of Jew hatred – to rise in the Western world.

Interestingly though, I have noticed an equally steep increase of Jewish pride and Zionism.

For decades, Jews have wanted a seat at the table in major universities, on museum boards and communal institutions. Today, Jewish leaders (and good moral Gentile ones) are quick to give up the coveted seat they once pined for if their Judaism is not respected or treated fairly.

Young Jewish adults, who were indifferent to their Judaism and apathetic toward Israel have been violently awoken to their history and destiny. Many have jumped headfirst into the moral and right side of this fight.

One thirty-something year old from our community, who lives in Manhattan, has since attended three rallies, and spent her Sunday putting up blue and white lawn signs that proudly declare 'We Stand with Israel.' This is a person who has yet to visit Israel and otherwise would make parsley jokes at the family Seder. Another individual of similar age has taken to the social media airwaves to fight back at haters, while countless of his peers have been collecting supplies and donating chunks of their paychecks that would otherwise go to bar tabs toward Jewish causes. Hillel on campuses have mobilized and swarms of students are stepping forward. Priorities are shifting. Values are focusing. Collective abuse to our tribe is maturing the younger ranks quickly. Hamas has rattled the peoplehood *into* young Jews. They are showing up in force. Yes, our haters have knocked on the door, again. But our supporters are answering in great number.

Next

I am having a hard time suffering fools these days. Truth is, I was never very good at it. But these times have whittled away any tolerance I *did* have for stupidity and thoughtlessness. Here is an example.

Yesterday, there was an old-fashioned sit-in in Washington, DC. Not at the Woolworth's lunch counter but at the Congressional office buildings. About 350 people, many Jewish, were begging for a cease fire in Gaza. Rabbis draped in prayer-shawls chanting Jewish hymns on behalf of peace, cried aloud to not invade the Palestinian strip of land and just 'give peace a chance.' They tied themselves to one another and demanded that the war – that has barely begun – stop immediately.

It would be hilarious if it were not so damn tragic.

The number of captives in Gaza is rising by the day. Hamas hijacked the limited aid that has come into Gaza away from the starving civilians to fuel their criminal activity. As one meme said, Gaza has run out of everything, except rockets and fuel for rockets. The leadership of Hamas will not budge an inch on negotiations. We have seen no proof of life for the 200 plus abductees. Accounts are unfolding about the level of ghastly and grisly deeds these sub-human beings did to women and elderly alike, within sovereign Israeli territory.

And they think the answer is to walk away? To put our guns down? To put the tanks in reverse? Are they serious??

I loathe war as much as the next person. But sometimes in some places, one *must* fight back. One *must* stand up to the aggressor. One *must* declare NO MORE! What has been proven for 75 years is if Israel lays down its weapons, we will be killed. What was established last week, is if we think our enemy has laid down their weapons, they have not. They are just pulling a trick on us. A devious tactic to make us think they want peace. When really, they want to catch us off guard and kill as many as possible. They so much as said so. Their goal and resolve are crystal clear.

These peace activists are more driven by social inertia then they are morality and justice. They put all wars and conflicts into the same box, and they respond in like fashion. How juvenile! Yes, all wars involve death and bloodshed, and they should be avoided when they can. But they all cannot nor should not be avoided. This is such a war. It is a just war.

Beyond deterrence, beyond security, beyond reassuring its populace, there *must* be a sense of justice that eliminates forever the evil of Hamas. The world cannot reach its potential with a terrorist group like Hamas on the loose. They are a threat to humanity, worldwide. How does tying your Talis to a pillar in a D.C office building fix that problem?

The lens of Judaism through which I see our texts instructs me, that a sage who is usually stringent on laws but, is relaxed on a particular law, or another sage who is usually relaxed on laws but stringent on a particular law, is a sage worthy of respect. The reasoning behind that mode of thinking is that the sage can compartmentalize. The sage can look at situations in context. The sage does not put everything into the same box.

The foolishness of these protestors is that they fail to see the context and differences between this war and what this moment means to the Jewish people and Jewish state. This time is not different because we are Jewish. Or because it is Israel. It is different because if we do not respond with the extermination of Hamas, they have telegraphed their gameplan for what we can come to expect as their neighbors in the months and years ahead.

Moreover, these same protestors were decrying the 'Israeli' missile that killed 500 souls in a hospital. They were silent today when the deadly missile was proven to be errantly fired by PIJ in Gaza. The peace advocates are silent when the death toll, as reported by AFP in Europe claims 50 souls (still too many innocent people) and not 500.

Most egregious to me is the taciturnity of these protestors about a missile that was made and aimed and fired to maim and kill innocent civilians in Israel. But when it misfires and kills innocent Gazans, activists can erroneously and recklessly criticize Israel for the act. Is not a core tenet of peace and justice, honesty, and transparency? The double-standard is astonishing. Why are they loud when they suspect Israel and quiet when it was proven to be Palestinian terrorists? Where is the passion for truth and justice and calling out murderers??

One Hamas sympathizer claimed on social media how imbalanced the two sides are because Israel has Iron Dome. They also went on to say Israel has bomb shelters and Gaza does not?!

Another fool I cannot bear.

Does this buffoon know **why** *Israel has Iron Dome*? Because Israel was subject to thousands of rockets on its citizens. These are not precision projectiles. These nail and ball bearing filled crude rockets land aimlessly, including playgrounds, nursing homes and schools. The dome offered protection to Israeli citizens.

There is no question of chicken and egg here. We know that the Hamas rockets necessitated Iron Dome. That is why Israel invented and procured it. To safeguard its people who love life and protect them from the years of rocket onslaught they were subject to. That is the same driving force for Arrow Defense and David Sling. As I am typing this report, I read of Houthi controlled missiles (read Iran sympathizers) who launched rockets toward Israel. The three rockets were intercepted by a US warship. Did Israel pick a fight with Yemen? The Houthis? Where and when does this end?

Has anyone cared to ask Hamas why there are no bomb shelters in Gaza? Hamas had the funds for terror tunnels, rockets and grenades. Why did they not invest in secure places for their citizens? This middle-aged, overweight rabbi asks, in a sarcastic tone, and his tongue firmly planted in his cheek. I think we all know the answer. Even the peace activists do. They just turn a blind eye to those inconvenient facts.

Speaking of hypocrisy, did these activist-rabbis tie their tefillin to the Capitol lectern when Assad butchered 500,000 Syrians? Was humanitarian aid demanded to flow from neighboring countries when thousands of Libyans and Syrians tragically died from mass flooding a few months ago? The world did not even know of this painful reality or worse, they did not care. No major news source even reported it. Ask yourself earnestly, why is the attention of the world fixated on this narrow patch of land and the so-called injustices, now?

Do we really think this is a tie-dyed, wrap our arms around one another, smoke a peace pipe moment? I most decidedly do not and would suggest those who aim to pacify today will have Jewish blood on their hands, tomorrow.

Last
In my house, we are having an ongoing discussion (at times, a heated debate) as to whether the innocent people of Gaza have the wherewithal to revolt against the evil of Hamas. If the statistics are right, Hamas is between 10-25% of the population. Clearly a minority. But they rule with an evil, iron fist. I concede that.

My argument has consistently been that the very masses which created the Arab spring and made a new reality overthrowing Mubarak in Egypt, and Khaddaffi in Libya, and Ben Ali in Tunisia, are also capable of overthrowing the wicked Hamas. The citizens either do not have the courage or do not have the divergence in views with the Hamas leadership, to do so. I dread knowing which is the real reason.

Originally, I thought I would write two or three of these blogs. Somehow, my fingers keep typing, my rage stays kindled and there is more to say. This is number 12. I think I will stop when I no longer can count in Roman numerals. Until then, thanks for reading and sharing. Putting my thoughts on paper helps me tremendously. I hope it helps you, even if a little bit.

Be safe!

13

October 18, 2023

Albert Einstein once defined the Jewish people as having a fanatical pursuit of justice. It was a great characterization of our tribe. Meanwhile, our enemy has a fanatical pursuit of injustice.

I am not sure how we reconcile those two differences.

When the enemy breaks every statute of the Geneva Conventions, upends international laws and ignores rules of war, how can we be expected to protect the living and avenge the deaths of innocents by the book?

I have been reluctant to listen to detailed accounts from Israel of survivors and first-responders. My soul cannot handle it. Not now. I did see one video by accident. It was a twenty-something year old woman who lived near the Gaza envelope. She was on a news broadcast where she explained that her brother survived October 7th, because he hid motionless for seven hours under a bed in a pool of his parent's blood until he was rescued by the IDF.

She concluded, "I apologize for not giving a damn about a humanitarian corridor. Where was the humanitarian corridor for me and my brother and my parents?"

There is no justice that could undo that *in*justice. There is no law to deal with that lawlessness.

Could you imagine a basketball game between one team who must follow every rule or the international whistle blows, and another that doesn't dribble, fouls at will and loads the court with more players than regulation allows? Salting the wound, the fans have the chutzpah to shrug their shoulders at the rule breaking thugs and scream in upset at the game plan of the rule following team?! The basic tenet between any match is that both teams abide by equal rules. If one cheats or disregards the rules, is there even a game to be played, or a field where both can square off?

Any group that is amoral, ruthless, unscrupulous or ajustical (I made up that word – but I gather you know what I intend) cannot exist in the same arena with those who abide by morals, follow ethics and have a fanatical pursuit of justice. This is what makes *this* conflict so much trickier.

Next

Last night I was at a fundraiser for Israel. Its focus was dialed in since the 7th, but the event had been on the books for months. As I was hunting for mini-hot dogs wrapped in phyllo-dough, I heard some smart, well-respected people gathered around spewing data that was totally inaccurate. I forsook my quest for hors d'oeuvres to insert myself in the conversation. I heard statements like *"Biden is forcing Israel to wait to enter the war and that is going to make Israel lose,"* followed by *"The Democratic party is going to tank this conflict and stop aid to Israel"* and then, *"We know Hamas has already killed all the hostages."*

I pushed back on these people - most I did not know well - with tons of questions that made them stammer in response. I then reminded them of the bipartisan 97-0 vote in the Senate in favor of

Israel and support from earlier in the day. After that, I repudiated the malarkey they were shoveling about Biden and debunked the facts they manufactured about hostages. I took out a small soap box and stood tall. I mustered the courage to rebuke this crowd and remind them we are not at a time to be fast and loose with facts and misplaced partisanship. It is reckless and dangerous. Too many people are ill informed. The worst antidote to that is to sell opinion as if it were truth and to spread falsehoods.

Most of these people looked at me with embarrassment and some shame.

The same goes to all readers of this diary. This is a Dragnet moment. Just the facts. Of course, we are entitled to opinions. Mixing fact and opinion is a dangerous cocktail. Its consumption could lead to confusion, misperception and in some cases, grave danger.

Speaking of facts and editorials – allow me to share some of both: In 2006, after the abduction of Israeli soldiers Eldad Regev and Ehud Goldwasser on the Lebanese border, and Gilad Shalit on the Southern border, Israel responded by instantly sending loads of troops into the North and South to get them back and wage a retaliatory war. While indeed, we left that war victorious, countless blunders and missteps led to the removal of Ehud Olmert as Prime Minister and deep resentment and upset with the military brass. Troops were not ready. They were missing supplies. There was a total lack of coordination, communication and massive death tolls for soldiers. How? Why? When?

My hypothesis for the pause before the ground invasion is so we do not repeat those hurried mistakes. I have no verification. It is just my hunch.

It also could be a strategy to release as many hostages as possible. The longer Israel procrastinates the tanks rolling in, the higher the chances of getting any of the captives back alive, or even being able to bury Jewish bodies with dignity in their homeland.

Maybe Israel is just playing a mind game with Hamas. Causing them to jitter with fear and fright and to catch them off guard.

Those who know why we have yet to go into Gaza have not told me and probably, they have not told you either. Let's not manufacture proofs or sell opinion as the gospel. It will not help.

Next
I just learned of the release of two American hostages. It caught me off guard. I cannot begin to fathom the trauma they have endured and the healing they will need. They are physically safe now. Their journey towards rehabilitation – physical and emotional - is just beginning.

Their release has left me confused. Of course, I am relieved that they are free and headed home. I suppose I should be grateful to their abductors for showing kindness, but that does not feel right. Not at all. There is nothing generous about Hamas. There are no positive or appreciative feelings I can garner towards them. I hate the idea that they did anything, even something so slight, that could reflect a kernel of humanity. Especially when their raison detre is about acting inhumanely.

I could easily swallow my pride and sing Hamas praises if it led to the release of every hostage. I could live with that lie if it brought some solace to the families and some hope to the country.

However, if presented with the choice of the release of all hostages on the condition of no retaliation against Hamas – no ground invasion and going back to the status quo, I am not sure if I could make that deal. Who could?

Honestly, I think I would accept the deal, get them home and then renege on the promise and invade without relent until every one of those vermin were eliminated. I guess October 7th has eroded *my* fanatical pursuit of justice.

Next
There is a forgotten reality that will be reminded to the Arab world, especially the Palestinians, in the coming days. Iron Dome saved more Palestinian lives, than Jewish ones.

Iron dome intercepting the dozens of rockets that would be lobbed over the separation walls gave a great source of comfort to Israelis. When sirens would blare, some would drink wine and naively go to their rooftops to watch the intercept, like they were fireworks. So long as Iron Dome worked and Israel could respond with targeted air assaults, the casualty rate on both sides was low. It was what people mistakenly called, 'proportionate.'

What has been preached for years and clearly forgotten by our southern neighbors, is that were it not for Iron Dome, we would have had to send troops to Gaza to clear out the terrorists, the launchers and the rockets which would have resulted in mass casualties and fatalities. I am reminded of the philosophical dictum; every solution creates a new problem.

Never did we expect that the enemy would break through a wall and wreak a day of horror like they did. When the Palestinians added guerilla and paramilitary infiltration to their arsenal of terror, they forgot that the reprisal would be numbers far greater than ever before. Not equal or 'proportionate.' Rather, massive. Enormous. Incalculable. After this monstrous act, it is unfair to beg for mercy. When elected members of congress and Palestinian sympathizers complain of the imbalance Israel has by employing Iron Dome, remind them that the technology saved more Palestinian lives than Jewish ones. And believe me, it saved thousands of Jewish lives!

I will close with a personal confession.

I am having a really hard time with prayer right now. I am still going to organized services. In the morning, I put on *Tefillin* and *Talis* but I cannot focus on the prayers. I am not saying the liturgy. My lips move and I mumble, but no devotions are coming out. I am not in the head space to thank God, talk to God or even plead to God.

If you see me in any house of worship and I am not reading from the prayer book or swaying along, deep in meditative thought, you should be allowed to know why. I have always encouraged my flock to show up and wrestle in their relationship with God. I am practicing what I preach. I doubt it will be like this forever. But it is for now.

When Moses came down from Mount Sinai, after receiving the greatest gift from God, the Torah (10 Commandments) Moses sees the Israelites dancing around the human made idol called the golden calf. Moses is filled with such anger, rage and disappointment that he shatters the newly given gift from the Holy One.

That story gives us license for our emotions. We are allowed to be mad, sad, confused, angry, pensive or any other word that you can think or feel. We are permitted to not say the words in the Siddur or, if we choose, to say them with even more energy. There is no correct response to this moment.

I hope we can all create space where all emotions are welcome, and all reactions are acknowledged.

May this Shabbat bring us peace, healing, hope and resolve. Shabbat Shalom

14

October 19, 2023

As the sun sets marking another week since the tragedy of October 7th, my anxiety and fatigue are wrestling with one another.

One thing I am becoming envious of, is the Arab world's sympathy for Palestinians. It is confusing.

Sympathy toward Israel was short lived. We gained world support for less than a week but damn, the price tag was so high. To paraphrase Golda, I do not want to pay that price. World sympathy for our cause is not worth it, even though we are deserving.

I was in Egypt, Morocco, UAE, Bahrain – all recently – and have met with countless members of those communities and senior officials. They each expressed excitement at the possibility of peace and bilateral relations with Israel. They were eager to move forward. Not a one of them lamented the challenges of the Palestinian people or the precondition of propping them up.

Now, Egypt, which has long prohibited public demonstrations have allowed protests in solidarity with the Palestinian people. Egyptian President Sissi hosted an Arab leadership summit today where they criticized Israel publicly for its treatment of the Palestinians. Interestingly, the summit could not come to agreement condemning the brutality of Hamas. That is telling.

Mind you, Egypt's border is still closed to any Palestinian who seeks refuge or safety. As are the borders of Turkey, Jordan, Syria, Saudi and Oman. Also, I do not think monies are flowing in to support the Palestinian cause. There is a lot of bark. Not a lot of kibble.

Recently, when asked if they would support an action that would allow any Palestinian to leave the Gaza strip for a better life elsewhere, Fatah leadership said emphatically, *"No."* The Hamas brass chimed in and said the same from the comforts of Qatar. *"We cannot leave the strip. We lose our ability to resist if we leave."*

I hope you all caught that.

There is not and never really has been a serious interest in living symbiotically. There is no desire of two states for two peoples. Whether it is done passively or violently, in onslaughts or drips and drabs overtime, there will consistently be resistance. There will be a continual denial of a Jewish State and its right to exist, a rejection of Jewish autonomy and a refusal to recognize Jewish sovereignty and the basic rights of its citizens.

If Palestinians could live in peace and security and create a country rich with trade, infrastructure and agriculture, along with a government for the people of Palestine, the leadership is announcing that they would still resist the Jewish right to live, breath, survive and be their neighbors. Regardless of borders. Regardless of Jerusalem. Regardless of the particulars of right-of-return.

It reminds me of the famous Khartoum Summit of the Arab League after the 1967, Six Day War. Israel offered to return the land it captured to Egypt, Jordan and Syria. Every single inch. The only condition was for those countries to cease their aggression towards Israel. Make peace. Allow us to live and be.

The answer was the famous 3 nos.

- **No** peace with Israel.
- **No** recognition of Israel.
- **No** negotiations with Israel.

In 2000 and since, those who have had to negotiate peace and dealt with mutually agreed upon land swaps, defined borders, resolution on return for Palestinian refugees, shared access on Jerusalem and other peace jargon, have been stymied by one condition that our Palestinian neighbors refuse to accept.

To me and you, it is both innocuous and crucial. I imagine that the details of borders and conditions of return would have been flexible if there would have been consensus on the following:

Cessation to ALL future claims.

Any deal that is reached, would be final. There would be no more claims either a week or a decade later demanding more space, new borders or demanding more Israeli concessions.

That has long been the deal breaker for Palestinians.

For the Israelis, their attitude was, why make these sacrifices, and create new vulnerabilities, fracture parts of the country only to have the other party be unsatisfied in short time and be forced to go back to the drawing board. That is a fool's errand. Israel is eager to make a peace – but a real and lasting peace.

For the Palestinians, cessation to all future claims really means they must redefine their existence. They can no longer be victims. They must be a victor. I do not think they are capable of such a narrative.

A few days ago, a Palestinian sympathetic news anchor, Ayman Mohyeldin, put on his Instagram feed two pictures, both of tents. One picture was from 1948 and the other, from 2023.

His caption under the picture read, *"To most people these are simply pictures of two refugee camps taken 75 years apart. But, for Palestinians, there is a direct through line from their ancestors who sought refuge in one camp to their descendants plight in another."*

I saw something different and tragic.

When Jews settled Israel 75 years ago, they too lived in tents. In fact, when I saw those 75-year-old tents pitched in sand, my first reaction was that might have been my ancestors' homes.

Jump forward 75 years and Israel is a blossoming garden in the Middle East. Israel leads in health, education, technology and security. Israel has a growing economy and are players on the world stage. Israel has such a functional sense of democracy that they have exercised their right in governmental dysfunction. A rite of passage earned over time.

Ayman, based on your picture and caption, I ask earnestly, how do you think we went from tents to homes? How did that fabric turn into concrete? It was not gifted to us, I assure you.

For our entire existence, starting on the actual day we declared statehood, May 14, 1948, to as recently as yesterday, people on all our borders have tried to kill Israelis for just being. Our singular crime has been our religious ancestry. We too have been oppressed. We too have struggled. We too have suffered incalculable loss and grief.

What allowed us to build from those tents and what has kept your people inside them is a mindset. We cherish life. We aim for victory. We dream about tomorrow.

You do not.

You speak of yesterday. You talk of injustice that fell on your people with no mention of responsibility for the poor choices made. You speak of the support of America to Israel but have done nothing worthy of your Arab brethren's real assistance. The Palestinian's devoted marriage to victimhood has yielded your reality, Ayman.

Palestinian refusal to agree to 'no future claims,' along with persistence on resistance and tears of victimhood all might garner short-lived sympathy. Of that, I have short-lived envy. But it offers the Palestinian people nothing for their future. Claiming Israel created this painful reality is more than patently false. It does nothing to get Palestinians out of the tent.

In case the world forgot, in 1948, when Jewish people were in those tents, we had good reason to wag fingers in the face of other countries. We could have cried and whined. The previous decade was not kind to Jews. But we dreamt of what could be, not what was taken away. Our entry to this neighborhood did not come with welcome cakes and invitations to Tupperware parties. We were attacked on all sides. We were suffocated by hatred. It never quit. Still, we anticipated the sunrise and did not mourn the sunset.

Of course, the Jewish people were pained, traumatized and angry. We channeled those emotions towards sifting the sand into a thriving homeland. We planted fruit trees and enjoyed its nectar. We invented baby tomatoes. We were forced to be security specialists. We plugged into technology. We stretched out a hand in partnership and peace to all willing to grab a hold. Those that did, benefitted quickly.

Most importantly, no one gave us what we have. No one. Israel and its people earned everything they enjoy today with elbow grease, grit, education, hard work, and dreams of what could be.

When you look over the border and weep for the tents Palestinians are still living in, cannot Hamas, Fatah and those marching in the streets of Cairo, Marrakesh and London ask themselves:

What has your victimhood done for your people?

Blaming Israel is such a cheap ruse from accepting responsibility for the Palestinian fate.

The best revenge to the long list of those who have sought our pain and demise is to show them how we suck from the marrow of life. To boast of our buildings, to brag of our technological prowess and marvel at our infrastructure. We dance at weddings and sing loudly at celebrations. When we do that, we signal to each enemy of yesterday and today, we are still standing. We are here. We are living and loving and being and dreaming.

The Jews have a thick dossier of crimes against our people. Dating back thousands of years, from expulsions, to being burned at the stake, to violent pogroms, to Holocausts to wars and terrorism, and now, even butchery inside of our homes, beheading babies and torturing the elderly. Our list is long. We too could easily fall on the sword of victimhood. We do not. We will not. Mainly because victimhood achieves little for our future. It does not fuel our growth. We use our tears to irrigate our homeland.

In the past 36 months, the tide had begun to turn in unimaginable ways. Palestinian's most vocal allies began to suppress *their* plight and dream of a future. The Abraham Accords was indeed the greatest threat to the 75-year narrative of the Palestinians. It finally debunked the paper-thin argument that Palestinian peace in the Middle East was the obstacle to other relationships.

October 7th was as much an attack on the Abraham Accords, the supportive countries and the Palestinian need to gain control of the narrative, as it was a smaller scale Holocaust for Israel.

The two greatest motives for the timing and scope of the Hamas attack were the visible fault lines of the Israeli government and the blossoming relationship between Israel and Saudi Arabia. If peace were to be made with the leading Arab country in the Middle East, that would mean curtains for the plight of the Palestinian narrative and its people.

I think the two greatest acts to avenge October 7th is first, for Saudi Arabia to continue in its pursuit of peace with Israel. Let the Hamas militants see that peace and its possibilities are more potent than hatred and victimhood. Let the Hamas leaders in Qatar witness a treaty. Let the masterminds of this terror see mature countries that dream, make peace with Israel and grow. Let every blind-following terrorist who were accomplice to this unprecedented terror, see that their brutality did not stop our pursuit of tomorrow and what can be. Let them all hear the rumbles of tractors cultivating the soil of peace.

Then, we should capture and kill them all. Each Hamas operative. From the generals to the sergeants to the secretaries in offices. We will find them in Gaza, Qatar and any hole they hide in. Because, let's face it, we can dream of peace, but we cannot live with those Hamas terrorists next door. Our survival necessitates their permanent removal from this world.

But they should die knowing of their failures. Each of them should leave this world knowing that they botched widening the fissures in the Israeli government and dividing its people. Just the opposite. They should have run through their minds before they meet their maker, that peace is more potent than terror. The last question I want each of these terrorists to consider before they leave this world is, *"How has victimhood helped their future?"*

Please be safe. The hardest part of this episode is still ahead of us. Their protests will be strong. Our unity can be stronger. They will be loud. We can be louder. They will point at civilian casualties. We have pictures too.

Do not cower. This is our moment to do our part in this war against Israel and Jews, worldwide.

Shavua Tov.

15

October 20, 2023

There is a curious case of dissonance when it comes to antisemitism in the Western world.

Much of today's Stream is assembled from a few different sermons I delivered, or posts shared over the years that address this strange place in time for us and for the 'not-us' of the world.

There is no question, antisemitism and Jew hatred is out and about. It is lurking in many suspecting and unsuspecting corners. Masks have come off and some friends have proven they are not really friends and other acquaintances are closer aligned than we knew.

One meme said, *"I now know which of my friends would hide me in the Holocaust."* It was a bit twisted, but I totally understood it. You did too.

So why do so many people not understand our victimhood, sense of fear and fright? It is more than our history. There are legitimate issues that could confuse a well-educated, thoughtful person.

These three statements are ALL true.

- Antisemitic crimes in America reached a record level during the past 2 years.
- Jews are the target of 58% of all hate crimes in past 33 months.
- Jews have ranked highest in the past decade and are viewed most positively by Pew Research.

To add to this confusion, Time Magazine did research with Pew and found Jews ranked as the most positive religion in our country.

Robert Putnam, the famed Harvard Sociologist who penned American Grace and Bowling Alone concluded his sociological research with this gem:

The religion that most people in America felt least intimidated by was Judaism. 80% of Americans said they would have no problem voting for a Jewish president if he or she were the best candidate.

They did not say the same about Muslims, Mormons, Quakers or non-believers.

Those facts probably did not knock us off our chair. In fact, we know that Congress, the Senate, Fortune 500 countries, University Presidents and other industries have plenty of Jewish representation. For our small representation of the US population, 2%, our strength is the real meaning of the word, disproportionate. We punch far above our weight.

Yet the hatred numbers and rise of antisemitism and anti-Zionist incidents are skyrocketing. How do we square the circle of being a group that has off the charts numbers of being respected and off the charts proof of being hated at the same time?

Anti-Zionism and antisemitism are like a Havdalah candle. The wicks are twisted to and from. They meld together. It is virtually impossible to dissect them. As they burn, they are a single flame.

To complicate things more, before October 7th there was a large group of people in America who were proud of Jews and Judaism and ashamed of Israel. At the very same time, there was another large group of people in America who despised Jews and loved Israel. (If you are struggling with who fits into these categories, think (INN) If Not Now – and Steve Bannon as examples).

Those groups tried to dissect the Havdalah candle.

The former group were big proponents of the BDS movement, which attracted Jew haters from oversees and helped their cause. What I had noticed about many BDS supporters is that they were as much anti-Israel and barely, if at all, pro-Palestinian. Meanwhile, the latter group falsely thought that by being pro-Israel, true Jewish Zionists would turn a blind eye to their xenophobia and moral cloudiness. They were dead wrong.

There is one relatively decent thing about BDS. It is not violent. Considering October 7^{th,} I appreciate the BDS form of warfare much more. However, the biggest flaw with BDS is it presumes with the stroke of the pen, the 75-year conflict is over. BDS refuses to take into effect six overtures throughout time that serious gestures for peace were rejected.

This generation of Palestinian youth has inherited a crappy fortune from the choices of their ancestors. That does not need to be Israel's fault. From what I am hearing and reading, that seems to be a choice Israel will divorce themselves from in Gaza. Declaring that they will have NOTHING to do with Gazans welfare or well-being or survival, as part of the end game of the

Hamas dismantling and this war. I will bet you, dollars to donuts as my dad would say, that somehow the international community and the Palestinian people will still come to blame Israel for any misfortune and mistreatment they are subject.

What I think I am really trying to get at is, anti-Zionism **IS** antisemitism. They are the very same. It is impossible to love the Jewish people and despise the Jewish state. And I do not want the love of the Jewish State from anyone who cannot love the Jewish people.

Now let's get to the issue of dissonance. Many have trouble seeing you and me as victims, persecuted or as 'other'. That stems primarily from Jews being white (mostly), successful, well educated, affluent, influential and with access. None of those traits fit the classic characteristics of 'other.' Yet we are.

In our home, we have an additional member of our family. Our nanny. She has been with us for eight years and she helps with everything. She cooks meals, tidies the house, helps with laundry, and walking the dogs. When the kids were little, she was a built-in babysitter too. We all love and adore her, and she is included as a full member of our household. She is a black woman, originally from the Caribbean.

We eat most of our meals together in our home. All five of us.

One dinner, we started talking about attacks on Jews and I said something along the lines of *'we are hated and discriminated against. It is just a fact.'*

Our nanny, this devout Christian, black woman from the Caribbean said nothing. She did not need to. Her face said it all.

Her expression said to me, '*You live in this house, your tribe is not denied jobs anywhere, your kids have access to fantastic education, they can apply to any college, not once does your religion interfere with your acceptance at ANY college except maybe Brigham Young. You drive a nice car, live in an affluent neighborhood and have some shekels in the bank, and you are claiming victimhood? Really? I can tell you and your kids something about victimhood and being the subject or racism and hate.*'

She is right.

And she is wrong.

She is right because – heads of industry in retail, food, aerospace, and finance are proudly Jewish. Elected officials are Jewish. 2% of America is comprised of Jews and 10% of Congress identifies as Jewish. No other group is represented that disproportionately.

She is right because every major city in America has a Holocaust Museum. More than 200 universities have a Jewish Studies program that students can major or minor in. What are we denied as Jewish people? Putnam was right. Jews have arrived and are respected.

And she is wrong.

When you walk into any evangelical church in North America, visit any Catholic cathedral in the northeast, can she tell me how many security officers are there? How much are they spending on safety? Did they have police with machine guns out when congress people who are vocal in support of Jews are visiting a synagogue? Do bomb sniffing dogs come to Catholic or Mormon day schools when tensions are high in Israel? Why does our temple spend 15% of our budget on security? Why do we have to lobby congress for homeland security grants? Why are all synagogues, thankfully, crawling with police on the holidays and during these tense days?

Professor Deborah Lipstadt, the czar against antisemitism in America, lasers in on this dissonance.

She says, the radical left refracts their views through two lenses: ethnicity and class. In that image they see Jews overall as white and privileged. How could someone white and privileged be the victim of hate?

And those that sling hatred towards Israel with tools like BDS or make rude comments about 'the Benjamins' or compare moments in society to wearing Yellow Stars, they defend themselves with the shield of it being impossible for them to be prejudiced. They claim, *'Look at my record! My life has been shaped by fighting for justice for the persecuted.'* It is a fantastic forcefield to sling accusations and be protected from accusations.

Meanwhile, the radical right does not see Jews as white at all. They see Jews in evil cartoonish depictions thirsty for money and willing to do anything to advance their cause with no care for what it does to others.

The one place where the radical right and the radical left agree, is in dislike of the Jewish and Zionist soul.

Part of this challenge comes in the uniqueness that is *us*. We are a religion. We are a people. We are a culture.

As a religion, we are open to any soul who seeks to join us in faith and prayer and belief. We are comprised of men and women, straight and gay, people of color, born to and by choice, Jewish. We are open to all.

We are a people that are connected to a sacred land that is ours – called Boca Raton. And another land – like Boca, 5000 miles away called Israel, which has historical connections. Our people, indigenous to both places love to bargain, always assume they know best, and fight for their survival!

And we are a culture. We fight for the oppressed in South Africa and help refugees from Ukraine and march in Washington for freedom of Soviet dissidents and put-up lawn signs declaring Black Lives Matter. We are a tribe that is connected to a calendar, whether we pray three times a day or three times a year. We are bound by whitefish, hummus, herring and babka and all speak a shared language of *kvetch, shalom, shlep, nachas and shule.*

But because our identity is tied to **any** one of these things, a religion, a culture and a land, we are not necessarily **all** those things but are some, and that connects us to the greater whole.

I hope that made sense?!

In this moment of increased tension and concern, and growing unity and solidarity, some would rather assume they are hated and build up walls and be on defense. I think that is a fatalist and an imprudent pathway forward.

Some would like to believe that hate is pointed elsewhere and enjoy the fruits of happiness and prospects for peace. I think that is naïve and a careless pathway forward.

I am not sure of the best way forward. But I am pretty sure, it is not following either extreme.

This is indeed a rambling rant – a stream of anxious consciousness that validates the notion that if you and I struggle with who we are and how we are, I imagine others are struggling too.

The one thing that *has* happened because of this horrid attack on Israel is it has inched us all a little closer to one another. Some moved from the right and others from the left.

I am sickened that tragedy is Judaism's greatest glue and yet, I am heartened each time we draw closer. What a warped reality and itself, a strange dissonance.

Stay Safe. Pray for our soldiers. Pray for the end of Hamas. Pray for innocent civilians. Pray for peace.

16

October 21, 2023

I try and write these Streams of Anxious Consciousness each day. I do not use canned materials or pen them days in advance. Like a good chef, I want to serve up what is fresh on my mind, and not pull things out of the freezer. That is why these streams are an amalgam of the events of the day, the news cycle and where I am emotionally.

Today was a really hard day for me.

In July of 1981, I was 8 years old. Adam Walsh was just a year younger than I and had gone missing a couple hundred miles away from where I was living in Florida.

His poster was plastered all over the schools and ice cream parlors that I would ride bikes to with my friends.

I was petrified.

A boy my age taken away from his parents was more than my eight-year-old mind could handle. I spent at least a week sleeping in my parent's bed and was frightened that every stranger I saw could abduct me. I am not sure when my fears dissipated or if I just absorbed them into my being.

This morning, I met with people from Israel who survived the attacks on the 7th of October and/or have loved ones that are being held captive by Hamas. I cannot imagine a worse nightmare. Except, now, as an adult, I can see it from both sides; from the side of being abducted, and the terror of living with the reality of your loved one being kidnapped.

Knowing of the barbaric behavior of the Hamas infiltrators, I tremble to let my mind wander as to what might happen to those we love.

A story I heard about a man who was relieved that his 9-year-old daughter was found dead shocked me without surprising me. His story has gone viral. No one is relieved, so to speak, that their loved one is dead, even more so, a nine-year-old child. But to think they are alive and being held by Hamas, death is a more welcome consideration, and thus his reaction was understood.

I have suffered through the pain of having my kids hospitalized. It was during those times, I made serious negotiations and concessions with God. I know what it feels like when Life 360 stops transcoding my kids' whereabouts for an hour or what happens to my heart when they fail to check in at a given time. Whenever this happens, it causes unbridled anxiety. I cannot begin to imagine what each of these humans whose loved ones are captured are dealing with. It is beyond words and comprehension.

My frustration grows hourly at the barrel Hamas has Israel over. They are holding the entire country hostage. They are pussy footing with hostages and flirting with their release and stopping a full-on ground invasion. It is all psychological warfare and a continuation of Hamas' manipulation. Two more hostages were released today. Two more. Less than 1% of those who are being held. The choice Israel is faced with of what to do next makes Sophie Zawistowski (the lead character in Sophie's Choice) envious.

I understand America trying at all costs to get the hostages back alive. I really do. Were my loved one there, I would do the same. If my son or brother were Gilad Shalit, I would have released 2000 prisoners! There is no price tag too large for my parent, or child or spouse.

Hamas has a firm grip on our most sensitive and vital nerve. It only adds to their ruthless criminality.

To green light the ground invasion and let the tanks roll into Gaza, would be tantamount to signing a death warrant for each hostage. Each hour lost for the ground invasion allows Hamas terrorists another day to live, breathe, see the sunrise and contemplate their defense. The conundrum is a continuation of cruelty and injustice that has not ceased since the 7th.

The second event that winded my soul today was a clergy meeting where only one Imam in our local community agreed to attend. The other three Imams refused to come, out of protest. And at the clergy meeting, the Protestant ministers could not condemn Hamas without equally condemning Israel. I was flabbergasted.

For the record, the Protestant ministers and Pastors upset me less, but still caused major frustration. They equated Israel and Hamas because they lacked the vocabulary and history to be conversant in the matter and assumed they were equal. If being foolish was a crime, we would have *way* more overcrowding in our prisons.

In my world, I know what I know, and I also know what I do not know. If I were convened for a meeting to discuss the ongoing tensions between China and Taiwan, I would sit, listen and learn. But I would hope to shut-up because I am not well versed on the topic.

I do not fault my fellow clergy for knowing less than Jewish clergy about the Israeli Palestinian conflict. I hold them in contempt for speaking and acting on topics they do not know well. Our process of learning begins with not knowing.

I was gut punched at this meeting by the local clergy member of the Muslim faith who could not muster the courage to condemn Hamas - in front of me or for his congregation. He insisted that Israel is committing war crimes and crimes against humanity. He argued the years of oppression by Israel led to the events of October 7th and justified those heinous acts. For a tribe that bandies the words "proportionality" around a lot, I struggle with the occupational proportionalism that allowed the barbarism of October 7th.

I along with my fellow Jewish clergy member were relentless in breaking down any form of equivocation or condonation to the entire group. We did not give up. We asked in what name could we allow the brutality that took place on innocent people? What religion permits that? What God allows that? Which liturgy chants those terrible things?

Each statement we made was rebutted with what about-isms, yeah but, and faulty reasoning. Each statement was an equal condonation of innocent people on both sides, with an insistence that more Gazans are dying right now than Israelis. Exact statistics of how many bombs have been dropped by Israel were provided but ignorance prevailed on how many rockets have been lobbed over from Gaza. Assertions of occupation by Israel in Gaza were maintained but ignoring Israel's unilateral withdrawal in 2005 were glossed over. Facts were used conveniently but not universally.

The two Jewish clergy at the meeting were chasing our tails. We were never going to get this Imam to accept reason. I mean, how do we reason with the unreasonable? How do we converse with the irrational? It is as impossible for us as it is to expect Israel to have exchange with Hamas. To do so, is to legitimate them. To ignore them is to leave the hostages in peril. And what is most frightening is this religious leader has the ear of so many people in his community. What scares me most is, he was measured for our meeting.

The other maddening moment in our clergy meeting today was this Imam spewing untruths. He asserted that he is positive with verifiable proof that the hospital bombing came from Israel. He was hesitant to show that proof, but of course, he had it. He asserted that Israel is specifically targeting civilians. That Israel is carpet bombing all of Gaza. That Israel is targeting mosques and schools to kill babies, by design. That Israel tells people to evacuate and then kills them while they are fleeing. He went on and on. He joins a long line of those in the Muslim faith right now that pile on about Israel and defend the indefensible from their own ranks. These are old fashioned blood libels. Nothing new. It is shocking to see one up close, and personal, though.

My daughter received some emails and texts from her friends who are Palestinian in Israel, days after the tragedy. Some were full of condolence and lamenting the terrible turn their global relationship has taken. Others were more pointed and blaming Israel. When my daughter claimed that Hamas raped women and beheaded babies and asked how that could be condoned, they replied that Islam forbids touching a woman and hurting a baby, so that is a lie and it never happened. I would not have believed her were it not for her showing me these communications and me witnessing on my own social media feeds hundreds of hateful trolls claiming Israel was dishonest and those terrible things never happened. That these abhorrent attacks were disproven. That Israel was deceitful to garner sympathy.

It took about twenty years for Holocaust denial to surface. It took less than twenty minutes for it to bubble to the top after October 7th.

Israel was compelled to release the dreadful videos, captured from terrorist body cams, to prove the barbarous level of atrocities that happened. Read that sentence again. And then again. And again. Let it sink in.

I doubt the footage will persuade the nay-sayers. They are just haters. Deniers. Enemies. People who would rather blame someone else or excuse them instead of taking any responsibility and owning the truth, regardless of its sting.

What enrages me, though, is most of these truth deniers were the fiercest activists against the Big Lie. They were the same passionate liberals that warned of the dangers of election denial and January 6th and contended against those who said, *'It was a just a tour of the Capitol by peace loving, patriots.'* They were the loudest to surface climate change awareness and using the facts of science to shut down the opposition. They were the brashest when dealing with flat-earthers. But if the lie advances the Jewish hating narrative, well then, by all means, use it. Tell it. Sell it. Share it.

Hypocrisy drives me batty. This duplicity is so damn thick, a chainsaw could not cut through it.

I do not liken this moment to Holocaust denial lightly.

When I heard the accounts of those who survived October 7th and those who did not, and those taken captive, I could not stop thinking to myself, 78 years after the liberation of Auschwitz and these stories are identical. One group wore black and green face masks, the other SS uniforms with leather boots but, they had the exact same agenda. Terrorize, brutalize, maim and kill Jews. They were both painfully successful. It was déjà vu.

Whenever someone told me their story of survival from the Shoah, I marveled at how it was 20% cunning and 80% *mazal* (luck). The same could be said of the cases I heard this morning, and I heard less than .05% of these stories. Like September 11th, for every person who miraculously missed their flight that day, there were those who flew standby and got on the plane they were not scheduled for. There is no one to tell the stories of those who had the cunning but were without *mazal* on October 7th.

I had a stiff drink tonight. I hope it helps me sleep. There is no pill or concoction that my brothers and sisters in Israel can have to help them sleep. How does the mom who saw a video of her 20-year-old IDF soldier son being abducted from his tank and dragged into Gaza, sleep today, or ever again? What is she praying for? His release or his death?

Even if the miracle comes true and he runs into her embrace again, (please God may it come true) the nightmare will never dissipate in her heart and mind. She can never be whole again.

There is a phrase in Hebrew I said over and over today. *Ayn Meelem*. There are no words. There just are no words.

17

October 22, 2023

The scariest scene in the movie Schindler's List for me, was when the Jewish residents of Krakow were forced from their homes with only what they could carry on their backs. They were moving from beautiful, well-appointed homes to rodent infested slums in the newly designated Jewish ghetto. These finely dressed people, part of the higher echelons of society, were now full of fear as they marched down the streets to their new living quarters.

The Polish citizens of Krakow lined the streets to catch a glimpse of the Jewish humiliation. Spielberg focuses on a pig tailed, blonde girl who jeers in disgust and satisfaction, *"Goodbye Jews. Goodbye Jews. Goodbye Jews."*

Those four seconds were the most haunting part of the entire movie.

The girl did not kill any Jews. She did not vote for legislation to migrate Jews to a ghetto. She did not deny Jews trade or business. What she *did* represent was a population that was more than a witness. They were accomplices. Perhaps not in the most grotesque and vulgar ways that Nazis and some Poles were. But they did worse than merely turning away. They lined up for our expulsion like it was a parade and taunted us like we were sports players who let our city down.

The loneliness the Jews of Europe must have felt in those moments are beyond depiction.

The two elderly women who were released by Hamas last night, began to tell their stories. These are Savtas, Bubbies, Nanas, Mimis, Gigis. In one glance you can taste the sweetness of cookies they baked and wisdom they shared and the warmth in their embrace. They endured seventeen days of a living hell.

One of the released hostages explained that she was beaten as she was taken captive. She then went on to recount that as she, at 85 years young, was tossed over the back of a motorcycle and driven through the streets of Gaza to a pre-ordained, subterranean hiding spot, passers-by and citizens on the streets slapped her on the head, hit her body with sticks, spat on her and heckled her.

Read that again.

An 85-year-old grandmother, taken hostage from her home on a Shabbat morning, thrown sideways on to a motorcycle, is beaten and hit on the head and spat upon by random citizens of Gaza.

Hearing this, my mind went to the *"Goodbye Jews"* chant.

I am sensitive and sickened, at the same time, by the comments and concern for the good citizens of Gaza who are subject to Hamas' evil grip. Sensitive because innocent people are dying in Gaza, and more will surely die. The children of Gaza were born into this reality. They did not choose it. My heart aches for them and the fortune they inherited. Woe to me if I ever lose sympathy for people like these.

I am sickened because not everyone in Gaza is opposed to Hamas. Even the so-called innocent civilians.

If a person walking down the street who claims they are not supportive of Hamas or affiliated with their atrocities, and did not take part in the terrorism of October 7th, yet they slap a Jewish octogenarian on the head while she is abducted, are they fully innocent? Are they really disassociated with Hamas and evil? Do they carry no hate in their heart?

The doctor who checked on the health of these hostages does not fit into the category of an innocent civilian. No more than Mengele was just trying to keep his Hippocratic oath. I'm sure if captured though, that is the claim he will make.

A few years back, during the war of 2014 between Israel and Hamas, I was asked to speak at a large rally before the United Nations. I recited the following lines:

"If you wear blue jeans and a t-shirt but carry an AK-47, you are not an innocent civilian, you are a combatant.

If you welcome Hamas into your living room to fire off rockets, you are not an innocent civilian, you are a combatant.

If you vote for Hamas, aware of their charter and chant to kill Jews and the Jewish state and support their success, you are an accomplice to their terror."

I was raked over the coals by left-wing, peace-loving folk for those remarks. Ironically, many categorize me as left wing and peace loving. Sometimes, I like to see myself that way too.

I do not know how anyone can associate with criminals and thugs and cohort with felons and support their crimes, and then claim they are innocent. It is a very thin line that seems to allow for hatred, corruption, criminal activity and protect from prosecution and responsibility at the same time. It is kind of like holding a baby and firing a weapon.

In our world, if your pal and you go into a coffee-shop, and that pal pulls out a gun and robs the store and shoots the clerk, you are an accomplice, *UNLESS* you try and stop them. That is how our legal system works. More importantly, that is how our value system is structured.

This makes the already impossible task of decoding who is on the good team and who on the bad team in Gaza, exponentially harder.

My daughter shared a profound thought yesterday. She has reached that age where she has as much to teach me, as I do her. Bias aside, I am wildly impressed with her depth and thoughtfulness.

She said, *"Dad, I am so much angrier with the supporters of Hamas, than Hamas themselves."*

I understood exactly what she meant.

The Hamas terrorists are evil incarnate. They were indoctrinated, lied to and manipulated. They are cruel sheep. They are unchangeable and unforgiveable.

But the people on the sidelines, those chanting, dancing, demonstrating, supporting, equivocating, arguing for, lying and misleading should know better. Should do better. Just as we are soldiers in this war for Israel's right to exist and Jewish survival, those supporting Hamas are licensing terror and brutalization as acceptable and advocating for barbarism and excusing savagery. How do faith leaders, teachers, physicians, Ivy League professors and their students along with industry heads condone terror and support antisemitism?! It is profoundly non-liberal.

Did anyone condone flying planes into buildings in New York and Washington, D.C.? Blowing up theaters in Paris? Bombing trains in Madrid? Since when is terror acceptable in any Western society? Yet, there are those who dare to defend the indefensible. The disappointment in those people is overwhelming. And the proximity these people share to our communal orbits is terrifying.

Ironically, the majority of Israel supported a Palestinian state. The Settler Movement and the current Knesset are not representative of the nation. The kids shot up at the Nova dance festival were peaceniks. So were the residents on the Kibbutzim along the Gaza border. Hamas murdered the greatest proponents of peace.

Hamas didn't care. They still don't. They claimed for years and proved in their despicable actions that their enemy is every Jew and the Jewish State, not the right-wing coalition or the conservative settler branch or ultra-liberals and peace advocates.

Most tragically for us and perhaps successfully for Hamas, these events will tilt people rightward. They must. Defense will be the singular and principal issue for Israel for the foreseeable future.

Tal Becker, another one of my rabbis on all issues Israel, regularly says that Israelis and Palestinians are in a perpetual fight for victimhood. This is playing out on every newspaper and television screen today. In fact, much of the airwaves of our synagogue WhatsApp group and the bickering between me and the Imam of which I wrote yesterday, is really a contest over suffering and deserved empathy.

My mind keeps going back to the dais of survivors of the 7th I met yesterday. Each story horrid, detailed, tragic and piercing. But, amongst them, there was no worse or better. No one person fought for more sympathy or warranted more compassion. Each person is unenviable.

On the cover of one of the news web pages I subscribe to, was a teenage Gazan boy burying his parents who were killed in an airstrike. My heart hurt for this boy. Even if his parents were part of Hamas or were Hamas sympathizers, he is now alone to fend for himself. His prospects of escaping the clutch of Hamas or PIJ after these events are slim.

Then my mind jumped to a boy I met yesterday. Really a young man. He is a few years older than my son Maybe he is 19 or 20. He is tall, slender, handsome and soft spoken. I imagine he likes sports, music, has love interests. He struck me as a typical 20-year-old until the events of October 7th.

He retold his horrific story of survival from that painful day. He lost contact with both of his parents by text. His mom around 9 AM on the 7th and his dad around 11 AM. He does not know their whereabouts, their health, their emotional state. He is pretty sure they were taken over to Gaza and not killed because they have yet to be identified amongst the dead.

I was 49 when my mom died. While painful and sudden for me, she lived a full and beautiful 85 years of life. Entering orphanhood was hard. Anyone who no longer has parents can appreciate of what I am writing. Those who cannot, may you not know for many years.

Just a few days ago, the father of one of our congregants died, peacefully. He was buried with honor. At the Shiva, the mourning daughter who is tickling 60 years young cried to me, *"I have no parents."*

As someone who is also an orphan, I knew the loneliness and pain she was experiencing. She and I had the blessing of many years between the death of our parents. Me, 11 years since my dad died, and her even more from her mom's death. We both have financial independence, professional stability and maturity, and still, its pain is immeasurable.

This poor 19-year-old is without parents. Without maturity. Without independence or financial stability. His pain and fear are beyond comprehension. Yet, I hope, and chances are favorable, that this boy will lean towards peace. What creates that divide between him and his Gazan counterpart?

Don't feed me occupation. Do not peddle oppression to me. It is bigger than that. It is a mindset. A value system. An ethos and one that I am proud to be part of, even if it paints me as pollyannish and naive.

I have much more to share but there are more things for us to collectively help with in this moment. We have kids from Israel landing soon to live with aunts and uncles and cousins while parents are deployed to war, and school in Israel is cancelled. They need warm clothes for a harsher winter than they are used to. They need to be hugged and loved and supported and to know they are with a communal family that loves them. We have local family members whose spouses, siblings and friends have been called up to military duty and are on the Gaza or Lebanese Border. We have simchas to still celebrate and classes to attend. We have so much teaching and advocating for Israel still to do. October 7th was not only proof of

Israel's security failures, but it was also evidence of our failing to equip our most strident supporters and students on college campuses with ways to defend Israel and Jews in word and deed.

The day is short, and the tasks are many! Onward and upward!

18

October 23, 2023

I have spent the last 12 months immersed in feelings of grief and mourning. I had hoped to slowly break away from many of those feelings. Instead, I have been forced to dive deeper into them.

The Jewish world is mourning and grieving on a few levels:

- We are mourning the loss of lives of our Israeli family.
- We are mourning the loss of innocent civilians used as pawns by Hamas.
- We are mourning the loss of security Israelis felt in their country.
- We are mourning the loss of progress towards more stability and lasting peace.
- We are mourning the loss of reality, which was violently shattered on October 7th.
- We are mourning the loss of relationships of those we thought were allies friends and supporters but have proven they are not, and most painfully, *were* not.

This is an immense sense of loss that we are all just starting to come to grips with. We will be grieving for a while.

In the most practical way, Israel is still identifying the dead. Not until that honorable process is complete for every person, can each body be properly buried. To date, hundreds have not been interred. A family cannot sit Shiva and begin formal mourning until that happens. *Shloshim* doesn't start until the formal burial occurs. If the identifying process takes a few more weeks, the actual mourning will last for weeks. The mourning period will go on way longer than 11 months following the 7th of October. It will be generational.

Whenever we are broken, it is hard to imagine that we can ever be whole again. If we can, we struggle with what that wholeness will now look like, feel like, taste like. We are an impatient lot. Only time will tell us how these events will shape us. It is too early to know at this date and place.

I described to someone recently that I feel like I am watching a movie I have never seen before, but I know all the characters and am familiar with the plot and the directions of each scene. It is all original and modern, but nothing is new. It is a surreal and spooky feeling.

The stories of grandparents and warnings of worriers are happening in technicolor. They told us these stories. Now we are seeing them.

Confession
There is little more satisfying to me than being able to say, *"I told you so."* I know it is childish, but it reaffirms my confidence in my theories, beliefs and my own knowledge, that I often second-guess.

And as satisfying as it is for me to say that line, it is equally annoying for me to hear it said to me.

I hate, (not sure that is strong enough) that this moment has licensed an entire group of people to say to me, *"I told you so!"*

The people saying this are hard liners, right wingers, worry-warts and *kvetchers*. This moment has validated their beliefs and crazy theories. It has tilted the scales of correct versus incorrect in their favor. It is morally deflating to me and adds to my deep sense of loss.

I can live with defeat. I can even live with being wrong. What hurts so damn much in them being able to say, *"I told you so,"* is that it proves I was a bad judge of character and situations. I was naïve. Stupid. Simple. It makes me question what else I got wrong and what else they got right. It makes me self-interrogate my judgements.

Further, it creates a pretend ledger where I find people who are supporters on Israel, but who I disagree with on so many other domestic policies. Are we on the same side of the ledger? What else do we share on that ledger? Today, I need those friends to stand with me on that side of the record. What happens tomorrow?

When I use my voice in favor of a woman's right to choose or support government helping those who cannot help themselves, will these people standing with me feel abandoned? Will they jettison their support of Israel? Will it force me to compromise on values that I was before, unwavering on?! What will become of my moral identity and ethical code?

I am feeling abandoned. Alone. Sad. Worried about my identity and my choices.

Next

18 days later and I am still astounded at how otherwise educated people can be so stupid.

Yesterday, I asked our 7th grade Temple students to raise their hands if they love their parents. Every hand shot up. I then asked while their hands were still up, *"Raise your other hand if you have ever been really mad at your parents and even said words like, 'I hate you' to your parents."* In seconds, each of the 40 kids had both hands in the air.

Each kid quickly understood that we can love a parent and still have anger toward them. As we mature, we can replace 'parent' with 'spouse' or 'child.'

Why is the educated world unable to hold both hands up? Why can they not condemn Hamas and love Palestinians? How are they equivocating the evil of Hamas? How are they falling prey to Hamas and their propaganda and manipulation? And how and why could anyone think that by condemning Hamas, you are against any innocent person – especially children – in Gaza falling victim?

It is not complicated. Yet, faith leaders cannot raise both hands. University faculty cannot raise both hands. Industry heads cannot raise both hands. Some journalists cannot raise both hands. Many college kids cannot raise both hands.

For years we have been pushing a paradigm that to support one thing is to hate the other. To hate Donald Trump means we love Joe Biden. To root for the Yankees means we despise the Mets. That is a broken paradigm.

Are we not able to hold two truths? Truths do *NOT* have to be at odds with one another. I can condemn Hamas. I can seek their eradication. I can be hopeful that their extinction provides the best future for Israel and Palestine. I can also support a Palestinian right to sovereignty, safety and a future. I can also be critical of the Israeli government. For me to be right, you do not have to be wrong. That is a faulty structure for any argument.

Still, I do not want to be naïve to the tribal nature of the war that is happening and the imperative to demonstrate solidarity. Of course, I want to save Jews and protect Palestinian civilians. Of course, I want to eradicate Hamas and plant seeds of peace for a future with a prosperous and real neighbor.

But at the very same time, when I run into a burning building, the first person I am looking to pull out will always be my family. My flesh and blood. You would do the same.

When there are two children that need to be saved, but time limits us to only save one, I am saving the Jewish child and I am not apologizing for it. When I must decide if I am shooting the person holding the gun behind the baby and being accused of a crime or being killed, I am taking the shot. I do not relish that decision, but it is the one I am taking. *My* life will take precedence.

I am still coming to the painful reality that no one else, or at least very few, are standing up to protect me. I must protect myself and my family right now, first.

So too, Israel unapologetically is choosing to save itself, even though that will inherently mean the loss of others and condemnation from many. What matters in the wake of that loss is our mournfulness and not glee. Our relief and satisfaction, not delight and celebration.

1

Much of life allows us to hold two truths that do not need to compete with one another. We can raise a hand of loving our spouse and raise our other hand they can madden us.

However, there are moments and crossroads where we must make a binary, either/or choice. Today and tomorrow, I am choosing my family, my people, my country, my land, my tribe. And I do not feel any sense of shame or embarrassment for doing so. You should not either.

I think that brings me back to the astonishment of people and the piss-poor choices they are making of neither being able to hold two truths or picking the wrong side of the binary, either/or equation. People who claim to be woke yet condone the murder of Jews. A group that advocates for women but is silent about rape in Israel. A population that marches for human rights and freedoms yet ignores the rights of 242 hostages in Gaza and tears down posters raising awareness to their plight. They seem to be incapable of holding both hands up.

If they are becoming tribal and choosing one side or the other, they are choosing Hamas even though it defies every one of their liberal, woke and left-leaning values. To me, that sounds more like Jew hatred and Israel bashing than it does standing for a cause that does not line up on your ledger. It sure plays out that way.

I vacillate between hope and despair, energy and exhaustion. Right now, I am smack in the middle of both. Tonight, when I pray, it will be to God to lean with me towards hope, towards energy, towards love and peace. May that fuel me for the morrow.

19

October 24, 2023

These streams of anxious consciousness are really an expression of my feelings. They are raw, sometimes undigested, but sincere and authentic.

I start with that preamble today because I am feeling frustrated and discouraged.

My morning began early, with a radio show dialogue between me and an Imam based in Brooklyn. This is **NOT** the same Imam that I had breakfast with earlier in the week, which was the source of pain and frustration.

I hate that I need to state for the record that Islam is a beautiful religion, based on peace, love, tolerance and goodness. What a sad reality of the need to lead with such a declaration. My beef is not with Islam. It is not with Arabs. It is not with Palestinians. It is with Hamas and its supporters, its enablers and enthusiasts. How can anyone conflate the two?!

The dialogue began when this Brooklyn based Imam refused to condemn the atrocities of October 7th. This is the second Imam in less than three days that I personally encountered, who refused to condemn the murder of Jews. I was very tempted to leave the interview right then and there. How can I have a meaningful conversation with someone who is not well meaning? I do not want to hold space or dialogue with any person who cannot mourn the death of my people. At the same time, if I left the room, then the listeners would only hear one side, a false and biased one. Thus, I stayed. I might regret that decision.

The discussion – if you call it that – was downhill from there.

When someone lies and makes accusations, we spend more time repudiating their lies than we do disseminating the truth. It is exhausting and futile, especially from people that are divorced from reality, detached from facts and disconnected from truth. It is a never-ending game of whack-a-mole.

This Imam asserted I support ethnic cleansing and called Israel a genocidal country four times in a matter of minutes. That cooked my grits!

I do not tell black people what racism feels like. I do not try and mansplain gender equality to women or simplify sexual orientation to the gay community. Do not call me genocidal! My people know about ethnic cleansing, expulsion and genocide. 1/3 of my people, 6 million Jewish souls, were exterminated not so long ago. Stay in your lane, Imam.

Further, the hypocrisy is exceedingly thick.

'From the River to the Sea' is a genocidal chant. It is echoing Nasser, who proclaimed in Egypt that he would drive the Jews and the Jewish State into the Sea. The chant is about making the land, *Juden Rein* – a German phrase meaning Jew-free. It most certainly is not about two-states for two-people. Murder of kids at a concert, because they are Jewish, male or female, white or black, religious or secular, is the very definition of genocide.

Rallies in Dallas, Englewood, Chicago, New York and elsewhere that gather people waving Palestinian flags and swastikas, chanting 'Gas the Jews.' 'Hitler was right' is what genocide is about.

Sadly, I predict that most people chanting 'From the River to the Sea' could not tell you the name or location of the river or the sea of which they are singing about. Proving it is more about hatred than a value set. How pathetic.

Don't assert *'humanitarian crises'* to me. Thousands of Jews in the North and South of Israel have been forced from their homes and displaced for who knows how long? Israeli kids are coming to the States to enroll in school and get a small taste of normalcy. Do not talk to me about food insecurity and crippled economies when most of Israel, including its places of education, have been shuttered for three-weeks and will for months more. Families are broken apart by members called to service. I also know of a humanitarian crisis happening in Israel that is being glossed over.

Gaza does not own the narrative on victimhood.

Next
Lately, I have been realizing how wrong I was about many things.

Recently, I wrote that I thought Biden's solidarity mission to Israel was a bad idea. I was totally wrong. In hindsight, it was brilliant, necessary and game-changing. I also legitimized Israel's fence sitting when it came to the war between Ukraine and Russia a few months back. Huge mistake!

Russia controls Syria. Israel tried to appease Russia by not picking a side, at least not publicly and keeping Syria and its border, quiet. Many in the Diaspora were embarrassed by Israel's mollification of Russia. But I claimed that those people did not understand the geopolitical realities of Israel's choice and its need for safety.

I was wrong. Again. Morality matters. We need to stand with ethical and decent partners and those that demonstrate a moral code aligned with ours. We need to be less worried about those with no morality.

Today, Russia hosted leaders from Qatar, Iran and senior leadership of Hamas. They were literally given a red-carpet welcome. They had an audience with Putin. These are birds of a feather. The new axis of evil, North Korea, Russia and Iran are the very entities supporting Hamas, Isis and Al Qaeda and demonizing America and her allies, namely Israel.

Israel tried to stay neutral on the Russia – Ukraine war front. Lots of good that did!

This was a wake-up moment for me that there are no 'sides' to consider when it comes to sovereignty, safety and morality. We stuck up for the bad guys. We were silent about the good guys when they needed us most. Now the bad guys open Moscow for evil summits and embrace the masterminds of murder. What a colossal blunder.

There is no substitute for morality. Ever. Lesson learned. The hard way.

Next
For the past two weeks, I have been wrestling with the Tree of Life Shooting in Pittsburgh and October 7th and the distressing divide between local and world response.

Only five years ago this weekend, a gunman targeted and killed Jews praying in a synagogue. It was chilling and scary. It created a sense of profound dissonance for me.

On one hand, Jews were targeted in their places of worship for the crime of being Jewish. The dead were Holocaust survivors, the elderly, people with special needs, and those who could not defend themselves. It was a moment of helplessness. A remix of a familiar song.

At the same time, the faith-based world came out in a wide embrace of Jews in our moment of agony and fear. The Pittsburgh Steelers team attended the funeral of Cecil and David Rosenthal and added Jewish Stars to their cleats in solidarity with the victims and the global Jewish community. The cover of the Pittsburgh Gazette printed the first two words of the *Kaddish* prayer in Hebrew font, *Yitgadel Veyitkadash* on the cover of its paper. It earned the journal a Pulitzer Prize.

We were targeted, and yet embraced. Victims of one person yet, healed by the greater community. We were equal to George Floyd, of sorts, where are lineage made us targets and our death enraged the good and moral people of the community to stand with us in unity, faith, friendship, love and harmony.

What changed in those five years?

The number of dead was 130-fold in Israel. The enemies were many, as opposed to one. The slayings gorier and more gruesome than imaginable. But condemnation was slow, if at all. Empathy was weak, if at all. Support for Israel's right to defend itself was tepid, if at all. Corporate and University denunciation of antisemitism was feeble, if at all?

What differentiated the Tree of Life from October 7th?

For me, as a Jew, nothing. It was a rehash of that same song of antisemitism and Jew hatred. It was another target, this time louder, more painful than ever in my lifetime. Both sets of victims were innocent. Both groups were in their safe spaces. Both groups did nothing wrong, except being Jewish.

But for the rest of the world these two horrors were different.

Why? What made the difference? Is it Israel? An attitude change on Jews? A world stage versus a U.S. one?

I am trying so desperately to solve this riddle. Mainly because if I can learn what captured empathy in Pittsburgh or what repelled it on the 7th, well than I can utilize those findings to get a better result. That is the social scientist, alpha-male in me who is constantly trying to fix everything broken. I know deep down it will not be simple. But perhaps, we can all ask ourselves the same question and come to a collective answer.

Last
I wrote my very own meme today and flooded social media with it. I was proud of my cleverness.

The meme was about the shooting in Maine last night and the manhunt to find the shooter.

It read:

- I will not condemn the shooter unless we can condemn those he killed too.
- The shooter was under occupation for years.
- These victims deserved it.

- The manhunt that is happening to remove this shooter is unjustified. It is infringing on the civil rights of all Maine residents. It is genocidal. For shame!
- The shooters acts are justified. Maine and the people of the bowling alley are the real terrorists.
- Both the shooter and the state of Maine are equally to blame for this.
- This shooting did not happen in a vacuum.
- From the Atlantic to the St Lawrence, Maine will be free.

Read these statements and realize how ridiculous it sounds – until of course you are talking about Jews.

For some in my community it did not land right. It came across as harsh, insensitive and not the tone we want to take regarding a mass shooting and another people's tragedy.

For those it landed wrong with, I am sincerely sorry. I had no intention of being inconsiderate of the death and horror the citizens of Maine are dealing with today.

What this meme and the response from some highlights, are the spectrum of emotions and feelings our community is experiencing.

For me, today, I am feeling angry, snarky and fed up with the hypocrisy. I wanted to point out the absurdity of comments made in a context that could highlight our feelings. That is where I am today. It was different yesterday and will be different tomorrow.

That is what grief and tragedy do to people. They take us on a roller coaster of emotions and none of them are wrong, per se.

For one of the congregants who I spoke with today (and mind you, she could offer a clinic on how to disagree with respect, kindness and love) her worry was that memes like this are devoid of the empathy that this shooting in Maine demands from our people. The subtext of her comments to me was, *"Are we no longer empathetic, kind, compassionate people? Are we no longer going to lead with our values? Does our pain permit our snark?"*

It is a legitimate worry and one that I think is rooted in the fear that our identities might be changing.

We bristle at change. Yet, this moment is more powerful than our will to stand firm. October 7th will undoubtedly change us. How? Will it sway our moral code? Will it recalibrate our responses to tragedy? Will we analyze if one group abandoned us if we should do the same to them, (which was not the intention of my meme)?

I sure hope not. I wrote when this trauma first hit that being left alone by those I thought were allies has been a deep cut. But it never means that I will stop advocating for what I believe is morally right.

At the very same time, we cannot be passive about hypocrisy, silent in the face of antisemitism or hushed when facing equivocations. We now have been forced to wear battle fatigues. It is hard for many to don them, yet alone engage in combat. It is a new frontier. A sad and lonely one.

My meme was an attempt, perhaps a poor one, at fighting hypocrisy and tackling double standards. My empathy, or lack thereof, was the casualty.

I am still learning how to manage both simultaneously. We all are.

20

October 25, 2023

I marveled at colleagues who hours after October 7th turned to text and tradition for solace and answers. I was not there. I was too filled with rage, questions, hurt, shock and grief. I did not think the sages of old could help me.

Now, almost three weeks later and I am turning slowly back towards texts and tradition to soothe me. There are not many manuscripts made for this moment. Ironically, with a rich history of torture and pain, we struggle with why bad things happen to our people. Theological answers are either cheap or unsatisfying. It has left me sputtering for explanations and comfort.

I then turned to the Torah portion. This week we read the story of our first connection to the land of Israel, what was biblically known as Canaan. Abram makes a journey to this place and God emphasizes that Abram will leave all that he knows and is familiar with, to explore and settle this new land. There is tremendous emphasis on the new and unknown.

I do not have any formal psychological training. Still, as a pastor for almost 25 years, I have done my share of counseling and understand better than some, what lives underneath many people's feelings.

What I am witnessing is unprecedented anxiety. There is a tremendous fear of the unknown and this moment is *somewhat* unknown.

October 7ᵗʰ did not simply crack our belief of reality and belonging. It did not make a small fissure of our place in the world. It violently shattered that perceived reality. We are coming to grips with that violence and the irreparable nature of the destruction. This is all new.

Undoubtedly, our Jewish world will not be the same. It will not be business as usual for any Jewish organization, Hillel on campus, Israel support mechanism or Jewish house of worship. Our Jewish identities in the Diaspora and in Israel, the shared DNA that contributes to our identity, will permanently be altered. That is for certain.

What is not certain is *how* it will change for the Jewish world. In what ways it will be different? Where will it pinch and where will it comfort?

Not knowing what will be is reason for our unease and angst. For those history buffs, if we turn to our old playbook when faced with a reality like this, the forecasts for our future seem dark.

In the world of biblio-drama – where we project the emotions and feelings of biblical characters into our conversations – I imagine Abram would be loaded with anxiety for his impending journey. Will he be hungry, welcome, challenged, happy or fulfilled?

Anxiety, especially amongst Jews, can bring out the worst in us. We go to dark places. We assume the worst, (not always by character – often by experience). Remember that old joke? What is the difference between a Jewish optimist and Jewish pessimist?

The Jewish optimist says, 'It cannot possibly get worse than this.' The Jewish pessimist says, 'Yes it can.'

This is a time that demands neither optimism or pessimism, rather realism; calling balls and strikes and being honest with ourselves and others, even in the face of the uncertain and unknown.

Someone earlier today said to me, *"Rabbi, I never thought we would be looking down the barrel of another Jewish Holocaust here in America. Yet here we are."*

I did not say anything. I just hugged him. I know those words come from a real place of fear and anxiety.

At the same time, I disagree with his assessment. This does not feel like another Holocaust to me.

In 1939, the German Government were the powers enacting the laws against Jews. Today, the United States Government has been full throated and unwavering in their support of Israel, and Jews nationwide.

The horrors of the Holocaust barely harvested world sympathy for the Jews. Today, when faced with loss, we have universal sympathy from those who share our moral coordinates.

During the Holocaust, there was universal apathy. Today, we are facing antagonists and indifference, but we are also welcoming fantastic support.

During the Holocaust and before, we were limited in our influence, access and resources. Today, we hold that trifecta.

In 1939 we had no state of Israel. Today, we not only have a State, but the State has powerful friends and can unleash immense power to repel many enemies. It is not impervious to enemies, but Israel is far from weak.

As a population, we seemingly can look at an art installation of a two-thousand tile mosaic and focus on two tiles that are missing. We are a kvetchy lot. A worrisome lot. A fearful lot. An anxious lot.

We do have much working for us, even if not ideal or perfect. Much of the international world stands with us. Some publicly, others privately. There are many assemblies and rallies where Palestinian sympathizers have gathered. Some have been violent, like in New Orleans yesterday. Most of those gatherings have as many or more Jewish supporters present. As hard as it might be to fall into a familiar posture, we must stand firm in realism.

I do not think we are on course for another Holocaust. I do think the Middle East is becoming a tinder box and needs to be dealt with carefully, and thoughtfully. It is a delicate line to walk and a new path for all of us.

What makes people use phrases like the one the congregant shared with me, is because we do not have a vocabulary for right now. We are fluent in pain and past, and conversant in hopeful and future. But what is the expression for this moment?

Abram had no vocabulary for the moment. He did have grief and anxiety. His dad had died as soon as he started the journey, and he offered his wife up to the Pharaoh out of fear he would be killed,

STREAMS OF SHATTERED CONSCIOUSNESS

demonstrating both emotions. But the language Abram could have used in the face of his uneasiness is missing from the text.

All this is to say, that from the time of the Bible to today, new and uncharted is difficult. Creating a new language is complex and appreciating a new reality is challenging. This makes an already hard moment, event harder.

Next
I really have not written much about the hostages. Maybe unconsciously my mind cannot go there. I cannot fathom to think.... just cannot imagine the heartache and sickness these families are enduring, which might be as painful as the treatment of the captives.

What I do not understand, regardless of what your upbringing is, irrespective of if you were opposed to the occupation or wanted to establish more settlements, is how anyone can deny the hostages plight or our collective demand of their release.

I do not know how to unpack students and faculty at universities along with people on the streets tearing down these signs. What could motivate a person, especially one that traffics in 'wokeness' or inclusivity to deny any human suffering?

These are not *I Stand with Israel* lawn signs. This is not about unabashed support for Israel. It is about humanity and suffering. Who would be opposed to that? They are women, children, elderly and the infirm. For God's sake!

I wish I had a solution to this level of hatred and blatant antisemitism. I do not. But it really hurts to witness in real-time.

Last

For years we were worried about who we were offending in our words and actions. We tiptoed through statements and proclamations and had our antennae up for anything that even rhymed with offending us. When Bernie Sanders said *"All Lives Matter"* he was excoriated for being insensitive to minorities, Black people in particular. I can call Bernie lots of things. Insensitive to suffering of others is not one of them.

We wore kid-gloves. We were governed by fear and not virtue. What that timidity did was threaten our ability to use our moral voice. It made all types of different groups vying for the sole rights to suffering and did not create more chambers in our heart for shared empathy and compassion.

My old boss used to say, when we stand for something, some will be with us and others against us. When we stand for nothing, we will always end up standing alone.

We are beginning to witness the veracity of her statement. We must learn to stand for what is right, good, moral and meaningful. It might offend some, but it will allow our heads to sleep in a soft pillow. We cannot stand alone.

The past decade or more has been a strange time where people's knives have never been sharper, and our skin has never been thinner. That is a dangerous combination. We need to blunt those knives and thicken our skin. We need to laser in on the intentionality of the person uttering the words or doing the deed, and less on the single broken tile in their spoken mosaic. We can be better. We must.

As the sun sets this Shabbat, I will gather with my community not at my Temple but, in the town square where a Shabbat table of 222 empty seats will be made. It will have highchairs and wheelchairs to signify the age disparity amongst the hostages and the emptiness and brokenness that exists. I saw the organizers setting up the scene, and it already cracked my heart in half.

I do pray that at this vigil, our diverse community unified in our love of Israel and our commitment to bringing the hostages home, lifts my spirits, connects me closer to God, and affirms my hope. I really need that right now.

I wish you a Shabbat of peace and light.

21

October 26, 2023

As I start the 21st episode of Streams of Anxious Consciousness, I have lost track of what I have already said, or maybe I just thought it and never wrote it down. Perhaps I said it at some other class or sermon. My brain is like oatmeal these days. My apologies. If anything is redundant, I hope it either reaffirms the statement or, reminds you of the sentiment.

About 25 years ago, I was at Ben Gurion Airport waiting impatiently at the El Al check in counter. A man was cutting the line, person by person. He was not leapfrogging dozens at once. After one look, each person moved their luggage to the side and allowed this man to pass in front without a word being said and no scene erupting. Israelis can have sharp elbows. Seeing this go down without any cuffuffle was strange.

As he got closer, I noticed that this man's button-down shirt was ripped wide open over his chest, a Jewish sign that this man was a mourner. No one in line knew him. We all knew he was grieving, and we responded individually, by allowing him the courtesy of not having to wait longer than necessary.

That moment highlighted the brilliance of the Jewish custom of *Kriah* – the tearing of clothing or pinning the torn black ribbon that adorns our chest when one of our relatives die. It is an outward sign to the world of what we are feeling inside.

There is no ribbon or tear for this moment. I feel like I am hemorrhaging and people around me are walking by, wishing me a good day, offering unsolicited smiles and cheer. Can't they see my wounds? My pain? My hurt? My sadness and grief? It feels like such a part of me, but still not visible to the naked eye.

When men or women lose hair on their head and eyebrows from chemotherapy, it usually is an outward emblem of a tumor that is not visible to the naked eye. It is a sign of a disease that is wreaking havoc inside our body.

This moment feels like a virus has taken over our feelings and controlling our emotions, but there is no tell. No giveaway to the person on the street.

Last night before Shabbat, I attended a vigil with Jews and Zionists from our area. There must have been 5,000 people assembled. Many were wearing shirts that read, *"Bring Them Home."* Others gathered were draped in Israeli flags. We held 222 red balloons that were released at the same moment for each hostage. There was a long Shabbat table with a seat and picture for every soul that is being held captive.

That gathering hugged my spirit. It was exactly what my soul needed and exactly when I needed it most. It was a balm to my aching heart because it reminded me, I was not alone. *We* are not alone. Much like when I drive up and down the local streets or when I frequent shopping centers and I see signs that read, *"We Stand with Israel,"* I am reminded that it I am not a singular soldier against a mighty battalion. We are many. Those numbers give a boost of strength and invigorate our spirit.

The vigil was also a moment where all congregated could see through the outside layers of the feelings we were experiencing inside our bodies. Everyone there was suffering a similar pain. Our shirts and flags we wore on our backs, were figuratively torn. We could see each other's wounds and taste each other's agony. We were with those who were able to see our scabs on the outside and know our anguish on the inside.

Next

This Shabbat we read the story of Sodom and Gomorrah. Abraham begs God not to destroy the town for fear that the good will perish with the bad. Abraham begins to barter and beg God that if he can find 100 upstanding people inhabiting the town, that God will not destroy Sodom and Gomorrah. They barter all the way down to ten righteous people. Abraham loses the negotiation and God destroys the corrupt town and the wicked people therein.

This biblical story blasts haunting echoes to our modern world. For those protesting the bombing of Gaza today, giving you the benefit of the doubt, you are like Abraham asking Israel to pull its finger away from the trigger because the righteous and good should not die with the wicked. That is a worthy request and a noble ask. It is consonant with Jewish values and mirrors the expressions of Abraham.

I have great pride being connected to those seeking peace. I am honored to be part of an army that responds surgically to terrorists in response to the indiscriminate butchery they subjected my people to. I am grateful to support an army that protects its civilians and does not target innocents. I am proud of my people that worries and weeps for guiltless souls.

124

I am also not naïve enough to purport that the innocent will not be the casualty of Israel's actions. Some will be. They have already been. Children did nothing to earn death by bombing. My heart cries for them and for the reality that Hamas has subjected them to. It is excruciatingly painful. What the protestors and I really disagree with each other about is *who* is to blame for those deaths. Not whether their deaths cause us hurt and pain.

Next

A few days before October 7th Israel was in its 3rd trimester of protesting the current Knesset and the right wing, authoritarian direction the government was headed. What many of my Israeli friends expressed to me this summer was that if more tax dollars go to the Ultra-Orthodox who do not serve in the army and who abuse the welfare system, and if we lose the democratic nature of the state, and checks and balances in the regime disappear, that they will leave the country. Officials were afraid of 'brain drain.' That is where the best and the brightest realize their potential is maximized elsewhere and they leave Israel. It was a serious concern that lurked prominently during the judicial overhaul protests. Hundreds of thousands of Israelis were prepared to pack their bags and no longer live in Israel, serve in the military and pay taxes to a place that does not reflect their ideals.

One month later, and the country is facing a second fear of 'brain drain' – though radically different in nature. If Israel cannot respond to Hamas with a devastating blow that will make them wish October 7th was never carried out, and if we do not scare the fecklessness and shamelessness out of Hezbollah and Tehran and all its proxies, these very enemies will be emboldened, and Israel will be weaker.

She will become weaker because no one will choose to live and raise their family in a place that is not secure. I would not stay in a hotel, regardless of how many stars it boasted if it was not safe for me to sleep and night. Neither would you. Nor should anyone. Our safety must be paramount. Who would live in a country that has an unprecedented level of evil and savagery at is doorstep and let it continue to live, breathe and exist? Who would ever be able to sleep at night in Israel again, if this threat is not eliminated? We cannot afford to lose one soul more in Israel because of our lack of security. Not only must Hamas and all terrorists be wiped out, but we must remove the element of fear, as best possible, from every Israeli psyche. We do that by not only eliminating Hamas, but by doing so emphatically and forcefully to evoke fear in our enemies. That is a language that the Middle East speaks fluently. It is foreign and grotesque to the Western world. Bridging that gap is no easy feat.

Related

I have often wondered if Columbine never happened, would there ever have been a school shooting in America? I think that the second most horrific result of Columbine was emboldening the dozens of copycats that have followed. Uvalde, Parkland, Sandy Hook were all impregnated in the minds of evildoers *after* Columbine.

I worry about the Palestinian Islamic Jihad, Hezbollah, the remnants of ISIS and Al Qaeda who not only celebrate October 7th but who will use it as a portal to expose the porosity of our vulnerabilities. That is the most compelling reason to eliminate Hamas so damn hard, that those slivers in the portals of vulnerability our enemies salivate over, are closed fiercely and swiftly.

My last thought today is from an ancient fable about a prince who turned 13 years old. For his birthday, his father, the King gifted him a horse.

The country folk announced how lovely that the prince now has a horse.
The town sage said, *'We will see.'*

A few weeks later, the boy fell off his horse and broke his leg.
The country folk announced how terrible that the prince was injured.
The town sage said, *'We will see.'*

A few weeks later a war broke out, and all men over 13 with a horse were drafted to the army to wage battle. The boy had a broken leg and could not serve.

The country folk announced how fortunate that the prince's injury prevented him from service.
The town sage said, *'We will see.'*

A respected and revered rabbinic colleague reminded me of that story when he scolded a group of people on his social media page who were strutting their *"I told you so"* to the world. His terse response was, let's just see how right you really are. Time will indeed tell.

This is not a moment for intellectual haughtiness. It most certainly is not a time for arrogance or overconfidence. It is a time for unity, humility and kindness. It is a time for all of us to channel our wisdom and pause and to utter the words, *'We will see.'*

Shavua Tov.

22

October 27, 2023

My definition of fanaticism is when people manipulate words or weaponize religion for unintended intent.

Fanatics are running rampant and co-opting words that used to be benign and are now seen as evil. Meanwhile, evil words have been sanitized, all in a fanatical pursuit of distorting truth and manipulating narratives.

I want to reclaim a bunch of words, express their true intentions and make clear delineations of what we could and should say. I also want to take note of words we need to use sparingly or should trash, because they belong at the bottom of our lexicon.

The word Zionism originated as a pursuit to establish a Jewish State. It now refers to the development and protection of a Jewish nation in the land of Israel. Zionism is all about the right of a Jewish people to have a homeland. It is *not* a bad word. It has been co-opted by haters as a weapon and used as a derogatory term. Ironically, it is a badge of honor. A word of praise. It should be used loudly, proudly and freely.

The term 'Woke' stems from African American vernacular English that alerts people to racial prejudice and discrimination. It has evolved in recent years to represent a liberal leaning bias to be supportive of LGBTQ awareness, racial justice and social inequalities.

This word has also been co-opted, but by a different extreme to devalue social justice and denigrate those who seek to help the downtrodden and are politically progressive.

The essence of these words and the movements behind them are good at their core. Why would we allow anyone the right to hijack these words and manipulate them to serve their goal, especially when they do not represent the definition?

I should not need to use a semicolon in defining myself as 'woke' or a 'Zionist.' Why do I need to apologize or give detailed explanations when using those words? I know what those terms mean. I do not need or want crazies and fanatics to ascribe their definition on to me. Shame on them. And I do not want fringe elements of those groups to define what we do and do not stand for. I know what we are all about.

At the same time, there are a few bad words we all need to be reminded of too.

Antisemite is more than Jewish hatred. Semitism as first used by a German historian in 1781, comes from the idea of languages from a Middle Eastern origin. Almost 150 years ago, a journalist referring to the hatred of Jews coined the phrase, antisemitism. The phrase stuck because the idea was prevalent.

Today, antisemitism means more than Jew hatred. It connects historical, political, religious as well as social streams of Jewish identity and advocacy and bundles them as one. Because Israel is a Jewish State and the indigenous homeland of our people, to be anti-Zionist is to be antisemitic.

One of my favorite illustrations of this comes from Congressman Richie Torres. He says, *"Could anyone imagine saying I hate Puerto Rico. It is a horrible place that is riddled with horrible things, and I do not like the way people behave there. I despise their terrible policies and are cruel to the animals and the indigenous people of the land. It deserves to be wiped from the map. But I love Puerto **Ricans**!"*

That is beyond absurd. The place and the people are intrinsically connected. Anti-Zionism and antisemitism are one and the same.

Of course, Israel and Zionism is rooted in democracy, which allows us to question and take umbrage with our leaders. We are encouraged to disagree with our government when it does not suit us. Some would say, it is a requirement of Israeli citizenship. But being critical of a government is not being opposed to the existence of a state. Most Americans can explain that distinction easily.

We need to treat the label of antisemitism with disgust and revulsion. It should hold similar weight to terms like racist, rapist or pedophile. The very lowest scum of the earth traffic in antisemitism. Its degree of offense needs to be elevated.

Ironically, many who play in the sandbox of wokeness, and social justice are not thinking twice about playing in the world of antisemitism. I cannot get past the hypocrisy. To call a woke activist racist is a great crime to their character. So too, must we do the same with calling them antisemitic, when they behave in that manner.

Many such people misusing the term woke feel invincible against such labels. They see the world refracted through two lenses; oppressor and oppressed. Oppressors are usually wealthy, white and have entitlements. The oppressed are usually of color, economically challenged and stretching to achieve. Oppressors have power. The oppressed are powerless.

If you look through these lenses only, like so many activists today do, with no history, facts, nuance or understanding, one could wrongly deduce that Israel oppresses and Palestinians are oppressed. But that is not the case.

Many of these naïve foot soldiers might have received an education in top notch schools, but they are stupid. They march blindly for causes they know nothing about. When anyone who claims to love liberal values tears down signs of civilian hostages taken against their will because they loathe Israel. Or they falsely call Israel oppressors, it boils down to nothing more than antisemitism. It is that simple. It is not complicated. They *must* be called out for their unashamed hatred.

These so-called activists are stooges. A stooge is someone that does evil people's bidding for them, without even realizing how they are being manipulated. They foolishly correlate that supporting the oppressed Palestinians means they should stand with Hamas. They are clueless. A stooge cannot contemplate for themselves. The stooge thinks vilifying Israel and claiming the hostages are deserving of their fate is morally sound. It is preposterous if it were not so sad.

I am going to try to add a new word to my lexicon and you are free to use it and disseminate it widely. It is an antisemitic stooge, or A.S.S. for short. Allow me to share some examples of who an antisemitic stooge, (ASS) is.

If you decried the bombing of a Palestinian hospital by Israel but were silent when evidence proved the missile came from Hamas, you were never really angered about the death of innocents in a hospital and children dying. You are an antisemitic stooge, (ASS) who unfairly targets Jews and Israel.

If you want Israel to be found guilty of war crimes in the United Nations but are radio silent when Hamas headquarters are uncovered smack in the center of, and underneath a hospital, you are an antisemitic stooge, (ASS).

If you scream in frustration that Israel is blocking fuel from arriving in Gaza, but your voice is squelched at the endless fuel used to propel rockets towards Israel by Hamas (which requires hundreds of gallons of fuel for a barrage to get airborne), you are an antisemitic stooge, (ASS).

If you wag a finger at Israel for bombing civilian targets and are speechless at the 25,000 rockets to date, that have been launched by Hamas on civilians in Israel, you are decidedly an antisemitic stooge, (ASS).

If you blame Israel for a paralyzing siege over Gaza that has denied food, aid, supplies and restricted travel for Palestinians but conveniently ignore the materials that were at the disposable of Hamas which were used to assemble thousands of rockets and mortars that were brought into Gaza, the 100,000 machine guns in the hands of terrorists, the thousands of pounds of dynamite, the scores of grenades, the millions of tons of concrete used to build terror tunnels, and the at least 500 Gazans who as recently as last month were able to freely travel to Iran for terror training, you are an antisemitic stooge, (ASS).

If you fault Israel for stifling technological advances or limiting trade in Gaza but seem to forget the elaborate ventilation systems used to oxygenate tunnels or the access to millions of cell phones, iPads, and truck loads of Go-Pro cameras strapped to the bodies of terrorists, you are an antisemitic stooge, (ASS).

If you claim Israel is lying about the atrocities that occurred in Jewish homes and deny that people were tortured because you have seen no proof, even though Israel was compelled to disseminate pictures and videos, yet you take the word of Hamas on numbers of injuries and deaths and how many of those are civilians and not terrorists, you are an antisemitic stooge, (ASS).

If you senselessly claim that 230 hostages deserve their fate, and you equate their captivity to the 4300 Hamas terrorists in Israeli jails. Yet, you ignore that those terrorists in jails were given a fair trial in a democratic judicial system, they are served Halal food, are offered prayer mats and prayer space five times a day, a chance to study the Quran daily, given medical care and attention as needed, are afforded opportunities to talk and see family and walk outside, when none of those things are given to the 230 Jewish hostages, you are a raging hypocrite and an antisemitic stooge, (ASS).

If you have repeatedly tossed the phrase, 'proportionality' around but are fine trading 4500 felons for 230 innocent civilians, you are an antisemitic stooge, (ASS).

If you are sure of the pain inflicted by an Israeli bomb but question the veracity of the stories Israeli victims of terror endured, you are an antisemitic stooge, (ASS).

Most of the antisemitic stooges I see are mired in hypocrisy and steeped in double standards. Not being able to treat situations equally adds proof of the viral crime of Jew and Israel hatred.

It is time for us to reclaim our vocabulary and draw distinctions between good and bad, right and wrong in those words. We should not be ashamed of being Woke, Zionist or activists. Whereas antisemitism should be a label of embarrassment, shame and disgust. If anyone claims the above, make sure they know the title they wear. They really are an A.S.S.

And anyone who uses the former part of any of the arguments above needs to be rebutted with their hypocrisy and shamed for double standards and their silence. They can and should be labeled loudly, an antisemitic stooge, (ASS). Feel free to use ANY of these examples to print or broadcast media, social streams or around the lunch table. We can be loud too!

I wish all a week of peace. May gladness rain and joy increase. We need that so badly!

23

October 28,

Today I am sharing three disparate thoughts which are indeed streams of consciousness that have me quite anxious. I will start with a controversial thought.

Before you judge that which you are about to read, please pause. Three short disclaimers.

First, I have no shlep. I'm just venting an opinion to the atmosphere. This is not me making direct suggestions in the ear of the Secretary of State.

Second, I have no idea if what I am about to suggest is the right thing to do. I feel it in my gut. But I am not positive.

Third, those who disagree with me surely have every reason and historical basis to argue their point. There is no right answer. I certainly understand the other side.

I think Israel should accept Yahya Sinwar's (Hamas' second in command) <u>offer to swap</u> all of the hostages for approximately 4500 Hamas felons currently in Israeli prisons.

Yes, many of those felons have bloody hands. Yes, most of those felons are sworn to Israel's destruction. Yes, most of those felons and Hamas will celebrate their return. Yes, releasing those felons in essence, is rewarding Hamas for their savagery. Yes, most dangerously, it licenses and emboldens Hamas to do it again. Yes, it is wildly disproportionate – an ironic term these days.

I understand all of that. It sickens me to my core.

But I'm also a son, a brother, a husband and a father. And if it were my family member, I would do anything - and I mean anything - to bring them home.

There would be a few conditions of this exchange in my pretend diplomatic world.

- The prisoners would go to Gaza and not the West Bank.
- There would be no cease fire.
- Returning each captive includes bodies of the Israeli dead.

Why am I suggesting such an unequal swap and why such a radical approach of negotiating with sworn enemy terrorists who have done the unthinkable to our people?

Because we need hope, and we need it badly.

Hope is like a trick birthday candle. You can blow it, wave at it, whistle its way and it will never go out for long. It will flicker and burn again. We need to add fuel to our hope.

Israel's fortification right now will come from hope. It is not an accident that *HaTikvah*- 'The Hope' is Israel's national anthem.

Judaism is based on choosing life. It is focused on asking God every year to be inscribed in the <u>Book of Life</u>. We are a people that read in Psalms the importance of dreaming about tomorrow. We wake up each morning trying to turn those dreams into reality. We are a people that pine for weddings, births, B'nai Mitzvahs because they reaffirm life. That is core to our canon.

Hostages are deprived the ability to dream. Their hope is like that trick candle being doused in water. It will not flicker any more. It will not burn again. So too, will the flame of the families of the captives burn out. They deserve to have their hope restored.

Israel failed in its most sacred task of keeping its citizens safe. Let it redeem its mistake as best as possible and make this deal and bring them home.

Hope is the source of our eternal energy. It is what we need. It is why we are in business. It is what we cherish most. We need to see these sons and daughters, husbands and wives, moms and dads, bubbies and zaydies, back home. Those that were killed and brought to Gaza and those who died in captivity, need to be brought back and afforded burial in their homeland with honor at a place where family can sit and bring flowers and say prayers. We need them home.

Hamas dialed in to the most sensitive artery in our bodies. Life. I'll cede that win to them. We must preserve life and fuel hope with the hostages home.

Next
This Shabbat, we celebrated a Bat Mitzvah. That is no big deal. Thank God, our community has a Bar/Bat Mitzvah or two practically every week. But this family originally came from Israel and much of their family that had anticipated coming for this simcha were unable to leave the country for reasons like being

drafted to service or they were needed on the home front, or lack of flights going and coming to Israel.

When we have celebrations at the Temple, we share honors in our congregation. A dear family friend of the family was asked to lead the Prayer for the State of Israel.

This man leading the prayer made me look tiny. He was tall, strong and fierce. His presence was intimidating. He began the first words of the prayer and took a long pause. I looked his way and saw he was crying. The moment grabbed his emotions. He could not hold back his tears. The entire service paused for about 120 seconds until he could gather his composure. The pain and power of the moment was palpable for all present. It brought home the centrality of this moment for Israelis who are on the front line of a multi-layered war.

Another fascinating phenomenon happened in that moment. Cantor Singer and I were flanking this man when he started the prayer and broke down. We gave him his space. After two minutes, both the Cantor and I encroached the man and softly put our hands on his back. It was then, that he gained strength.

I am sure there is a name for this psychological phenomenon. It was powerful to witness in real-time compassion and touch giving another human strength and hope.

Shortly after that moment, a man walked into the synagogue, not really dressed for the occasion. He said he was watching services online but needed to be with us in person. I understood exactly what he meant.

We need each other now more than ever. We need to be close and physically present. We need to give hugs and hold hands and be patient with one another. We need to allow tears, anxious laughter, and giving the benefit of the doubt where we can. Humans and physical presence are the ingredients that will enable us to persevere this sad and familiar moment in our Jewish history.

Next
I am writing this Stream from Poland. It is my 24th trip to this country and it had been on the books for months. I regularly lead delegations from our synagogue here to take testimony to our history. When here, we learn about the thickness and prevalence of Jewish life in this region from the 1400s until 1945 with a focus on the events of 1939-1945.

October 7th has added a strange filter to the lens through which I am seeing this familiar place.

In two-dozen visits, I had become somewhat desensitized to the harshness and biting memory of the Holocaust. Of course, the potency of standing on the largest Jewish cemetery is never lost on me. But the shock and awe of physically being in that place has evaporated over time.

Standing under the signs of *Arbeit Macht Frei* was different today. It would be dishonest and unfair of me to tell you how it felt different. I am still metabolizing this visit. In time, I will share. But it was different. Not better. Not worse. Different.

The first undigested thought to surface for me, comes from Theodore Herzl. In 1902 he wrote a book called *Alt Nue Land*, German for *'Old-New' Land*. Herzl's angle was that developing Israel and claiming it as our homeland was an old and familiar place, at the same time. It is new and undiscovered. True! Every visit to Israel is a balancing act between trips to the Wall or Masada and learning about a tech start up and how Israelis have engineered growing cucumbers in sand.

Standing in Poland while my family is in America and my heart is in Israel, feels a bit *Alt-Nue ish*. There are eerily familiar echoes of ancient days, and the rapid and frightening rise of Jewish student hatred on campus feeds those channels of memory. There are different realities of the situation on the ground in both American campuses and Israel that do not make this an even comparison but enough that tickles those dark memories.

Like A*lt-Nue*, this moment seems known and new at the same time. That is comforting and scary, all at once.

Last
A college professor of mine once taught, the most complicated ideas can be made simple and the simplest ideas, are often complicated. Allow me to take something complicated and pose a simple rhetorical question to all of us to ponder.

On college campuses there have been groups like SJP (Students for Justice in Palestine) and others like it, for decades. Their primary focus has been registered as an advocacy group for Palestinian people and statehood. OK. A noble cause, on paper.

Each time a conflict arises in Israel, SJP and like-minded organizations get militant and target Jews on their respective campuses. Yesterday, at Cornell University, a group of students connected to SJP or one of its sister organizations or like-minded clubs, threatened Jewish students on campus and told them not to visit the Kosher dining hall or the Hillel because they will be tracked and *"raped, beheaded and even killed."*

Students in college who identify as Jewish are shaking in their Keds. They have been literally locked in their dorm rooms, afraid to venture to the halls to visit friends, or study in the library out of existential fear.

How in the hell does Jewish existence in upstate New York threaten SJP? Why does a conflict in Israel necessitate physical violence to a sophomore in the dining hall anywhere in the world? Is SJP about Palestinian Statehood and equality or is it about denying a Jewish state and a Jewish presence outside of the State? Based on this action, there is no debate. It is the latter.

I have strong feelings about how these students that are threatening Jews need to be handled. They need to be made an example of, loudly, that reverberates through every campus in America.

I also think we need to get bodyguards on campus for our students, at least for now, at the expense of these well-endowed schools so our kids can eat, study and enjoy college like any other student could and should. Being locked in a room for justified fear of being jumped or killed, is insane. What if one Jewish student on campus is seriously hurt or killed? What will we do then? Schools need to get smart quickly and nip this in the bud. Right now, the inmates are ruling the asylum. Students must feel safe on campus. College should be a place to explore, have fun, develop thoughts. Not a place to barricade oneself in a room for fear of danger outside.

I know that if threats to women were posted and those who identify as female had a fear of being beaten or raped, we would pay for protection on campus, as we should. Same if Black people or Muslim people were the targets. This is not tolerable. Threats against Jews needs to be handled equally.

It is time for every SJP member and all the protestors on the streets swinging poles over the heads of Jewish people and throwing punches on the boulevard, to pause and ask, why the militancy? Why the violence? Why the threats? Is it about building your future State or erasing our current State?

I know what answer it feels like.

24

October 29, 2023

I am penning this note from Poland. To be here now is in and of itself, surreal. To visit a painful Jewish memory while we have large and fresh wounds is strange, to say the least.

Today's Stream connects the dots of history and modernity and the murder and memory of Jews.

A few people, including Yehuda Kurtzer, wrote early on in this sad saga about the permissibility of using Holocaust language and imagery. It always was taboo to use the word Holocaust or to correlate any event to the years 1939-1945 that was not connected to the Shoah. But October 7th seemed to give license for Holocaust language and imagery. I suppose that is because of the gruesomeness of the terror and the genocidal nature of the terrorists. Also, as we have heard, it was the single worst mass killing of Jews since the Holocaust. Those seem to green-light comparing the two events. If that did not suffice, Gilad Erdan, Israel's Ambassador to the United Nations, choosing to wear a yellow Star of David on his lapel, seems to give us an OK to correlate the two moments in history.

This trip to Poland was missing something.

I am in Poland often. Every time I visit, there are busloads of Israeli kids walking down the tracks of Birkenau and being taught specifics about the camp and its history. It is reassuring to hear Hebrew when here. Coming to Poland is part of the mandatory High School curriculum in Israel.

Usually, at the end of the tracks these kids gather in groups, and they drape themselves in Israeli flags and sing *HaTikvah*. It is emotional. People witness that moment with wet eyes and soft hearts.

Today at Birkenau, there were no Israeli kids present. I did not hear one syllable of Hebrew spoken. Not an Israeli flag was to be seen anywhere in the miles of camp we traversed. There is an obvious reason those things were missing but its absence was eerie and felt. I had become used to it. I could not help but wonder if and when they will come back.

My rabbinical school classmate and friend Adam retold a question asked innocently on October 8th, 2023, by his young son.

"Dad – we have a day to remember the destruction of the Temple. We have a day to remember the Holocaust. Will there be a day to remember October 7th?"

Out of the mouth of babes. The subtext of his question is, if our historical anchor has been the Holocaust for the past 80 years, does October 7th supplant that, especially for Israelis? Will it join a long list of days we remember dead Jews? Will this day become part of that exhaustive inventory of groups that tried to kill us and failed?

When these high school-age kids draped in their flags would march at Birkenau, it was an outward expression of the most horrible time in Jewish history. Simultaneously, human witnesses - the actual fruit of this horrible time - coming forward to declare that we were victorious. Israel's existence was the unspoken declaration of *Never Again*. But it has happened again and again and again since 1945. In Rwanda, Darfur, Bosnia, Ethiopia and to now, to Jews. Just never in such grandness and never since the Holocaust for Jews.

Will Auschwitz now lose its potency for Israelis? Since October 7th has ignited the kindling for antisemitism, will October 7th replace Auschwitz (and its symbolism) for Jews worldwide? Will it cause its potency to diminish? I wonder.

When I lead trips to Birkenau, I always encouraged participants to pick up one of the millions of stones on the rail tracks and to put it in their pocket. If going directly to Israel after Poland or perhaps in the future, I instructed everyone to take the stone and press it against the *Kotel* (Western Wailing Wall) and share a kiss from rock to stone. Doing so would fulfill a dream that those who perished during the Holocaust could not taste the sweetness of. I know it is a bit kitschy, but it worked. It was my *shtick*.

My mind raced today. Where would we gather stones in Sderot or Kibbutz Be'eri? Where would we bring those stones to kiss? What would be the unfulfilled dream of those who died?

Next

Poland is loaded with memorials and monuments, and each have deep significance. Umschlaggplatz, the final deportation spot for Jews of the Warsaw Ghetto had always been one of the memorials that struck me. It is black and white, symbolizing the stripes of a prayer shawl (*Talis*). It has a large piece of granite hanging overhead to denote the load that awaits the journey. A sliver in the monument allows a tree to come into focus, signifying the narrow hope for those who could see it. On the wall of the granite monument inside the small, rectangular space, are about 200 inscriptions. They are common first names of people who lived in or near Warsaw and were sent to their death at Treblinka.

When I came to Poland as a father, I noticed that my kids' names, not wildly common, both made the list. I took my hand and gently touched the etched names of my kids, as if I were caressing their soft cheeks. Much like I see people in my synagogue do with the bronze *Yahrtzeit* plaque on our surrounding walls. Seeing my children's names brought a new potency to that memorial for me, ever since.

Umschlaggplatz Memorial, Warsaw, Poland

After October 7th, our Temple has included the names of those who have been injured, are missing or have died since the fateful day in Israel in different roll calls, memorials or prayers we have offered. The list had both of my kids' Hebrew names within the first 10 lines. I welled up and paused. My kids who have been to Israel more times than they have years of life. My kids who are fluent in Hebrew and in Zionism. My kid who spent a gap year living in Israel. My kids who know as many Prime Ministers of

Israel and the order of their service as they do American Presidents and their party. My kids who have spent more time in Israel than any other place besides their home. It is literally their second home.

Names on the Memorial

This is a long-winded way of explaining that the death of Jews, whether at the Tree of Life synagogue in Pittsburgh, Kibbutzim near Gaza, or at Majdanek and Treblinka death camps, feels frighteningly near.

Next

On June 14, 1985, TWA flight 847 was hijacked from Athens, Greece by Hezbollah operatives demanding the release of 700 Shia prisoners in Israeli jails. Shortly into the flight the hijackers realized Jews were onboard the plane. They demanded the flight attendant, Uli Derrickson, a woman of German descent, collect all the passports and separate the Jewish names so they could be divided amongst the passengers. Uli refused to do it. She courageously said to the terrorists, it felt like Germany and the selections all over again. She could not be part, even unwillingly, of a second generation of Germans who selected Jews for punishment and death.

I am sharing this story for two main purposes: First, the past repeats itself. Hezbollah is still a threat to innocent people. Ironically, the torture of innocent people for the release of prisoners is accepted by Hezbollah and Hamas, and the world seems to be silenced. If Israel were to collectively punish the Palestinian people for the crimes of Hamas, that would be wholly unacceptable. What a wild double-standard.

The second reason this story hits home now, is about the next generation fulfilling a similar trajectory to its ancestors, and the pain that path brings to society. An illustrative story to further the point.

In Krakow, there is a permanent memorial installation in what was the center of the Krakow ghetto, called Krakow Heroes Square. It is a large platform, flat with cobblestones that has an assembly of 70 empty chairs. It is illuminated at night, and the chairs are separated and organized in order. The emptiness of the chair is loaded with symbolism. In Polish tradition, every Christmas a chair is left empty at the family table for those who we want to honor and whose physical presence is missing. In Judaism, we have a similar ritual on Passover where we ask all who are hungry to come and eat and opening the door for Elijah. The emptiness of the chairs in the exhibit clearly represents the death and loss of life that the ghetto and World War II created for the city of Krakow and the Jewish world. The square is a regular stop on our Jewish history tour of Poland.

Except yesterday, most of these empty chairs in the square had a sign of a missing person kidnapped by Hamas on October 7th. Most of the signs were in Polish, while some were in English and a smattering in Hebrew. Locals passed by and read them intently and with empathy. I saw one man read the sign and cross himself. That got me.

My mind jumped to the TWA flight and Uli. Another generation making selections and another generation in Poland bringing a new symbol to the emptiness of the chair. Will that cycle ever end? Will those seats hold signs 20 years from now about Jews who are no longer? Is history really the circle game? If so, how do we end this vicious cycle?

Last

Speaking of the past repeating itself, inside the former barracks at Auschwitz I, there are quotes from SS leadership about their stated desire to rid the world of Jews, Gypsies, Romas, Sintas and other non-Aryan groups. The actual language that was used in German translates to 'exterminate', as if these humans were vermin. It was a genocidal decree that was the intention of Nazism. They were almost successful in their quest.

Genocidal chants and decrees are dangerous. For many, especially those who follow blindly, the words land on the ears of the listeners and are understood as doctrine that must be fulfilled and followed.

The phrase *"From the Land to the Sea, Palestine Will be (or must be) Free,"* is a genocidal chant. In 1967 Nasser said he will drive the Jews to the Sea. He was referring to the Mediterranean and hinting that with the help of Jordan and Syria, the three sides would encroach Israel from North, South and east and force Israel west into the Mediterranean. It was a decree calling for a mass genocide of the Jews in Israel.

The borders of Israel are such that whether we look at maps from the partition plan of 1947, or the post-Independence War armistice lines of 1948, or 1967 borders after the capture of Sinai, The Golan Heights and the West Bank, or 2005 when Israel evacuated all of Gaza, the land was, could have been or is partitioned for two peoples. To wish that Palestine extends from the River Jordan to the Mediterranean Sea is channeling the decree of Nasser and having a single country that is free of Jews. It does not ask for the peaceful relocation of Jews. The chant does not talk about two lands for two peoples. It is a genocidal ambition and should be treated as such by all those who are against genocide. Each time we hear that chant we need to call it out for what it is, a call for genocide. We must shut it down.

I close this note with a sadness and a glimmer of hope. We just learned as I write this Stream of the reunification of a female IDF soldier who was abducted by Hamas. It really is a miracle. The prayers of her family were answered. At the same moment, a similar age girl's family received confirmation that her lifeless body was found in Gaza, and the sad news was shared with her loved ones. We thank God for our miracles, and we hold tight our neighbors, both who are shedding salty tears, but for different reasons.

25

October 30, 2023

Shortly after the October 7th attack, I published three succinct talking points that I believed every major Jewish organization should have been pumping out to its constituents. I called it, <u>Sing from the Same Hymnal</u>. Making sure we are in concert with our messaging is critically important, not only to us, but in defeating our enemies.

Almost four weeks later, those original points still stand. It is time to add more to the list. Here is my attempt:

1. We mourn the loss of innocent life. There is no celebration over the death of any innocent child, of any background or religion. Jews worldwide and Israel lament the death of every innocent soul in Gaza.
2. There are more than 230 hostages being held against their will in Gaza. They have been in captivity for 26 days. They have had no access to the International Committee of the Red Cross (ICRC), which is a violation of the Geneva Conventions and International Law. Their families have been given no signs of life or well-being. We have strong suspicions about the physical and emotional abuse the hostages have been subject to. These hostages are children

as young as nine-months and senior citizens in their 70s and 80s. There needs to be a universal demand by all United Nation countries for the immediate release of each hostage, without preconditions.

3. There can be no cease fire. Not now. To put our weapons down today would be a victory for the terrorists. It would embolden the intentions of other evil doers. It would allow Hamas to recruit, rearm and renew their call for Jewish destruction. War is horrible. Still, sometimes, war is necessary. This is a just war. This is a necessary war to drain out a horrific evil and remove the oppression of the people of Gaza and the threat to the State of Israel. When Hamas is eradicated, we can have mature conversations about cease fires. Not today.

4. Humanitarian Aid needs to flow to the region. Food, medicine, drinking water, baby formula and toiletries must be made available for those in need. An international force should be deputized to ensure those supplies are not being hijacked by the terrorists, who deprive the needy, enrich themselves, and blame the starvation of children on Israel. The Jewish community joins the international world in its pain witnessing the suffering and malnourishment happening in Gaza and blames Hamas for their plight.

5. Anti-Zionism is Antisemitism. Full stop.

Feel free to disseminate as desired and necessary.

Next

If a picture is worth a thousand words, the pictures I am seeing are worthy of millions of emotions. Two pictures are dominating the see-saw of my emotions. They are flooding social media. The first is a lion, large and fierce, roaring with flames behind it and a tattered Israeli flag waving in the background.

To most, it denotes strength, vigor, independence and the Jewish State's ability to defend itself with immense power. I liken it to an image Rabbi Danny Gordis invoked long ago, of a young Jewish boy on top of an Israeli made tank praying with Tallis and Tefillin, immersed in prayer, a black M-16 rifle slung over his back.

Juxtapose that picture with Gilad Erdan, Israel's Ambassador to the United Nations who has controversially chosen to wear a yellow star on his Italian made suit.

His added accouterment is reminiscent of well-known picture of the young boy in the Warsaw ghetto wearing a tattered jacket with a yellow star sewn to its lapel, his hands in the air and fear painted on his face.

Meir Dagan, former head of the Mossad of Israel used to keep that picture in his office. When asked why by reporters, he would always reply, *"Because we are not going back to that!"*

The back and forth from those two extreme pictures and their connected narratives can cause vertigo. My entire life, from a young age until today, my Judaism and my Zionism has been shaped by equal parts of those narratives: strength and weakness.

We heard *"whisper the word Jewish,"* or *"wear a cap instead of a kippah,"* or *"all the world hates Jews – we have to stick together."* Those phrases have been abutted by a radically competing narrative.

"Israel is the only place that has planted more trees than they have removed of all the nations of the world." "Israel is the only nation that sends field hospitals and first aid to enemy countries to help in the wake of natural disasters." "Israel is leading the way in technology and medical advances to cure diseases." We can add to both lists.

In the center of what was the Warsaw Ghetto a large granite monument is situated. It is known as the Rappaport Memorial, named after its chief designer, Nathan Rappaport. It is two-sided. One side is a large carving of Mordechai Anilewicz, the leader of the Warsaw Ghetto uprising. He is holding a grenade, shirtless and mighty. He is flanked by men and women, religious and secular, some who fell and some who were fresh from battle. All wide eyed, wielding weapons.

On the other side of the monument is a depiction of Jewish men, women and children being exiled. Their heads are lowered and their eyes, heavy. One is holding a Torah scroll and another holding a baby. The Nazi helmets and bayonets are visible driving the Jews on their forced exodus, but the oppressor is easy to exchange, depending on when in our history we are hearkening back to.

This one monument is the duality of our existence and the polarity of our narrative.

I once penned an article called <u>Mr. Blue Bird and Chicken Little</u>, about two characters who were amalgams of two camps of thought in my congregation. One who only sees the blessings of our people and the other who would proclaim daily, the sky is falling. At the risk of quoting Billy Joel, we only go to extremes.

Why can't we construct a radical, solid, fierce and thoughtful center that lives proudly between our polarities? Why can't we see our strength and our fragility in the same eyeshot? If we can walk and chew bubble gum, defend our land and shed tears for the price of that defense, remember our past and be humble of our accomplishments, together we can live in that center where we belong and find balance, albeit wobbly at times.

Marcia Linehan developed DBT (Dialectical Behavioral Therapy) for people who struggle with an all or nothing approach. *'I love you and I am taking a break from you.'* *'It is raining, and the sun is out,'* are two examples of finding two truths, at the same time.

Much of our infighting comes from a collective inability of the people who are part of the polarities refusal to see the other side, coupled with radical dogma. Those extremes can be seen, heard, understood and appreciated much better if the vantage points are centered.

Related to power and weakness, most people 40 years old and younger have never experienced antisemitism before this moment. Those 50 and older, most likely have. That means that more than half of our population never knew that before 1967, and the miraculous victory of the Six-Day War, most Jews did not wear a Kippah in public. They either wore a cap, a hat or did not venture outside with a yarmulke. I am familiar with many households that as soon as the man and the boys of the house walked over the threshold of the front door, they took off their coats and donned a Kippah. It was a safe space. The reverse happened when they left the house.

The strength and seeming invincibility of Israel deputized Jews worldwide to feel secure and safe on the other side of that threshold.

Right now, Israel feels compromised, vulnerable and weaker. Jewish families worldwide are questioning whether we should remove our Mezuzahs. We can claim it is from threats, but it is as much from fear. There are no known cases of homes with Mezuzahs being targeted. Still, we want to be careful.

What does all this mean? To me, it is demonstrative that the State of Israel's very existence reflects the comfort we display in our Jewish identity in the Diaspora. The equation is simple; the stronger Israel is, the more comfortable we are showing off our yarmulke in public, so to speak. The weaker Israel is, the more fearful we are of having our Mezuzahs seen to the world. This is another obvious example of the connective tissue between Israel and Jewish identity that crosses rivers and seas and applies to Jews worldwide.

October 7th removed a blanket that we took for granted which had kept Jews outside of Israel warm for decades. Its absence has caused us to tremble in chilling fear.

Next
Partisan crap is starting to clog the pipes of aid for Israel. Rumor is that some in the House of Representatives want to divide the aid package between Israel and Ukraine so to pit the challenge for most Democrats of supporting Israel and showing support

for President Biden. It is a narrow-minded, childish, politically motivated stunt that plays games with life saving measures. This is not a new tactic invented by Republicans. In fact, Democrats did the same ridiculous move not long ago when they bundled an aid package with support for Iron Dome in it, pushing Republicans to vote against the protective funding.

These are all silly antics. Political theater. Childish games. Jockeying for Sunday morning highlight reels and C-Span airtime. They do not move the ball down the field. Much like our enemies today, too many members of the House seem more focused on pointing out the dysfunction of their colleagues across the aisle and creating litmus tests for them to regularly fail, then they are committed to finding common ground on legislature and moving forward. Shame.

House of Representative Members, if you care about America, stop these partisan shenanigans and get the aid package passed, quickly. You have already lost enough precious time, and this is not a moment for antics.

Last

Our fears were realized when news hit the airwaves of two soldiers that died in battle inside of Gaza. Then this morning, eleven more faces, names and families devastated. I do not know if Israel can handle any more funerals. And there will be more. We know that. If we are on the ground, rooting out the evil door to door, soldiers will be hit by IEDs, sniper fire, booby traps and gun shots. It is the heaviest price to pay, after our emotions and hearts have been taxed beyond our worst imaginations. It was one of the many reasons we paused for so long before going in with tanks. As Yoav Gallant said, *"We are making significant gains but paying a very heavy toll."* We do not praise the death of an IDF soldier. We decry it as a reality foisted on us throughout history and indeed, in this moment as well, by those who rather kill us than accept our existence. It makes our heavy hearts, heavier, our tearful eyes, wetter.

May their souls be bound in the bond of Life. May their families find comfort in the peace we shall pursue today and always in their memory.

26

October 31, 2023

They got him. The violence inciter on the campus of Cornell threatening to gruesomely kill Jewish students and causing students to convert dorm rooms into bunkers. Thanks are needed to law enforcement for their speedy response to this menace.

The suspect is not Palestinian.
He is not Muslim.
He is not a white nationalist. In fact, he is not white.

This is the new face of antisemitism in 2023. The honor student next door.

Patrick Dai is an Asian American from upstate New York. A National Merit Scholar with an off-the-charts intellectual quotient.

I point out this heritage to highlight the lunacy of this moment. A man who recently would have been targeted by some during the Asian hate escapades, someone who himself is a minority in America, targeted Jews on campus in the most vicious and threatening manner. Where in the hell does that hatred come from? How can one minority demonize another for being, well, a minority. Is the hypocrisy not screaming out at most of you?! It is non-sensical.

We cannot call this kid stupid. Not if he is a merit scholar and straight A student. He was studying engineering at one of the most prestigious schools in the country. He might have received an academic education, but he is failing morality.

What was glaringly missing from this kid's hateful threat to Jews was the Asian, white, Christian and/or Muslim band of sisters and brothers that should have knocked gently on the doors of their Jewish classmate and said to them, *"I'll walk with you to the dining hall. I will come with you to the Hillel. We are safe if we are together. If they hurt you, they will have to hurt me first."*

I think that sentiment is a microcosm for what has been missing from society right now. We could have used a friend to walk with.

Random but related to Dai.
The sale of Italian flags on Amazon has quadrupled in the last 27 days. People are logging on to purchase Palestinian flags and mistakenly – perhaps naively – are selecting the Italian one. The flags share some of the colors but none of the design. Why does this matter?

Because supporting the Palestinian plight is a cause célèbre for ultra-leftists and liberals. Most of these people could not tell you where Palestine is located on a map, how many Palestinians there are in the world, any shred of its history or what its flag looks like. It is really a false flag, excuse the pun.

I am all for standing up for the Palestinian people if that is your jam. Support Palestinians right to statehood, independence, liberation from Hamas if you choose. If you are buying an Italian flag because you know so little about the cause, are you really advocating for the Palestinian people? Most who are standing for the Palestinian cause via Amazon are just rooting against Israel and Jews in a not-so veiled act of antisemitism. That is why so many silly souls wrongly conflate Hamas and the Palestinian people. None of their ambitions are shared. It reminds me of the line in Hamilton, *"If you stand for nothing, what will you fall for?"*

Next
Last night at the hotel bar, CNN was playing in the background. One of the IDF spokespeople was interviewed about the bombing and targeted attack of terrorists in Jabaliya, in the heart of North

Gaza. The interviewer asked the question with judgement and scorn to the Israeli soldier, *"With civilians imbedded in the areas, you still pulled the trigger?"*

I was so annoyed at the question and its tone, I walked away before I could hear the soldier's answer.

I think what he should have said - what I hoped he had responded was - *"Yes."* Nothing more. *"Yes. We did drop that bomb."*

All that could be added is why would any journalist put the onus of morality on the IDF for choosing to remove the threat and not on Hamas who uses those civilians as shields. The bad guys should hold that burden and responsibility. Those questions should be asked to Hamas, Hezbollah, PIJ, and asked to leadership in Egypt who has announced that it is willing to sacrifice millions of lives to ensure Gazans do NOT enter Egypt. It could have been asked to leaders in Qatar who are holding the keys to the hostages in Gaza. They should answer these questions, not Israel.

If Hamas can shoot at Israel and call "base" like kids playing tag with children and civilians as shields, how can we ever remove the existential threat they pose? It is a perpetual forcefield that we must break.

It would be easier and safer for our soldiers and protect the grieving country from more death and bloodshed to only drop bombs from the air over most of Gaza. The collateral damage would be unfathomable. Israel's commitment to protecting civilian life in Gaza is felt most by parents, siblings, spouses and children of the dead soldiers who were killed because Israel values saving civilians in Gaza from Hamas. If we did not, we would not be on the ground there at all. I wish all sensationalist news outlets would recognize that fact and report on it, properly.

Before my wife and I had children, Sunday mornings consisted of us enjoying a leisurely brunch at the kitchen table and playing a game we invented called, The Ethicist. It was based off the column in the New York Times. We would read the case to each other printed in the paper and offer our best ethical solution to the question posed of the moral guru, before we read The Ethicists response. We loved when we got it right and took issue with The Ethicist when he failed to see it our way.

How would The Ethicist slice this Jabaliya problem? Hamas masterminds hiding amongst children? Terrorist headquarters in hospitals. Keeping fuel for rockets and food for terrorists and hiding both from citizens. Denying civilians passage to safe zones. What is a warring country to do? How would the Ethicist handle such cases?

The question is rhetorical because it is a new form of warfare and reality that, Israel is the first to face. We are the canary in the coal mine, again.

In 2000, when Israel named, targeted and assassinated Hamas leadership, the country was regularly chastised by the United States and other countries for what they deemed unnecessary action. Mind you this was during Intifada II when busses were exploding and Hamas suicide bombers were detonating themselves at cafes and pizza parlors all over the country, killing innocent Israeli civilians, living life.

Then 9/11 happened. The United States took trillions of dollars of resources and made playing cards to track down the heads of Al Qaeda along with Osama bin Laden.

Ethics are subjective to our pinch points. If it hurts, we feel permitted to do what is necessary to make it stop. If the pinch point is distanced from us, or not throbbing, the need to address the pinch wanes. I relish *and* dread the day when the pinch points draw near to those who chastise us now.

Last

After George Floyd's senseless death, people were reawakened to continued racism in society. My tribe was horrified and stood in solidarity of a painful reality for black people in America. We stood together to be more aware and work towards eliminating the societal disease of bigotry.

This event is different. It has felt different. When Jews die, some have the unspoken feeling that we had it coming to us. It was deserved. Jewish blood is cheaper. Evil weighs less when it is against Jews. We can philosophize for years on why that is and the crossroads of white and privilege and religion and ethnicity we find ourselves today. This intersection is the silence of companies speaking out and the hesitation of university leadership using a moral voice.

I cannot tolerate any more of the *'why'* or unpacking the history and root causes of Jewish hatred. I do not want a sociological experiment or an expensive study. I am fed up. The hatred and hypocrisy and double standards just need to stop. For good. Forever. We must institute a zero tolerance towards antisemitism and force at worst the law and at best, the scarlet letter on those who cannot follow the needed moral code of society to which we sadly belong.

27

November 1, 2023

A <u>fantastic video</u> has been circulating the air waves. It is a must-watch clip! A young "good trouble" maker walked around New York City holding a clipboard titled 'petition' to help Hamas free Palestine. The unsuspecting passers-by gasp in excitement at the opportunity to lend their name and signature against the oppressive Israel and go on the record for Hamas with their support.

He asks, *"You are all in?"*
Each person replied emphatically *"Yes,"* or *"Uh-huh!"*

The "good trouble" fella then says, *"I have to read you the terms and conditions of the petition, just so you know what you are signing."*

He continues in front of each person who was chomping at the bit to put their John Hancock on the clipboard. *"By supporting Hamas to free Palestine, you agree to the following: you agree that every Jew, Christian and non-Muslim in the world must be slaughtered."*

The camera pans to a new suspect while our "good trouble" maker explains more of the not so small print.

"By signing this document in support of Hamas, you endorse making homosexuality punishable by jail or death. Are you ok with Iran using Hamas as radical puppets to spread jihad and destroy the West?"

"You support strict Sharia law which bans women from showing their knees, their hair, forbids them from playing sports in public, and disallows women from being able to travel without a man's permission. You want a terrorist group that beheads babies and rapes women to replace the only democracy in the Middle East."

The clip closes with all the people saying they are not comfortable signing this "petition" and a credit block appears that reads: Facts for Peace.

I LOVE IT!

I forwarded it to thousands of people. It was a clever maneuver to highlight what Hamas really stands for. Two other things came out of this creative caper.

First, it showed how wildly uneducated most people are about Hamas and what the terrorist group stands for. It is the irony of the century that so many left leaning liberals and woke activists are loudly supporting Hamas which calls for the death of their friends, eradicating their social circles and destroying their value systems. They still ask where to sign.

The second item the "good trouble" maker pointed out to the world is how eager society is to add their name to a petition against Israel. If you do not know about Hamas and what it stands for, then most people were really vocalizing their dissatisfaction with Israel. He did say, after all, the purpose was to help Hamas "free Palestine." Unless you have been living under a rock, most should know what Hamas did on the 7th of October and why they did it.

When Hamas came out from their tunnels to attack us, they also unlocked the cellar doors and gave light to viral antisemitism and Jew-hatred that has been infecting the world. It is shameful and so damn hurtful, still.

Next

Near the entrance to Jerusalem, on one of her seven mountain tops, Har Herzl, Israel's national military cemetery and Yad Vashem sit side by side. There is a little-known and even lesser taken path that connects the back of Har Herzl which is like America's Arlington National Cemetery and the famed Holocaust Museum and Memorial. It is called, *HaShvil Hamechaber* – The Connecting Path. It is an ironic name considering its purpose.

After World War II, when entire families were decimated by the Nazis, some lone survivors emigrated to Israel. Shortly after, Israel's War of Independence broke out in 1948, many of those lone survivors who were the last heirs of a family, a legacy and a name, died trying to establish the Jewish State. That sacred 'connecting' path lays honor to those forgotten souls and gives tribute to the names which were disconnected from living, growing, and rebuilding in Israel and continuing the legacy of those who died in Europe.

The name of the path would be more fitting if it were the '*dis*connected path,' since individual and family heritage was arrested from carrying forward. To me, that path twists and turns towards perpetual sadness. Situated between two places of historical and modern death, in most cases of both places, murders because of our mere existence. Those who survived were taken at the next turn and were denied being the continuing link in the chain of our people.

OLYMPUS DIGITAL CAMERA

That path has been on my mind because of two painful pictures. Each time I saw it yesterday, I had to fight back tears. Yossi Cohen, former head of the Mossad is pictured consoling a 15-year-old named, Pedayah Mark at the funeral of Pedaya's father, Michi, who was murdered in a terrorist attack in 2016.

The next picture was the same Yossi Cohen, sitting by himself, at the funeral of Pedayah Mark, a Givati soldier, who was killed in Gaza two days ago, defending Israel from Hamas terrorists.

The links in the chain were broken again. Who will continue the Mark family name? The Mark family legacy? The Mark family customs and traditions? The Mark family jokes and banter? A family wiped out in two different spurts by hatred, terror and intolerance.

A path that has been broken. Here we are again, with the same abomination leading to the identical result. Death and paths that are shattered and ended before they reach their destinations.

When will these broken pathways be paved? When will there no longer be generations killed prematurely by animosity, venom and violence? It cannot come soon enough.

Next
Ismail Haniyeh, the leader of Hamas, a multi billionaire who lives luxuriously on the Palestinian's embezzled money in Qatar, announced today – in direct contradiction to his colleague's assertion yesterday that Hamas will carry out October 7th like attacks again and again until Israel is gone – that he wants to

begin immediate political negotiations that calls for an immediate cease fire and a two-state solution. That headline should tell us one thing: Israel is kicking military ass! The last (few) times something like this happened, namely in 2006 with Hezbollah, was after Israel offered such a crushing blow to the enemy that they were begging for mercy. The idea that Haniyeh would raise the balloon of two-states publicly speaks of how desperate Hamas is right now.

A few related thoughts.

We have learned the hard way from Iran and crippling sanctions, this is not the time to take our foot off Hamas' neck. To give Hamas even a small pocket, is to allow evil to continue to fester and breathe. We must make sure the regime has no air in its lungs, no pulse in its evil heart. It must die.

We also have learned from Hamas that we can only believe one thing they say: They want to kill all the Jewish people and remove Israel from the map. That is the *only* statement we can accept at face value.

My dad used to say, *"A liar needs a good memory."* Hamas lies so often it is impossible to decipher what is genuine and fake. But I can assure you that Jewish statehood is not to be taken seriously by Hamas now or ever. This gesture is a sign, that indeed, they have woken a sleeping giant in the IDF and Hamas is worried about their future.

It also unpacks the utter chaos that is Hamas. One spokesperson for the group says we did not harm civilians, while another prides himself on the havoc and barbarism they wreaked. One says we will commit these atrocities over and over while the next in leadership makes a gesture for peace within hours. This is a *dis*organization that can only agree on one thing. Sadly, we all know what that is.

Last

I am writing this Stream from my hotel room overlooking Brandenburg Gate in Berlin. Speaking of ironies! Just today, Chancellor Scholtz announced a formal ban on any public support for Hamas or any terrorist entities in Germany. That includes Isis or Hamas flag waiving, marching, chanting or announcing support for any form of terrorism. Fantastic leadership. Thank you, Chancellor.

My first gleaning from this announcement was who could have thought Germany would be the pacesetter for stopping hateful rhetoric? I do not think many who lived through Pearl Harbor and Kamikaze missions on navy boats in the Pacific would believe that Japan is one of our staunchest allies today and has been for decades. Heck, Saudi Arabia was (and hopefully still is) on the precipice of normalization with Israel. The naïve and wildly hopeful side of me sees a glimmer of possibility that one day, my kids and grandkids will be the same inheritors of goodness from those who housed the worst enemies and espoused the worst hatred.

I also applaud how well Germany walks the fine line between arresting fascism and allowing free speech. My dear friend who was born in Israel but has lived in Germany for almost two-decades told me a story today from a moment in 2017. A neo-Nazi group wanted to commemorate the anniversary of the death of Rudolf Hess, Hitler's deputy, and march to Spandau where Hess died in prison.

Germany wrestled with the two modern foundational ethics of the country: freedom to assemble and speak and, Never Again on this soil.

The city and country leadership walked the line as follows:

The group could bring flags, but they had to be German flags. No swastikas or hateful flags, banners or signs could be seen or shown. The marchers could say and do nothing that would intimidate others in any manner. Counter protestors were welcome to display their distaste for this gathering and disgusts for those still proudly displaying the dirtiest stain on German history for all to see.

The curved line drawn is not hard to follow. Yes, we can assemble, and we can have free speech, but we cannot have speech that glorifies hatred, advances racism or promotes ethnic cleansing or its cleansers or intimidates any group. They can do nothing that provokes violence or leads to violence. It is not hard to follow *that* line.

The United States is struggling with these two issues as if they are in contradiction to one another. The clashing of two competing values is growing rampant on college campuses, discussion groups, and even on my Temple list-serve. I think we should follow this simple line and learn from those who made grave mistakes and learned generational lessons of what they can never go back towards.

It is far too high a price to pay for any country to make those mistakes again to learn and grow.

28

November 2, 2023

The leader of Hezbollah, Hassan Nasrallah's long anticipated speech was more worthy than on face value. It was a blustery rant and fearful admission that Hezbollah does not want to share the current fate of Hamas.

There are a few reasons for this announcement, in my estimation. The citizens of Lebanon will be far less sympathetic to Hezbollah turning their country into an active war zone and eventual rubble than the people for Gaza are for Hamas. If Israel were to face off in a full-on war with Lebanon, I suspect Hezbollah would be fighting internally with locals who want nothing to do with the guerrilla regime and externally against Israel.

Add to that the bruises and scars still stinging from 2006, after Israel went into Lebanon to retrieve two of our captured soldiers. Israel was not well prepared for that incursion and still, it set Hezbollah back decades. If Hezbollah *and* Hamas were to be pulverized simultaneously, the terror investment of Iran would be decimated. Look at this decision by the Nasrallah as actually Iran the puppeteer, choosing to diversify and protect the few remaining assets against Israel it will have.

The groundhog Nasrallah lives under ground, (hence the moniker, groundhog) unable to see the light of day since 2006, for fear of being assassinated by Israel or like-minded operatives. He heads a world recognized terror entity and is persona-non-grata east and west. The loud statement that this war is a Palestinian issue only, is telling those in Qatar and Gaza, they are on their own. I would not trust much of what any terrorist leader says. Haniyeh, Sinwar and Nasrallah are on the same level as Goebbels and Eichmann. Thus, Israel is not removing troops or letting its guard down, nor should they.

One thing worthy of exploring though: If Sinwar and Haniyeh, Hamas chieftains are claiming Israel occupies Palestinians, and Hamas' dispute is over land, what is Hezbollah's beef with Israel?

The answer is simpler than you would think. Nasrallah and his minions are not contesting borders or the 1967 war, which did not involve Lebanon at all. They are not opposing 1973 and Yom Kippur gains, which were none. Hezbollah is contesting having Jews in the neighborhood. Whether every Jew lived solely in Tel Aviv, Eilat or Haifa is more than the radical Islamic group could handle. They do not want Jews in the world, and most definitely not on their border. Hence their determination to eviscerate us from their proximity for now, and eventually from the world.

Of course, I do not want to see Israel face another front of the war. But I would be curious to see world opinion chant, *"Free Lebanon"* and *"No more occupation of Beirut,"* to further point out the stupidity that is abound amongst the supporters of terror, who are just antisemites in poor disguise.

In the Arab world, every country is jumping on the bandwagon of demonizing Israel. Algiers and Turkey have been creaming us in the press, recalling ambassadors and equating Israel to Satan.

Sayeed Kashua, the Palestinian Israeli author depicted a similar moment in time in his book, <u>Dancing Arabs</u>. Any time Israel was backed into a corner militarily, Kashua writes about the Palestinian jubilation and commentary at the dinner table with the inter-generational family. Adult members of the household would proclaim that the Arab world has finally found the nerve of the Israeli. Jews will be defeated and will learn humility and shame. These words are shared around the television and newspapers and coffee houses. Excitement and anticipation ensue.

Then, the tide of the war changes dramatically. Israel dominates and defeats the Arab enemy. Kashua jumps to the same people who now curse the stupidity and arrogance of the Arab aggressors that even contemplated these terroristic moves and engaging in conflict with Israel. Kashua makes a point of highlighting the thoughts of the same family who scream out (in private) lambasting the thoughtlessness of the Arab world leadership as the root cause of stifling the growth of Palestinians, worldwide.

It reminds me of a plane full of eager people landing in Las Vegas, full of energy, excitement, hope. They are boisterous, mildly inebriated and naïve enough to think they are the first who will take the casinos down. Jump a few days later to their departing flight. The gate and jetway are silent, filled with people hanging their head low, wallets empty, and kicking themselves over their mindless hubris.

I think that image Kashua conjures up is happening in spades right now throughout the Arab world. The question is, when October 7th sets back the Palestinian people, and the residents of Gaza generationally, will they decry Hamas in what is left of their living rooms, like Kashua remembers? Will they blame Israel? Will it be one thought aloud and another in private?

I do wish most of the Arab world leadership and the masses would grow a spine and show courage. As I type, Secretary of State Antony Blinken is meeting with Arab leaders in Jordan. I would bet large sums of money that off the record, these leaders are appreciative of Israel rooting out Hamas. I am also confident these same leaders will declare adamantly; no Gazan refugees will be allowed in their countries. Lastly, they will mourn the loss of innocent civilians.

On paper, there is nothing to find issue with. *Off* the record.

On the record, these same Arab countries will decry the humanitarian crisis, blame Israel for the loss of life and insist that the International Criminal Court be waved as a warning towards Israel to stop their bombardment. They will demand from Blinken, on the record, there be a cease fire. They will beg Israel to stop continuing the humanitarian crisis in Gaza and blame Israel for creating a middle eastern calamity. They will recall ambassadors.

Ironically, Egypt will be in this conference, who shares a border with Gaza and refused to let one refugee inside. Egypt was responsible for filling discovered Hamas tunnels leading from Gaza to the Sinai with raw sewage, killing scores of Hamas operatives and civilians, not so long ago. We all must have missed the protests and world condemnation!

Jordan will be in this conference which is home to the largest population of people who identify as Palestinian. No refugees will be permitted inside Jordan.

Saudi will be at this conference, who has more resources in interest alone to support the people of Gaza and this humanitarian crisis than the GDP of some major countries.

Where is their courage to say what they think aloud? Why can't they condemn Hamas and share in the struggle for independence for Palestinians? Why are they silent in the face of terror on the record and spineless in calling it out before the cameras or with reporters?

Could these countries and its leadership just show some temerity to lead by example? I have been to quite a few Arab and Muslim countries in my life. Almost all the people I met are smart, thoughtful and considerate. Saying they mourn for innocent people, wish for Palestinian autonomy in a sovereign state and denounce Hamas is not a difficult statement to utter, especially on the record. But they cannot. They do not.

Just this week, the Ashkenazic and Sephardic chief rabbis of Israel issued a rare, joint Halachic (Jewish law) decree that prohibits bigotry, intimidation or violence from Jews towards Arabs. October 7th has brought a lot of racial divides in Israel to light. Some extreme actors have taken to channeling their anger and upset at Israeli Arabs.

That behavior is reprehensible. It cannot be tolerated in the Jewish State. To help curb such behavior, the two rabbis announced jointly, in a unified and booming voice, that it is against Torah law to behave meanly or violently against Arabs.

When I read this, I was proud to be Jewish. Proud that the tradition I use as a compass and the leadership of the people I am part of, use their platform to denounce demonizing any people and acting violently. I stuck out my chest a little that Israel printed this in the front of the newspapers and was clear throated that this bad behavior is not a Jewish ethic, and the State will not tolerate bad actors or bad actions.

Most violence in Israel happens on Fridays, which is a Muslim sabbath, of sorts. The religious go to the Mosque for prayer and the clerics get them riled up during their sermons. The youth leave, raring to go, setting tires ablaze and throwing rocks and ramming cars. The Madras and the Mosque are hotbeds of fomenting violence and directing anger to Israel and Jews. It should be the opposite.

Where are the Imams doing the same as the chief rabbis? Where are the leaders using their voice to find peace and not stoke hatred? Where are they, damnit!?

These Arab countries' pettiness is laughable. The Arab religious and state leadership is embarrassing.

Next
The college campus is on fire. The flames need to be tampered and safeguards need to be stablished to ensure that another eruption never occurs again.

A friend recently said that colleges need a Marshall plan. I agree.

After World War II, the United States spent what is worth about $190 Billion today, investing in trade, infrastructure and materials for Western Europe to rebuild. It was known as the Marshall Plan. It was a huge success, the fruits of which are felt anytime we enjoy the theatre in London, go to the top of the Eiffel Tower, shop at Champs de Elysses or eat pasta in Rome. The first purpose was to rebuild these countries and their cities so there could be a bright future in a post war world. The secondary and primal purpose was to ensure America stays a super geo-political influence and that Stalin and Russia do not seize the indigence and vulnerability of these war beaten Western European countries.

Colleges need a Marshall-like-plan so that every student can feel safe, regardless of where they are from or what they believe. They need to continue to be bastions of free speech while learning the responsibilities that come with speech. Universities need to be a forum for vigorous debate accompanied by shared respect. Schools should encourage curiosity and insist that facts matter. We can critique leaders and colleagues, but we do so with a baseline of respect and never advocating or encouraging violence. Opinions and beliefs are welcome on campuses. Facts, however, can never be supplanted for emotion.

Over the years, Jews have been forgotten as a minority. That is much of what we wanted. To be fully included in community, in society and at the workplace. It worked until now.

We are a people, an ethnicity, a tribe, a religion and we indeed are subject to bigotry, intolerance and indifference. This moment has brought the layers of our identity into plain sight. As a result, we are riddled with fear, feeling fragile, especially on college campuses. Students and faculty on campus need to be re-educated about Jewish history, and the basis of our ethnicity and background along with our intrinsic connection to the State of Israel.

The college experience has long offered education in and out of the classroom for countless other minorities and ethnicities. Jews had been passed over. Perhaps because many thought we had arrived or because our differences were rarely seen or felt. But it has risen to the surface, big time. We cannot hope that the tensions simmer down and go away. We must address this head on so if it does rise again, our response is different and better.

If we cede this moment to time and do not get in front of this crisis, then those who wish to write the narrative without us in it will ascend the podium and fill the void. We can never allow that to happen.

Like the Marshall Plan, we will need a quarterback to lead this endeavor. Someone like Ambassador Amy Gutman, former President of Penn and current Ambassador from the United States to Germany would be excellent. Maybe Lee Bollinger, former President of University of Michigan and then Columbia University. I think Ben Sasse would be a good candidate. Sasse is a former Senator and current President of the University of Florida. There are others worthy of being added to the list. Whoever *is* selected, it needs to be someone native to the topography of colleges and adept at policy. A person able to walk the line of freedoms and restrictions. A bridge builder who can dream of what can be and not just denounce what is and what was. This should be a collaborative between the Anti-Defamation League, Hillel International and the U.S. Department of Education.

I can think of no role more important than educating and modeling tolerance for our future. Let's get cracking on this initiative. The day is short, the task is great!

29

November 3, 2023

Hamas has been cooking up a pot of hypocrisy and lies and the world is eating up all they are serving. When did society develop an appetite for crap with a heaping side of false virtue?

Hamas launches claims against Israel but ignores the same laws and rules it says we violate which they openly transgress. I am bowled over by the double standard.

Every Hamas accusation against Israel is really an admission of their wrongdoing and guilt. Here are some of the most blatant and glaring examples:

- Hamas leadership decries the war crimes and crimes against humanity that are happening in Gaza while staying silent about the fact Hamas entered sovereign Israel and brutally murdered 1400 civilians and children and elderly and women which is a crime against humanity and a war crime, in and of itself.
- Hamas ascribes blame to Israel for violating the Geneva Conventions when bombing hospitals and ambulances. Meanwhile, the Hamas headquarters are located inside of a hospital and Hamas weapons and militants are ferried to

and from by ambulances. This fact was even announced by none other than Mahmoud Abbas, President of the Palestinian Authority. Those actions are a direct violation of the Geneva Conventions.

- Hamas uses children as a human shield. Hamas shot and killed innocent Palestinian civilians trying to flee to the humanitarian zone. Yet, when a child is killed because she was forced to be near a Hamas fighter pressing launch buttons on rockets, Hamas is impervious to criminal accusation or wrongdoing, only Israel is criminalized.

- Hamas begs for a cease fire yet goes on multiple media channels and proclaims the resistance of October 7th will continue to happen repeatedly. It was Hamas who broke the last ceasefire on October 7th. Still, many want Israel to pause now and wait for the next attack, which has already been intended and declared. Where is the onus on Hamas? When can they surrender to enable a cease fire?

- Hamas apologists claim repeatedly that the 240 captives and the missing posters hung around communities is a ploy by Israel to garner sympathy. Many of the same apologists claim no Israeli person is being held in Gaza. When Hamas is accused of kidnapping innocent civilians or barbaric brutality like raping girls and beheading children, they ask for proof and deny the charges. But when Hamas claims 500 were killed in a bombing, we should take their word without evidence. Of course, it was later proven those numbers were inflated ten-fold, and the bombing was caused by a Hamas errant rocket.

- When Israel is blamed for a humanitarian crisis, but Hamas is unscathed for their role in depriving children food or fuel or energy for cooking, why are they free from guilt for the humanitarian crisis they created and perpetuate? Why is Egypt free from blame for refusing to open its border for refuge adding to the crisis yet Israel is responsible for aid homing and coming? The hypocrisy is omnipresent.

- Why is Israel demonized for bombing Gaza with pinpoint precise rockets, yet in the last three weeks close to 10,000 rockets have been fueled and launched from Hamas into civilian populations that can land indiscriminately in grocery stores, kindergartens and nursing homes inside of Israel. The world is silent to that atrocity. Only Israel is committing crimes by being accurate. Really?!

- Why should Israel apologize for building bomb shelters and investing in Iron Dome while Hamas built tunnels for their jihad and left the civilians of Gaza to be unprotected. Is it Israel's fault for protecting its citizenry? Is it Israel's obligation to protect the people of Gaza when Hamas refuses to?!

- Why is killing an Israeli soldier acceptable but a Hamas operative who wears no uniform, wears no pledge pin to Hamas, yet fills his blue jean pockets with grenades, is categorized as an innocent civilian?

This is only a small sampling of a much larger list of these double standards, hypocrisies and false pretensions. It is stymieing.

Halloween is over. Stop the masquerade of humanitarian and Palestinian advocacy. It is really an anti-Israel, anti-Zionist and antisemitic aspiration. We can see through the costume.

Related and connected to that thought:
The language being used by pro-Palestinian advocates – who most are anti-Israel protestors – is designed to pierce the Jewish soul. It is not coincidental.

That is why almost every pro-Palestinian pundit and spokesman uses words including, genocide, apartheid (Jews were the fiercest advocates against the South African apartheid movement), ethnic cleansing, war crimes, colonialists and more.

These are weaponized words aimed to hit where it hurts the most. It is shameful and reprehensible. These words make claims about Israel that at one time, Jews were victims of themselves.

This cunning technique is utilized for two reasons:

First, it attempts to label Jews as hypocrites and lessens their original claims.

Second, it erodes the potency of the crimes and devalues the words if they are applied in cases against Israel.

For shame!

Otherwise, we would hear about Israel's right to live in peace. We would listen to sentiments from the Arab world, spoken in madrasas and mosques that Israel deserves a homeland. There would be a clear denouncing of violence. Instead, there is silence.

Regrettably, cynical suspicions have been confirmed. Palestinian upset is not about their state. It is about our state. Palestinians are not mad they do not have a homeland. They are angry that Israel does.

Related and connected to that thought:

Normally, I loathe Ben Shapiro. He is indeed smart but very arrogant and usually devoid of compassion. He seems to possess an inability to be wrong.

Yet, this week at Oxford I was heartened to see him take down person after person in a debate forum with the same and simple question he posed.

"When you say, 'Free Palestine' or say, 'Palestine is occupied,' which part of Palestine do you want free?" Shapiro asked.

Without exception, each one answered him, *"All of it."*

Bingo!

This is not about the right to Palestinian sovereignty. This is about one state without Jews.

For almost a month now, we have been writing and circulating memes about what has been missing from our non-Jewish coworkers and friends. For me, I have been hurt for not receiving any sense of empathy, compassion, camaraderie, holding me and my people close and checking on our welfare in our moment of crisis. Those things were noticeably absent, and it still pains me.

Along those lines, there is one thing missing from the Arab world now. From the countries protesting Israel's defense and from demonstrators waving flags to and from in Washington, Berlin, London and Paris and anyone demanding a cease fire. That is the declaration by these groups and people, that there is a Jewish right to statehood.

If any Arab leader, any passionate defender of the rights of civilians in Gaza, any advocate for peace and those marching for a cease fire could articulate the need for a Jewish State and the notion that the Jewish people have an inherent and legal right to a homeland, that the Jewish State should be uncontested and established in peace, I think we would exhale. A little bit.

But the silence during this time has really been about a denial of our right to a Jewish State. There has been a not so quiet desire to weaken Jews, take away our defense, deny our right to sovereignty, autonomy and independence, and most notably, statehood. A wish to turn back the clocks and erase the last 75 years and undo Israel's gains.

That is the greatest paradox and hypocrisy of all. It is claimed that the Jewish people are occupying Palestinians and denying them self-determination, but the answer for most on that front is to do the *very* same to the Jewish people. There is no recognition of the irony, hypocrisy or double standard that Palestinian apologists offer.

If you do not believe me, take a gander at the protests in front of the White House yesterday. *"We do not want a Jewish State,"* was sung out loudly and clearly for all to hear. The same was chanted in London and Paris.

I ask, earnestly, how does denying Israel statehood fix the Palestinian problem? Or is that not the Palestinian issue?

Those that protest do not seem to care what happens to the Jewish people. But the Jewish people and world are demanded to care about what happens to the Palestinians. Sounds unbalanced and one-sided to me. Or perhaps a better word is, 'disproportionate.'

If Palestinians want a state, side by side Israel, we have offered an invitation since 1947. We can offer another invite tomorrow. It has been refused repeatedly. Is it because Palestinians do not like the terms or is it because Palestinians really want a state without Jews in or near it?

If Palestinians continue to deny a Jewish right to live in peace and security, we will stop at nothing to move those threats further away from our population. Walls and checkpoints will be the least of Palestinian worries. The blame will again fall solely on those who seek to harm us, and with the silence of the population who has neither the courage nor intention to announce a Jewish right to exist in self- sovereignty.

After, it will only take days until the denigration of the lives of Palestinians will be blamed again on the Jewish oppressive force and Israel's occupation. Yet, those same people that blame Israel will conveniently develop amnesia when it comes to burying scores of dead Jews killed by terrorists.

We are not inexperienced to being asked to *"go elsewhere."* That has been the Jewish condition since Egypt. Jews had a dream and a long fight to establish Israel. We paid a hefty toll before and during the last 75 years.

Israel is not going anywhere else. Ever again.

We are not sacrificing those who died for a homeland to pack it up and start over somewhere new. We know how that movie ends.

We are not going anywhere else. Ever again!

After 2500 years, we are finally home. And while we might welcome the stranger in our home and cede land for a homeland for others, we are not forfeiting our right to our homeland in peace, security and prosperity.

We are not going anywhere else. Ever again!

We will not apologize for Israel's strength and defense, which is a necessity of that same condition.

We are not going anywhere else. Ever again!

I am going to tweak a familiar chant from the LGBTQ movement. *'We are here. We are Jewish. Get used to it.'*

The world needs to get used to the idea; we are not going anywhere else. Ever again!

We are home.

30

November 4, 2023

My family asked me when I would stop writing these Streams. I replied when I no longer have something to share. Thus, I continue. I know it helps me much. I hope it can offer you some support, education, perspective and challenge.

Until now, for some unknown reason, I chose to use Roman numerals for listing each Stream. I knew when I arrived at 30, I would change to natural numbers since I did not want any Google searches to yield Rabbi David Kirshner XXX. We are at 30. Thank you for going with the flow and understanding.

Friday morning, I went back to visit the villa that hosted the infamous Wannsèe conference. It was at that haunting place in early 1942, that German leadership enjoyed wine and caviar and listened to classical music, sitting with a gorgeous view of the picturesque lake behind them. Within ninety minutes time, those powers decided how they would deal with the "Jewish Problem" in Europe.

Birds chirping, trees and the surrounding areas littered in autumnal leaves, the stillness of the lake seen from the dining room window makes it look like glass, all lend itself to this feeling like you are walking in a painting.

Here, in this gorgeous place, while enjoying opulence, scrumptious foods and lavish décor, evil people decided to do unthinkable acts to Jews. Hannah Arendt wrote about the banality of evil – the limp reaction of the gruesome and barbaric acts of which Nazi leadership instructed underlings to complete. Wannsèe always underscores the banality of evil.

Being there now, I could not help but think of the masterminds responsible for the barbaric act of October 7th. It was not devised in a tunnel and was not funded from the taxpayers of Gaza.

It was devised and implemented and funded most likely by Iranian Revolutionary Guardsmen and Iranian leadership along with Hamas brass, sitting in billion-dollar, gold encrusted hotels in Qatar, and drinking fancy teas and sipping expensive coffees, savoring rare foods, all while discussing this maniacal scheme to kill Jews inside of Israel. Then, these planners and organizers implored their mindless henchman to carry out their dirty work. These Hamas terrorists belong in a category reserved for Ivan 'the Terrible' Marchenko, the Ukrainian guard of Treblinka, who treasured his gruesome task of killing Jews, or Adolf Eichmann who was part of the Wannsèe Conference and the Final Solution.

Soon, I am headed to Israel. I am already having nightmares about what I might see, who I might meet and the trauma my kinsfolk has, and is, enduring. To think some sipped from fine China with their pinkies in the air when mapping out this gruesome day is more than my mind or heart can accept. It was an encore of the banality of evil.

The headlines have been replete with calls for a cease fire. Two articles in two different news sources printed this week claimed that the window for action by Israel against Hamas is closing. The United States' tolerance for Israel's actions will soon evaporate. Other countries will join that chorus.

What is the statute of limitations on empathy? How long does morality get the spotlight? When do we move on from the 1400 dead and the 242 captives? Is there a time-length for each soul? Do murdered kids measure differently on the empathy meter? How about raped girls? Kidnapped babies?

The answer is never. It is seared into our minds, like numbers tattooed on our arms. For eternity. Perpetuity. Generations. Israeli resolve to live in peace and security will and must never end. We learned painfully, that when we take our hands off the wheel, even for a little while, there will be those who try to violently steer us over the cliff.

Furthermore, the idea that we should stop our war on terror soon is a mighty large sentiment by a country that spent a decade in Vietnam and cost 58,000 lives and billions of dollars. It is a hefty notion from that same country that spent two decades in Iraq and Afghanistan, lost thousands of soldiers and scores more were wounded physically and emotionally with no clear victory. Today, the Taliban is still in control and powerful, Iraq was crawling with Isis and the USA tells Israel to pause. Really? Is that the best course forward? The same country that is spending trillions (and rightly so) on aid to Ukraine to ensure that Putin does not try and conquer Eastern Europe, is telling us to pump the brakes? To halt removing terrorists from our porches and patios? Why? Because of a few misinformed and misguided mice that are roaring.

No. We cannot abide by such a request.

Israel is a country shaped by Munich and Entebbe.

In September of 1972, Palestinian terrorists snuck into the Olympic Village during the summer games in Munich and held eleven Israeli athletes hostage. The German police failed at protecting the

Olympians in the village, and after much negotiation, the terrorists and their Jewish hostages were moved to a nearby airport. There, a German attempt to have the terrorists eliminated and the hostages rescued was violently botched. It resulted in all the athletes being killed while some terrorists were captured alive and released just a few weeks later.

Frustratingly, Prime Minister Golda Meir had offered to send an elite Israeli commando unit to Munich to storm the village and try and save the athletes. German police said they would handle the situation on their turf.

The Germans failed miserably. Jewish blood was dripping on German soil, again.

In June of 1976, Air France flight 139 was hijacked. The terrorists demanded the release of dozens of Palestinian prisoners in Israeli jails.

Prime Minister Yitzchak Rabin and Minister of Defense, Shimon Peres immediately assembled a bold and audacious plan called Operation Thunderbolt. The crack-team of Israeli commandos would land in Entebbe and eliminate the terrorists, and then fly all the hostages back to Israel.

Entebbe's success was a modern-day miracle. More, it was a post-Munich declaration that Israel would never again relinquish responsibility to another nation to care for its citizens.

That is why this incursion into Gaza must continue. The cost of our cessation is a price no family or country can afford. We cannot leave our fate to Gaza, The United States, the United Nations or any other country.

America knows that Hamas will be on its doorstep soon enough if Israel falls back. We have a responsibility to remove them from our borders and allow Israelis to live and sleep in peace. If we learn from the United States' example and ours, from Munich and from Entebbe, we must see this through until our objectives are achieved. We need the US' blessings, endorsement and support. Words of pause and cease fire, especially while Hamas holds 242 Jewish souls against their will, are not helpful, not productive and not welcome.

Eventually, this war will be over. Gaza as it was will be a faint memory. The Jewish survivors of the Gaza envelope will have a long road of therapy, support, rebuilding and trauma to deal with. It will last far past the end of this century. Israel has already committed trillions of resources and will keep moving forward to make sure those who survived will be supported and the memory of those who were murdered, will forever be honored.

The people of Gaza deserve a future too. If we learn from the mistakes of America, we have an opportunity to see what we can establish in Gaza that will not yield the same result.

After the United States quietly and successfully funded Afghanistan's defense against Russian aggression, we had no endgame, no strategy for after Russia walked away in defeat. Fast-forward and the Afghans gave birth to the Taliban. Ironically, it was America who funded and armed much of the Taliban aggression we faced post 9/11.

Many Western countries think long and hard about how to win a war. They do not think as hard about how to prevent the same war from happening again.

This will be the challenge for Israel in a post Hamas Gaza.

I want to share some ideas we should aim for and others we should not.

Under no circumstances should the United Nations be deputized as a peace keeping force in Gaza. First, the United Nations is naming Iran as the chair of the Human Rights Council. That is like naming me the spokesperson for under-eaters anonymous or naming Donald Trump head of the humility commission. The United Nations does not miss an opportunity to miss the opportunity to remind the world why it is in existence. It's resolve and purpose diminishes by the day.

Even more worrisome is the poor track record of the UN. If you visited the Lebanese border anytime in the past 15 years, one could easily see a United Nations flag waving, demarcating a UN peacekeeping outpost. Within a few yards is a Hezbollah outpost, with flag waving. These outposts are lined up around the border of Lebanon and Israel and the flags and posts are just a stone's throw from one another. I am not sure if the UN peace keeping mission and Hezbollah are in cahoots, but it feels that way. Since 2000, when Israel left Beirut and since 2006, when UN resolutions insisted on a peacekeeping presence, hundreds of thousands of precision rockets have been amassed and are hidden under the noses of the UN, in nursery schools, mosques, hospitals and other protected sites in Lebanon.

This is all a long way of saying; the United Nations cannot be trusted with peace making or peace keeping.

Israel cannot and should not reoccupy Gaza. We cannot afford the cost. 'Cost' is a triple entendre. I mean financially, and the cost of loss of life for Israeli soldiers, and the cost of loss of dignity for the Palestinian people.

The Palestinian Authority cannot govern Gaza. The PA is brittle. Abbas has lost strength over time, and with his exit soon enough, who knows what will be of the Authority. To assume the PA are good partners in a hotbed like Gaza, is foolish and dangerous. Even the best intended PA officials will be overthrown, like they already have been in Jenin, Tulkarem and other West Bank enclaves.

Whatever mission is assembled, perhaps of moderate Arab countries who have no tolerance for mischief and can fund support, it MUST include a new educational system that speaks of possibility and not one that demonizes Jews and Zionism. Salam Fayaad is a noble person. He should come back and lead the initiative for the people of Gaza. Fayyad is a forward thinking, American educated, economic genius who served as the Prime Minister of Palestine for a while. He used his voice to advocate for education, investment, technology and growth. It was a harder sell than bombs and guns and he was quite literally, run out of town.

Fayyad, or someone of his ilk, along with a conglomerate of moderate peace keeping countries is what Gaza needs for a different future.

Dalia Scheindlin just authored an <u>article in the New Republic</u> on the least bad option for Israel. She advocates for something close to what was done for Kosovo, in 1999. But Scheindlin goes out of her way to explain this is the least-bad option, not a great option. There is a big difference. Regardless of which option is chosen or versions of different options that are cobbled together, refocusing on education in the Gaza Strip must be paramount.

When Ariel Sharon unilaterally withdrew from Gaza and Jewish entrepreneurs gifted millions of dollars of plug and play agricultural infrastructure to the people of Gaza, it was to give the Palestinians a running start towards growth. Instead, we know what they did with the sacred opportunity.

No one can tolerate more of the same or a repeat when we withdraw again. It is time to begin thinking about what can and should be in place in Gaza next.

Next

Nary a minute passes and I do not think about the Israeli hostages. Their personal plight in tunnels and darkness, disconnected from their homes and families coupled with the indescribable torture families are living through not knowing about their loved ones, hurts my heart and mind, simultaneously.

There are no words. My fingers hurt even typing these words.

Especially crushing is the idea that babies, toddlers and six-and seven-year-olds are in Hamas hands. What will happen to them? What will their fate be? Will they be kept alive? Will they be nourished? Fed? Clothed? Taught a new language? A new religion? Will they be instructed to hate Jews? To demonize Israel? To become shahids?

The dread and horror are unspeakable and unthinkable.

I was reminded of an apocryphal story in the aftermath of World War II. One lone survivor went back to his home to find rubble. At what was his workplace, he saw no remnant of his prior life. There was no evidence of the synagogue or the schools that once were bustling in his hometown. The person searched high and low for any survivors of his family there. Months turned to years with no success. The man was alone. He could not locate any other survivors.

In despair and defeat, he would shuffle to the town square daily and feed the pigeons, sing Jewish songs and weep.

One day, a group of kids from the local orphanage were in the square and the weak spirited man was spreading the crumbs for the birds to eat. He then began to sing the words of *Avinu Malkeinu* and the *Shema*. As he did, kids from the orphanage stopped frolicking and looked up. They knew that song. It opened a recessed vault of memory. There were Jewish children given to the orphanage so that they may survive the war. This man's song was awakening their identity and DNA.

I would certainly want my child to live and would offer them to the custody of Christians or an orphanage who would care for them, if God forbid, I were faced with that choice from WWII.

I am not sure I would want my children to stay alive and be in Hamas' custody. The choices are ghastly.

I can only pray that we can sing loud enough for those babies and toddlers and children to hear our voices and our songs. May their identities never wane and may those vaults of memory stay open forever.

May God bring them to their families' embrace immediately. Please, please God.

31

November 5, 2023

Much of my life and education have been shaped by cinema. One of the great classics for me is the Godfather. Two ideas from this movie have been on my mind as of late.

The first is when Peter Clemenza is in the basement of his home teaching Michael Corleone how to shoot the gun, he will eventually use to kill Police Captain McCluskey and Virgil Solozzo at Louis restaurant in the Bronx. In the moment of privacy and solitude, Clemenza tells Michael how proud everyone was of him that he was a hero during the war. Clemenza then riffs about how Hitler should have been stopped in Munich, implying the war never would have happened if he were taken out long ago.

Pete Clemenza, while a fictional character, sees the world through the prism of his experiences and way of life in organized crime. In the Godfather's world, little problems are solved, and big problems are removed permanently. To allow the problem to remain is to prolong the inevitable of it being an ongoing problem.

Clemenza was referring to November 9, 1923, when Hitler led the failed and infamous Beer Hall Putsch. That incident landed Hitler in prison and concretized his desire to overthrow the government and embrace fascism and hatred. It was his entrée on to the world stage through anarchy and anger. The world should have taken his maniacal aspirations seriously and nipped them in the bud. Instead, they let Hitler fester and his ideology grow like a weed, and he did more damage than humanly thinkable. Peter Clemenza's way of handling a problem like Hitler is to remove him permanently, so that he is never an obstacle or problem for any being, forever more.

A little more than twenty-six years ago in Amman Jordan, the Mossad took on a gutsy attempt to assassinate Khaled Mesha'al, head of Hamas' terror unit at the time. The decision to take Mesha'al out came shortly after a suicide bomber detonated himself in the Machane Yehuda Market in Jerusalem, killing 16 civilians and injuring over 160. The bombings were increasing in frequency and Israel needed to stop them hard and stop them loudly.

This was not going to be a shoot and run job or a big bomb in a car ignition. Mesha'al was living in Jordan at the time, finding safe harbor. The plan was that when Mesha'al exited his car to enter his Hamas office in Amman, a Mossad agent disguised as a pedestrian would open a shaken can of cola that would spray all over the area. At the exact same time, another Mossad agent in the role of pedestrian would spray Mesha'al with a deadly poison. The idea was that the simultaneous spraying of poison with the exploding can would make Mesha'al think he was hit with fizzy cola. Within hours of contact on the skin, the poison would take effect and the Hamas head would die.

The plan almost went off perfectly except, in the last second, Mesha'al's daughter called out to her dad from the car he was exiting. He turned away and the cover was blown. The agents still opened the cola and sprayed the poison, but Khaled and his handlers knew what happened.

Mesha'al was rushed to the hospital where his life shortly hung in the balance. The two agents were grabbed and held by the Jordanian authorities who were livid. To pull this move off in Jordan was a slap in the face to King Hussein and his country. He was fuming mad. The hit gave the impression that Jordan and Israel were in on the scheme. Israel had egg on its face and needed to save the two agents lives, who surely would be brutally tortured and then killed if they did not intervene. The timing could not be worse. This was just a few years after the peace treaty between Israel and Jordan. Botching this could make the whole pact unravel.

The price for the release of the agents was the antidote to the poison to save Mesha'al and the release of Sheikh Yassin from an Israeli prison. Yassin was one of the kingpins of fomenting hatred and advocating violence against Israel. Releasing the Sheikh was an enormous price tag. I am sure he sanctioned dozens more bombings and attacks and even more Israelis died because of his release.

I know this sounds like a script in a Spielberg film. It might be one day, but this is how it all went down.

I keep coming back to Clemenza and his background telling Michael that were he in charge of politics and leadership, the plan would have been to remove Hitler in '23 like they were doing with Solozzo and McCluskey. In fact, Puzo and Coppola are quite brilliant to add that subtle line in the movie as a subtext for how some handle problems.

Israel cannot pause the DVR and rewind back to 1997 and choose to let Yassin rot in jail and Mesha'al die. But Israel can learn from these missed opportunities and pray over the philosophy of Peter Clemenza and whether the Godfather needs to be the methodology moving forward. To quote Michael Corleone, *"Solozzo is going to kill pop. He is the key. We must get to Solozzo."*

Allowing Mesha'al to live saved two Jewish people. Indeed, that was worth it. Not putting the crosshairs back on Mesha'al immediately, surely led to more dead Jews as did the release of Yassin. Mesha'al is still living the life in Qatar and worth billions of dollars. He has enriched himself while the people of Gaza fall lower on the poverty scale.

On May 13, 1948, the day before Israel declared independence a group of Jewish pioneers prepared for battle from neighboring enemies encountered a lone Bedouin shepherd who spotted their hide-out. A practical and ethical debate of whether to leave the shepherd be, since he is innocent or to kill him, because he might tell their location to the Arab aggressors, ensued. The group decided to allow him to leave and let him continue herding his sheep and carry onward.

The next day all the Jewish fighters were ambushed and killed. That is one of the main reasons Israel's day of memory has always preceded the celebrations of independence. It is a commemoration of the mass murder of Jews who paid a hefty price for following morality.

Ethics and practicality do not always jive. Most times they do. Even though I always tell my kid to walk away, there are a few times when my kid must fight. My kid has a duty to fight. My kid should defend her/himself. Ethics are constant but not absolute.

Israel has some serious tussling with ethics and practicality to do. Maybe that is why the word 'Israel' means to wrestle with God.

Next

Inherent in a Jewish soul is a drive to live.

I still cannot watch any of the videos circulating from the 7th. None. I cannot handle kids dancing or babies playing or lifeless bodies on a lawn. It is more than my eyes and heart can digest.

I am reading though. A lot.

One account I read was about a young man, all of 20 years old named Hersh from Jerusalem, who was at the Nova song festival with friends. He had his arm blown off from a Hamas thrown grenade but was still alive. The terrorists took him as a hostage. They ordered him to climb in the back of a pick-up truck with other hostages. He took his one good arm and pulled his body over the tailgate and into the bed of the truck.

Reading this account, I was amazed and shocked Hersh had the ability and strength to pull himself into that truck. Why did he not fight off the terrorists? Why did he not try and hurt them, knowing he might die but resist? Maybe he would overpower one of them. Maybe he could have used his energy to run.

What catapulted Hersh to the back of that truck was an innate power to live. It is how we are all designed. No matter how much life we are given, most just want more. More time, more laughter, more experiences, more tastes, more memories made, and more memories created.

When Emily Hand's dad shared with the journalists his tearful sigh of relief when he found out his 8-year-old daughter was found dead, I understood most of it, but was still a tad puzzled. His reasoning of not wanting his innocent, freckled face, 8-year-old kid to have to live through captivity, and the barbaric torture she would witness or worse, be subject to at the hands of Hamas, would make me wish for the same fate her dad wanted.

Yet hope is a power that cannot be quantified. Even the terminal patient and the doctor who shares the diagnosis have hope. They hope for a little longer than the timetable says. Hope that she is free from pain. Hope he comes back whole, free, ready to live and learn and love.

My heart is numb today when I learned that Emily's family has been notified that they now believe she was indeed abducted and being held by Hamas. Because these savages mutilated and burned bodies, identification through DNA has been a long process and one Israel until now, was unfamiliar with, especially in volume.

What is this single Irish father, a widower whose Israeli wife died from cancer a few years ago, to hope for now? Does he hope she is dead? Does he hope she is alive? What can he hope. Each worst-case scenario somehow still gets worse for this family.

The Hand family had already mourned little Emily's death. They sat *Shiva* for her. They cried for what was lost. Do they still say Kaddish for the loss of her innocence? Her youth? The trauma that will kill a part of her soul forever, even if she lives.

Will we be able to say the blessing, *Mechaye Hamaytim*, bringing the dead back to life when she is returned? If she does come back, will she have a pulse? And if she has heartbeat and breath in her lungs, will she even be alive?

The part of my mind that still believes in goodness and hope sees little Emily in Hersh's embrace, deep in a dark tunnel. Hersh tells Emily stories to make her laugh and reminds her that the IDF and their family is coming to get them both. Emily makes sure

Hersh's wounds stay clean. Together, they keep each other's bodies and spirits strong. In my dreams powered by hope, they are alive.

My heart bleeds open for these poor people – both the ones in captivity and the one being held hostage by Hamas while agonizing over the fate of their children.

May whatever be the best scenario that brings hope and relief to the Hand and Polin families and Hersh and Emily, come to be. I am just not sure which scenario that is.

32

November 6, 2023

Rashida Tlaib was censured in Congress yesterday. She is only the 25th congressperson to be censured in the almost 250-year history of the House of Representatives. Many Democrats crossed party lines to call out the Michigan based representative. I am relieved that for some, morality trumped party loyalty.

Tlaib's censure is bittersweet for me.

I love that America elected a Muslim, Palestinian woman to Congress. I think it is proof of America that Ilhan Omar, a Somali born woman who wears a religious head covering, serves to keep America and the foundations of freedom, tolerance and openness it was built upon, alive and strong. I love that Congress looks like America; black, white, male, female, trans, old, young, straight, gay, Jewish, Christian, Muslim and non-believers. That *is* America. That is the secret sauce that makes this country unique and successful.

What gets me is when those two particular congresswomen use tropes that demonize Jews or invoke chants that are genocidal against Israel. When pointed out, they do not pause and reflect on their hurtful words. They do not absorb how their sentiments lands on a different people. They double down and refused to back away or apologize.

Tlaib has traded snide comments about Israel and Omar, about Jews too many times. What bothers me more than their hatred is that they are disconnected from facts.

For example, Tlaib claims Israel is an apartheid country. Nothing could be further from the truth.

- In an apartheid country, Israeli Jews and Palestinian Muslims or Christians could not marry. In Israel they can and do.
- In an apartheid country, Israelis and Palestinians could not vote. In Israel, Palestinians and Israelis can and do.
- In an apartheid country, Israelis and Palestinians could not serve in the army. In Israel, Palestinians and Israelis can and do serve in the army.
- In an apartheid country, Israelis and Palestinians could not represent the judicial system. In Israel, Palestinians and Israelis can and do serve on the courts and as advocates. One of the chief justices of Israel is Arab. In a further irony, the Chief Justice who sentenced Israel's President Katzav to prison, is Arab.
- In an apartheid country, Israelis and Palestinians could not live in the same areas or sell lands to one another. In Israel, Palestinians and Israelis can and do live side by side. Ironically, it is forbidden in Palestinian areas, including Gaza, to sell land or property to a Jew, under penalty of death. *THAT* is apartheid.

This is not to say that there are not problems in Israel. The way too many Israelis treat Palestinians needs to be addressed in a serious way. There are, I would contend, racist elements and behaviors within Israeli society that needs to be dealt with soon. Settler violence towards Palestinians is criminal and immoral. Each incident and actor should be tried and punished. To commit those acts of violence in some twisted and distorted interpretation of the Torah is fanaticism. It is one step away from what radical Islamic fanatics on the other side do. If not reigned in, I worry of what those fringe elements will become.

None of those actions justify Tlaib continuing with her chant of *'River to Sea,'* nor her claims of Israel being an apartheid country. Nor does it excuse Omar talking about *'The Benjamins.'*

Here is another ironic detail related to Omar's antisemitic claims.

It has recently been revealed that Qatar has invested billions of dollars around U.S. college campuses. Qatar has also been harboring the Hamas heads of terrorism in their country and elevating them. The United Nations, UNRWA, the European Union and the United States, along with Qatar have donated trillions of dollars to the people of Gaza for aid and relief. Those funds have been embezzled and pilfered by Hamas and used for terror and enriching Hamas leadership.

Perhaps Representative Omar was referring to the Qatari *'Benjamins.'* Maybe the UN or EU *'Benjamins?'* Or was she glossing over those funds and their misappropriations to focus on the age-old antisemitic image of Jews and money.

I do not care what gender you identify as, what religion you are connected to, where you are from, who you are attracted to, or what color your skin is. If you are an elected official, you should be able to call balls and strikes, know right from wrong, without challenge. Of course, we can have debate on when life begins and whether it is the responsibility of the government or the individual to provide health care. Brutalizing children, raping teenage girls, kidnapping Holocaust survivors, setting people on fire can never be justified, excused by antisemitic tropes, chanted over with genocidal slogans or ignored. Never.

Both Tlaib and Omar, along with a 'squad' of others have consistently voted against aid to Israel. Beyond the dangers this poses to Israeli civilians, including denying Iron Dome funding to protect the innocent, it is replete with ignorance.

If Tlaib, Omar and the other mimicking members of the 'Squad' bothered to learn about aid to Israel as is their responsibility as elected officials, they would know that in the Memorandum of Understanding (MOU), the $3.5B of aid that goes to Israel annually, more than $3.1 Billion of that is products and materials manufactured and produced in America. Thus, by voting against aid, they are really voting against American jobs, the American economy and American infrastructure, along with making Israeli citizens more vulnerable. That either highlights serious incompetence or frightening hatred that transcends their patriotism and oath of office. Either way, their actions and behaviors should scare us.

Ritchie Torres, a member of Congress who is Black, gay, Latino and Puerto Rican runs in many of the same circles as Tlaib and Omar. He is the darling of the Progressives caucus in Congress. Best of all, he is one of the fiercest defenders of Israel. As he says, *"I defend Israel not despite being Progressive, but **because** I am a Progressive."*

Congressman Torres should be the standard of what nuance, understanding and advocacy for humanity can look and act like.

I do not care which party Tlaib and Omar represent or where they are from or what religion they believe in. What I do care is that they have facts and a moral compass. They seem to be missing both as of late.

It was Congressman Ritchie Torres that drew my attention to a disgusting moment on the college campus from last week.

Before I share, a short proviso. I have been writing a lot about comparisons between what is happening now and what happened during 1938-1945. I know it is not a comfortable equivalence for some. I do not toss these Holocaust analogies around lightly. Whoever said the past is prologue was genius. Below is an example of a terrifying similarity.

At Penn, a well-educated, Ivy League college student took to the podium in a rally and was speaking fondly about the *"joyful"* images of butchered Israelis from the *"glorious"* October 7th, massacre. This student felt *"happy"* upon hearing the news of dead Jews. In what appears to be a call for violence, she tells the crowd to *"hold that feeling in your hearts and bring it to the streets."* Congressman Torres points out this is not a patient in a psychiatric hospital. This is a student at one of the most prestigious universities in the world.

There is a toxic and sadistic ingredient to anyone who can relish in dead Jews. I expect that from Hamas and ISIS. I will not tolerate it on a campus where my community members attend and learn. It is too dangerous.

When I read about this student, I was immediately reminded of two examples from the Shoah. The first is Franz Stengl, the former commandant of Treblinka who fled to Argentina after the war, where he lived for more than twenty years without being brought to justice. Eventually, Simon Wiesenthal tracked him down. He was brought back to Europe and tried in Germany. At his trial, a photo album from Kurt Franz, the second in command at Treblinka was found. The title of Franz's picture album from the death camp was called *"The Good Old Days."*

Treblinka was notorious for being the most efficient extermination camp. In its stride, they could kill 17,000 people in one day. In less than 19 months close to 900,000 Jewish souls were systematically killed and then burned on rail tracks.

Franz photographed these atrocities and referred to them, and his partners in crime, nostalgically and with fondness.

Ilse Höess, Rudolf's wife, raised her children in a luxurious villa abutting the Auschwitz Concentration Camp. While prisoners were performing menial slave labor, dying of starvation and disease, Ilse and Rudolf's kids were frolicking in their swimming pool and swaying on their seesaw. She stayed loyal to Hitler and Nazi ideology until she died.

She recalled her time living in that villa as some of the best days of her life, filled with happiness and laughter.

Jews and gentiles are being hung and tortured just seconds away, within ear and eyeshot, and she was a living the good life. How can a person like that live in the same moral universe as you and me?

Question: Is this University of Pennsylvania student different from the likes of Stengl, Höess or Franz? A person who delights in the sight of dead Jews and pines for more. What has history told us about such people? How should we deal with such amoral characters?

Here is a satisfying nugget of related comeuppance.

Many of these hateful kids and adults who share their happiness in dead Jews, threaten to hurt or kill Zionists, taunt students on campus, demean them in the classroom, or tear down posters on streets of missing and captive people, are getting retribution.

There is a daily list of people outed for destroying missing signs, professors put on immediate leave and government officials fired. Students will soon be expelled, as they should. Some have been doxxed (where their pictures and behaviors are made public and shamed) and having job offers rescinded and scholarships revoked. These people and their supportive circles are denouncing their terminations and expulsions. They call it unfair and wrong.

Yet, these are the very same circles who invented and implemented cancel-culture. Except, now that they are on the other end, it lands differently.

I have never been a fan of cancel culture. I believe it removes a fundamental tenet of repentance and forgiveness from society. I hold true to my beliefs. Those who spoke with glee of dead Jews or taunted students on campus or threatened violence at a rally or said October 7th was deserved on the Jews or tore down signs devoid of compassion for human suffering, should be given a path to penitence and forgiveness. They just need to understand that forgiveness is given by spoken apology accompanied by proven deeds and acts.

I anxiously await both.

33

November 7, 2023

I hate the phrase, 'fake news.' I hate it because of the originator of the expression. I hate it because of the damage it does to the idea of a free press. I hate it because it erodes the integrity of journalists that are compromised by slinging that accusation their way. I never use the phrase. Ever.

That said, much of the media has been fast and loose with the data they are sharing and the source of said data. It is dangerous since retractions are usually printed in the back of the paper, if you get my gist. It is difficult to forget information once it is shared, even if that data is false. Ask some celebrities and their gerbils about that some time. Sharing bad data and recapturing it is tantamount to putting toothpaste back in the tube.

In Spring of 2002, in the thick of the second Intifada, a suicide bomber entered the Park Hotel in Netanya and detonated himself. He killed 30 people rejoicing at a Passover Seder and wounded 164 others. It was the 13th attack in 30 days, and it was the last straw for Prime Minister Ariel Sharon and the Israeli people. They could take no more.

Sharon ordered the army to make a siege of the city of Jenin, the origin of most bombers and terror that had plagued Israel for the previous 18 months. Israel wanted to stop the attacks and attackers before they set out from Jenin. Incidentally, it was after the Park Hotel Passover bombing and during the siege in Jenin that Ariel Sharon implemented the plan of a security wall for the West Bank.

When the IDF reached Jenin, they encountered booby-trapped homes meant to detonate upon entering, sniper attacks and other tricks that were waiting to kill many soldiers. They knew we were coming.

During the siege, the media reported that Israel was committing acts of genocide. Some described the numbers of dead Palestinians in Jenin as north of 5,000 souls. A building that was a terror enclave was demolished and the BBC reported that more than 2,000 Palestinians were believed to be underneath the rubble, left to die. The real number was three, and all the dead were tied to the Al Aqsa Martyrs Terror Brigade. One British reporter said the town stunk of corpses and the numbers of dead were in the 50-100 thousand range. Tom Gross, a middle east correspondent coined the phrase *Jeningrad* about the IDF siege on terror.

Day after day Israel was charged by the press with 'war crimes,' 'crimes against humanity,' 'genocide' and filling mass graves to hide dead Palestinian bodies. The information steadily flowed in from the Hamas leadership and Jihad groups to the press, and it was accepted at face value. Israel was called Nazis, Al Qaeda and the Taliban. Meanwhile, Israel was tight lipped with data, information and casualties.

Arafat and his cronies sold a massacre that was not, and most of Europe and other media outlets bought what he was selling.

Jump ahead to the end of the siege in Jenin. 23 IDF soldiers and 52 Palestinians (of whom 14 were civilians) were dead. Ultimately the Palestinian Authority, Human Rights Watch and the United Nations corroborated these figures.

I never read the apologies, the regrets or the retractions from ANY major news source after the truth surfaced. It was sensational and it sizzled. It was man biting a dog. Big bad Israel with tanks and guns removing terror cells that were blowing up buses, cafes and holiday meals and *we* were the ones committing crimes against humanity?! Absurd.

Today, there are reports from the Hamas led media that more than 10,000 Palestinians have been killed from this war and most are women and children.

Based on the data the IDF shares daily of the Hamas militants killed in action, Hamas numbers are not in the hemisphere of truth. By the conclusion of this war, the numbers will hopefully yield a high number of Hamas deaths. At that point, when the sunlight shines the truth, these falsified reports that are over exaggerated and not correct (most deaths will be combatants and what Hamas calls a civilian would qualify as a terrorist) will not matter. The damage will have been done. It is another dance of blaming and accusing Israel and taking the word of known terrorists and liars to paint an indelible picture. It is reprehensible. The toothpaste is out and not going back in the tube.

21 years after Jenin and the media is behaving the same. At the risk of using mouthwash, dare I say that many media outlets and Hamas are kindred spirits who both traffic in fake news. It is pathetic how many media places that are usually the target of the accusation of 'fake news,' are eating it up.

Worse than that, while the world weeps over these numbers, Hamas officials from Sinwar to Mesha'al have acknowledged that the price of liberation is a high civilian death count. Hamas calls itself a 'martyrdom people.' They tightly grasp the ideology that many will die to achieve their goals. Yet, they will use those deaths to leverage a narrative that will generate sympathy and turn the media against Israel. A double shame.

Next

When the Mossad started using operatives to kill terrorists, namely after Munich, they needed experts in explosives. This was new territory for the Mossad. They took people from the field who were authorities in dismantling bombs, not building them. What did Israel know from needing to build bombs?! This led to plenty of mistakes made in operations because of lack of preparedness in the skill of bomb building. The understanding between dismantling and building was profound. Ultimately, the skill set for taking apart a bomb is fundamentally different from building one.

Israel is struggling with human remains identification. Many bodies have still not been identified and thus, not buried. Families are agonizingly waiting in the balance for information on their loved ones. Israel has called in a team of archaeologists from around the country who are accustomed to sifting through dust and dirt and bone debris to determine how long ago someone lived. Except now, they are being asked to determine if the mutilated or charred remains of a person is male or female, old or young, and which family they are part of. They are not doing ancient archaeology but modern-day forensics. It requires a totally different skill set to identify bodies than determine if a set of artifacts or silver coins are from the Byzantine era or early Maccabees period. These experts are the best in the world at uncovering the thousands-year-old history of Jewish life in Israel. They are not trained at sifting through the remnants of modern Jewish life from 30 days ago. It reminds me of the Mossad and the struggle to build bombs by those who were trained to defuse them.

The same goes with preserving bodies until they are identified. Israel usually buries its dead within hours. Keeping bodies in a morgue and for long enough to make proper DNA confirmations is a reality the country never prepared for. Why would it? There is no mass refrigeration for preservation or forensics department in Israel trained to deal with this scale. Today, the country is in uncharted territory.

This is a whole new world for Israel. One that is unimaginable. We do not have professionals for these tasks. We have had to reallocate skills and trades which are adjacent to these skills to handle the situation as best as possible. It has made this time in Israel even more challenging and painful.

Next
Our Temple brings trips to Israel often. One usual stop for us is a small Moshav on the Gaza border called Netiv Ha'assarah.

This community was established in 1982 by 70 families who were forced to leave the Sinai Peninsula where they lived for the previous 15 years, after the conquer in 1967. Following the Camp David Peace Agreement between Israel and Egypt was signed, all the Jews of Sinai were forced to evacuate the region.

We connected with this community because of the unique peace initiative it started. Near the separation wall with Gaza, the people of the Moshav created a beautiful mosaic of small pieces of pottery. Signs with personal prayers and pleas for peace were affixed to the wall. Our groups regularly visited and placed these shards of pottery on the barrier. It was much like adding our prayer for peace, except this was offered not on paper in a crack in the Old City, rather on a newer wall that enabled security and was the difference of what was and what could be.

One of the members of the Moshav has guided two of our congregational trips to Morocco and the UAE, both new countries in the Abraham Accords peace initiatives. How ironic. This person is a sweet and kind soul who has developed a deep friendship with numerous members of our congregation. This added to the connective tissue of our community and this special Moshav.

On October 7th, Netiv Ha'assarah was hit by Hamas terrorists. No surprise since Netiv Ha'assarah is the community closest to Gaza. 16 people were murdered in cold blood.

Netiv Ha'assarah has been shut down because of its proximity to Gaza, (400 Meters away from the city of Lahia in Gaza). Its inhabitants are refugees living in hotels or with family throughout Israel or abroad. No one knows when they will be able to return home.

Netiv Ha'assarah has been evacuated twice now. First by Egypt during the Camp David Accords, now in war with Hamas. They are contracting in size and moving further away from the borders they once enjoyed. For all of those who claim that Israel 'occupies,' and Israel creates living challenges for Palestinians and forces its citizens to relocate, I point you to only one of numerous examples where our enemies continue to encroach on Israeli borders and narrow the space where Jews can live and sleep in peace.

How much more shrinkage of Israeli land will happen in the years ahead if we do not remove Hamas with such force that no group even considers a reprise?! I tremble to think of the slow goal our enemies are achieving.

Equally, when we were creating mosaics of peace on our wall, what were the people on the other side drawing and dreaming of? Perhaps that explains all one needs to know about what we are up against.

34

November 8, 2023

Whenever I am wearing my pastoral or counselor yarmulke, I remind the people I am meeting with that I am bound by confidence with whatever they share. The only exceptions are, if they tell me something that could bring physical or emotional harm to themselves or another, or if they are part of or covering up a felonious crime. When people share with me that they are having issues at work, challenges in their marriage, or turbulence at home, I try and listen empathically and give counsel, when possible. If the person(s) ever talks about self-harm or harming others, they have crossed the line of what can remain confidential, and I need to concern myself with their(s) and others' safety.

That is not an unusually hard line to walk and not challenging to understand. I did not need weeks of ethics training or days of legal courses to help define the line. It is simple. Everything stays in the vault unless they are going to hurt themselves or others, or a crime is involved.

My ethical parameters are no different than physicians, therapists, teachers, counselors or attorneys. These guiding principles should transcend geography, politics or religion.

You can probably appreciate my rage, anger and disgust upon learning about photo and video journalists who seem to have been made aware of the October 7th attack well in advance, and then documented the barbarism in real time. Some even participated in the actual attacks and chants. These so-called journalists then sold their pictures to well-known media outlets.

These correspondents must be bound to the same ethics as the professions mentioned above. That would require them to not participate in an attack – or any crime – that would cause death, destruction and violate dozens of international laws.

Important to note, these journalists are free-lancers and are not formally employed with any of the major companies they have done work for in the past or sold to on October 7th. If media outlets maintain their relationships with any of these journalists, they should be tried in the ICC for harboring and aiding known terrorists. One of the video journalists rode on a motorcycle with one of the jihadists, documenting the rampage while holding a grenade in his hand. The evidence is clear as sunlight. He was incriminated from his own camera.

Could you imagine a journalist donning a parachute and boarding a plane with the Al Qaeda hijackers on September 11th? Could you envision a reporter embedding with the SS at the door to the gas chambers in Birkenau? How about a broadcaster taking pictures of Jim Jones mixing the poison and Kool-Aid but still staying silent?

Journalists have ethics too. Every human has a basic moral code they need to follow. These so-called photojournalists violated every human decency and tenet that is core to the profession they belong. They are beneath the lowest dregs of any society.

One article I read on this topic was titled, *"The ethical challenges of photos journalists as part of the October 7th pogrom."*

What in the hell is the ethical dilemma? There is no dilemma. These journalists seemed to have been so aware of the attacks in advance that on a glorious Saturday morning, earlier than 6:00 AM, they were just causally waiting with running shoes and loads of film at the separation wall between Gaza and Israel for whatever might occur. These journalists could and should have alerted the authorities. They could and should have shared with their superiors what was going down. They could and should have made a moral choice. Instead, they were amoral. They were dishonorable and they were complicit in the atrocities that took place. They are not journalists. They are not civilians. They are terrorists. Plain and simple.

Perhaps most disgusting is when these 'journalists' are apprehended, and they still hold a grenade in their hand, and the IDF neutralizes the threat, the international world will condemn us for killing a journalist. Let's stop the shame-calling and hypocrisy and fake protections before they are implemented.

If any of these journalists would have been killed on October 7th or immediately after, they would have died as a terrorist. They were more a part of Hamas than they are an employee of any news outlet. They were accomplices in war crimes, genocide and crimes against humanity.

Today I saw a video from a gunfight in Jenin between Hamas and the IDF. A terrorist was shot and killed. The video shows a medic, dressed in a protective orange vest, running to the downed terrorist. The medic does not give mouth to mouth resuscitation. He doesn't perform CPR. He does not bind the Hamas person's wounds. The medic grabs the fallen terrorists machine gun and runs it to another terrorist waiting in the wings.

Woe to Israel if that "medic" were shot by the IDF. Condemnation would pour in fast and furious. Of course, the "medic" was carrying a weapon and then ferrying a weapon to other fighters to keep the siege alive. But wearing the vest protects him from being targeted. What an unfair scenario for any group. How depraved and morally corrupt!

The timing of the revelation of the collusion between Hamas and these journalists could not have been more painfully elegiac. This is the 85th anniversary of Kristallnacht – the night of Broken Glass pogroms that devastated Jewish shops and synagogues throughout Germany. It was the darkest foreshadow of what the coming years would bring for Jews in Europe.

Most believe that the November 1938 pogrom was spontaneous. They would be wrong.

A young Jewish boy named Hershel Grynszpan went to visit an anti-Hitler Nazi embassy official named Ernst Vom Rath, in Paris. Grynszpan was sixteen years young. He came to the embassy to lodge a complaint about his parent's treatment in Germany after they emigrated from Poland. When Vom Rath walked in to greet him, decked out in his Nazi finest, Grynszpan pulled out a gun and shot him five times.

Way before Snapchat, Twitter, Facebook, instant messaging, email, cell phones or pay phones, communication took much longer to get from Paris to Germany. Yet, within a few hours of Vom Rath's shooting, word had made it to Germany that the embassy secretary was dead. Thousands of angry people came to the streets within minutes, ready to march, set fires and beat Jews with batons.

How could they organize so quickly? And isn't it curious that this all went down on the same date as Hitler's failed Beer Hall putsch, only 15 years earlier?! Hmmm.

Serious Holocaust scholars contend that Grynszpan was a patsy used to rid the Nazi party of a thorny employee. Young Hershel was someone who could innocently light the match of a night of terror, riot, destruction and Jew hatred, which was ripe kindling for Germany.

Not so coincidentally, this was a similar modus-operandi that Hitler and Goebbels utilized to create the Reichstag fire and gain legislative control of Germany.

The collusion of the Gaza based journalists leads to a conspiracy that the world is quickly uncovering. The only ethical question to ask, is can we use pictures from known terrorists who profited from their duality of terrorism and photo contributor?

Judaism tells us clearly that one cannot read from a stolen Torah. We are not permitted to shake a stolen Lulav. We cannot pray while wearing a stolen *Talis*.

Perhaps these pictures should be removed from circulation or noted that they were taken by terrorists, so no one can profit from them evermore. Of course, the problem is it would remove more proof of the crimes committed against Israel and Jews by the evil Hamas. That is a serious conundrum that will not be easy to solve.

This Saturday night, as soon as the sun sets, I will be on my way to Israel. My mind is racing and my heart fluttering for this trip. I will share more. Until then, I wish you a Shabbat of peace and love and please God, a Shabbat of reunification for our hostages that need to come home.

35

November 9, 2023

In a few minutes I am boarding a plane to Israel. I have never been more frightened.

I do not scare easily. If you are reading this and have never met me, I am 6'0" tall and 235lbs, (after fasting). I am not easily intimidated and do not cry quickly, unlike some of my B&H rabbinic colleagues.

I am not afraid of bullets and bombs when in Israel. I am not scared of sirens going off in the middle of the night. I am not anxious to fly coach. I am petrified about what I am going to see and what my eyes and heart can absorb when I land in Israel.

Israel is part of my DNA. Our family has spent our summers in the Holy Land for the past 14 years. Our kids have been raised and shaped there every June, July and August. We have a community in Israel. We have favorite places where we shop, the guy we trust to do our laundry, restaurants we frequent and parks to hang out in on Shabbat. We integrate into the fabric of Israeli society every summer, and throughout the year. In any given twelve-month span, I can go and come from Israel north of five times. When my wife and I talk about where we will retire, Israel is the place that is the top of our list. Our kids have each been to Israel more than twenty times. It is our home away from home.

But now, I am going to a place that I know like the back of my hand, but it is wounded and hurting. My stomping grounds of Jerusalem will not look any different, but I am sure it does not feel the same. That is because I am going to a place where every person in the corner market or at the flower stand has someone who was killed or knows someone who is being held hostage. Everyone is wounded. Every soul walking the streets will not be smiling. Each person will be scared. Israel is that small and that closely knit.

When in Israel, we will meet people whose children, spouses, parents and siblings are being held by Hamas in Gaza. What can I say to them? How can I bring strength and comfort to them? I am not sure my heart can handle what it will witness. I am terrified to be adjacent to that pain, anguish and worry.

We will meet people who are sleeping on cousin's couches because their home is uninhabitable. Hamas set it ablaze, and they cannot live that close to the war zone. They have no idea if or when they can ever return home. They are coming to grips with the reality that nothing will be normal again. What can I say to those people that buoys their spirits?

We will meet members from ZAKA who are tasked with cleaning up body parts and mopping up blood. They have witnessed what the most deviant minds could not imagine. How can I bring calm to the noticeable tremble in their voice?

We will meet with first responders who ran up and down the streets and checked for pulses the night of October 7th. They had to distinguish those people who were shot and those who were brutalized. They are still at a makeshift camp helping the wounded soldiers in the Gaza envelope. What can I bring to offer them solace for the trauma they are carrying?

We are making *Shiva* visits to the family of soldiers who made the ultimate sacrifice protecting our homeland. They were killed ensuring my rite to live and love and imbibe the beauty of our country. They died protecting Jews worldwide. What words of consolation could be uttered?

We will see soldiers who have comrades who have died in their arms in recent days, and they cannot mourn them properly. They have fellow soldiers who have been seriously injured, yet they cannot visit them. These soldiers know they will soon go back into the war zone, and they are not sure which of them will return to their families and country standing on their own feet or carried off in a somber walk. What can we do for these soldiers to express our appreciation or show our love? How do we best demonstrate our support?

We will be in hospital rooms visiting those who have lost limbs, have bullet wounds and others who are carrying emotional scars that weigh more than bricks. How can our visit bring them relief?

This trip has me so scared for what I will see. I quaver just considering how ill prepared I am to deal with these circumstances and this moment.

12 years ago, my mother called me out of the blue to say my father had suddenly fallen sick. He was taken by ambulance to the hospital and was in the ICU. He was unresponsive. The prognosis was grim.

I dropped everything and flew to Florida immediately to be with him and my mom. My brother picked me up at the airport and I remember shaking. I was scared. What was I going to see? The man who gave me breath, taught me much and was a larger-than-life force was lying in bed motionless, a machine breathing for him and tubes coming in and out like a highway intersection.

My dad was a man I knew better than most and he was in a condition of helplessness. Even though I visited the sick for a living as a rabbi, I was wholly unprepared for the moment. I had spoken to my dad almost every day. We texted and emailed too. But next to that bed where he was hooked up to beeping monitors and clicking machines, I had no idea what to say. How to handle the situation. What to do. I was lost.

I am having that feeling of walking into that ICU room again.

Related
One of my proudest moments as a rabbi was watching how our community responded to the war in Ukraine. We took our ballroom that seats 450 people along with a dance floor and filled it to the rafters with supplies to be shipped over to the refugees and those fighting against Russia. We assembled a small army of more than 150 individuals who came and loaded the toothbrushes, baby formula, deodorant, socks, sleeping bags, Tylenol, and other items into large camp duffels. Eleven of us brought 147 duffels on two planes to Poland and the Ukrainian border on a humanitarian emergency mission. Those items were used within hours of landing in Poland.

A few weeks later, a Christian Ukrainian family of nine souls ended up at our doorstep. Our family decided to house them for a couple of days. That quickly turned into six weeks. One of them had a baby and the family of nine overnight became ten, (one arrived pregnant and gave birth in America). They all became an extension of our family.

Eventually, Temple Emanu-El found and furnished an entire home for this family near our synagogue. We are still paying for the rent for them as they continue to flee from Putin and his evil machinations. Our community has adopted this family and spoil them with clothes, sporting equipment, household items, cars, sight-seeing and tourist moments and lots of food. We love them very much.

Helping this family speaks volumes about the combined ethic of our community. My wife and I say regularly to each other that we are so proud of the community we chose to raise our kids within.

For this family though, I cannot appreciate for a minute what they must think. While we stick our chests out a little and boast of our goodness, how do they feel? I know they are beyond appreciative. They have shared in word and hugs and tears regularly how much our beneficence has inspired them.

Yet, I do not know what it feels like for someone to wear only borrowed or hand me down clothes. I do not know what it feels like to sleep in someone else's bed indefinitely or live under a roof someone else pays for.

We at the Temple do not second guess our generosity for a moment. We also follow Maimonides rules of charity as best we can, to maintain self-respect for the recipients of our assistances. However, the beneficiaries of our largess must feel indebted, humbled, beholden and at times, inadequate for being unable to fend and provide for themselves. I imagine it hurts their pride and sense of dignity. Sadly, there is no end in sight for these and other Ukrainians, fleeing their home for safety.

This war in Israel has forced hundreds of thousands of people to live from the kindness of neighbors. Those making the donations do not pause for a millisecond at offering up their space or wares to help those in their time of need. That is core to the Jewish spirit. But the acts of wearing borrowed clothes and sleeping on someone else's couch and eating another person's food must bruise their pride. It would, mine. How long can that sting last? How long can someone continue to be supported by others without a sense of guilt or worthlessness?

I am sure this feeling is unilateral. When this war in Israel happened, my family instantly decided we would open our home again for a displaced Israeli family. It is a no brainer for us. We need less than five minutes to get ready for them.

But for those coming in the house and living as a guest, I worry for their loss of dignity and self-esteem. It is just another casualty of this vicious attack and deadly war.

I am bracing my eyes for what I am about to witness. I am opening my heart to those in need. I am prepared to lift any spirit and add love to help restore dignity and purpose to those whose lives were shattered into pieces. Wish me strength.

36

November 10, 2023

During my most recent trips to Israel, I paused and marveled at the international representation at Ben Gurion airport. Taxing to the gate you could see tail fins of plans from China, Korea, South America, two from the United Arab Emirates, Bahrain, Canada, Morocco and more. Not to mention the carriers and cities that were being serviced in the United States. United Airlines flew from Washington DC, San Francisco, Chicago and Newark, twice a day. American Airlines was flying daily from Miami and JFK. Delta had daily flights from New York and Boston and Atlanta. I did not even mention the dozens of carriers servicing all of Europe. The only airport in Tel Aviv was a bustling hub of energy that allowed connections to all four corners of the globe.

Today taxing in, it was like the clocks were set back to 1947. The only tail fins one could see was El Al. I felt lonely.

Image courtesy of author

No US carriers are flying to Israel. None of the major European carriers have been here since October 8ᵗʰ. The flags of the various airplanes represented, have figuratively been hung lower than half mast. They are not visible. Will they rise again? If so, how long will it take? Will it be different and how?

I sat next to a Saba and Savta on my flight. They looked out the window with me upon arrival to Israel, noting landmarks and calling them out, like a grandparent who sees their grandkids from a distance and calls out their names and how they have grown. They realize their hand helped contributed to that next generation. These grandparents calling out Netanya and Caesarea and Tel Aviv were part of the hands that shaped these cities. You could sense pride, accomplishment and deep love in each syllable of every city that was mentioned.

I deplaned gingerly. Everywhere I stepped, there was broken glass (not literal). Shattered dreams and broken reality in tiny pieces, strewn everywhere. What was lost and the hopes of what could be in 75 years, were littered on the floor not yet swept up. That was either because the powers that be wanted the brokenness to serve as a reminder, or because in the business of war, the priority of sweeping fell by the wayside.

We were greeted with shelter signs, should rockets begin to rain down. A cold reminder of where we were and what was happening around. This was not a war that was. It *is* a war.

Image courtesy of author

Image courtesy of author

The large windowpanes that look out into the airport fountain from the arrival hallway, where thousands of people sip their last cups of Israeli coffee and spend what is left of the shekels in their pockets, grabbing souvenirs that escaped them on Ben Yehuda Street, is empty. A ghost town. Vacant. Like an abandoned property. It gave me the 1980's, cold war vibes of the movie, The Morning After. Just chairs and shops, most closed. Not a soul could be seen, except the lone immigrant in a uniform issued jump suit, sweeping the same floor he wiped yesterday, that has had no traffic since his last rounds.

At our synagogue, like most, the walls in our sanctuary are lined with bronze *Yahrzeit* plaques. I never spent too much time thinking about those plaques and what it means to our community. It has new resonance for me.

For almost two decades I would see people meander up to their loved one's plaque and weep. Often, they would take their fingers and caress the raised bronze lettering as if touching the face of a parent or a spouse. I have come to appreciate the presence of memory in our sacred space is a testament to history and our journey. It is that sense of memory which propels us forward. It is a reminder to everyone in the room praying, celebrating a wedding, listening to a lecture, observing a holiday or coming to meditate, that the memory of their loved one is amongst us.

Ben Gurion airport has opposing ramps, both that are walked down. Upon arrival, one ramp is oriented towards passport control. Upon leaving the country, one ramp takes you through the duty free and to the gates. Ironically, coming to Israel is called Aliyah, which means to raise up. But arriving and departing is made simpler. There is no climb. Just a stroll down a ramp to, or from, the Promised Land.

Equidistant on both ramps (which are visible one to the next, regardless of coming or going) are picture signs of each of the 242 hostages being held in Gaza. One sign per person. Infants, toddlers, kids, people my age, grandparents, Americans, Thai workers and Israelis, all side by side. In a not-so-subtle message, the government and people of Israel are telling any visitor, first aid worker, government official or clergy delegation the reality and pulse of the country right now, in their first steps amongst the proverbial shattered glass. What is being said without words is, you cannot step foot on the soil or have your passport scanned without knowing the trauma you will be entering. When it comes time to leave, you cannot escape the reality that still lives and breathes here every second those 242 souls are held against their will and their families cannot know their welfare or well-being. You might be able to leave, but they cannot, and their memory should be the last thing you see, before boarding to leave Israel.

I saw pictures of people whose stories I have come to know. Noa Argaman's face is seared into my memory. I can see her eyes filled with fright as she was forced on to a motorcycle and dragged into Gaza. Edan Alexander's picture made me pause. He is a

19-year-old boy from our hometown in New Jersey. Seeing his face on that poster which is also plastered all around our hometown was surreal. I saw the pictures of babies and toddlers and grandparents, not much different than the couple who sat next to me, or the innocent children who clapped when the plane touched down. The pain and hurt was immanent.

Image courtesy of author

Image courtesy of author

יהל שוהם
YAHEL SHOHAM
(3)

BRING
HER
HOME NOW!

BUSINESS AND MISSING
FAMILIES FORUM

Image courtesy of author

Usually, the luggage carousel belts are humming, and the porters are frenetically running around. Israelis are returning from trips abroad wearing Lebron James jerseys and grabbing suitcases stuffed they can barely zip, filled with amazon purchases and technology that is cheaper in the Diaspora. Christian pilgrimage groups, wearing matching white hats, name-tag lanyards dangling, usually gather near skinny kids holding up placards collecting groups and marshaling them to their awaiting bus. Bar Mitzvah families land eager to watch their kids get called to the Torah at the Western Wall. Tune in your hearing aids and you can hear Russian, Hebrew, French, German, Spanish, Portuguese, Amharic and Arabic even though each of those native speakers break their teeth answering me in English.

None of those sounds or energy were present. Just emptiness and a haunting silence. In the High Holiday prayer, *Unetaneh Toqef,* the author describes a similar silence with the poetic words, *Kol Demama Daka, Yishama* – a quiet sound that almost forces you to hear your thoughts.

243

The ground crew were bored. They were lazing on a drivable conveyor belt waiting for our arrival with little else to do before or after.

Image courtesy of author

The arrivals hall was the most jarring to me. I am used to wading through the throngs of people holding balloons and flowers greeting cousins from their weekend trip to Cyprus to find a taxi awaiting. I always insist on *Cafe Hafuch* – the Israeli name for cappuccino – and a bite before I leave the airport, so I can get the flavors of the country into my bloodstream as soon as possible.

Today, smack in the middle of the day, the arrivals hall was empty. No one was there. No balloons were visible. All the flowers were wilted in the refrigerated vending machine. Most of the shops were closed. Between most of the workers being called to military reserve duty and so few people arriving every day, the lack of pedestrian traffic meant it is financially prudent for shops to stay closed.

I asked a security guard how to get to a particular exit door where my driver was waiting. His face was tired, but he looked me in the eye and gave me detailed directions. He was more focused than usual. There was no typical dismissive words or body language.

When I thanked him profusely, he just looked at me. No, *"you are welcome,"* was uttered. He didn't even nod. Just a look.

Israelis cannot fake it very well. They always sucked at being disingenuous. I guess this was his way of saying, of course I can help you, but I, and we, are in no place for pleasantries. That is fair.

Image courtesy of author

Cabbies are camped out in the trunk of their car hoping for a fare. They look eagerly my way. When my eyes tell him I have ordered a ride, they hang their heads low again while taking a long drag of their cigarette. They go back to waiting.

The Israel that I had come to expect and know had all the same bones and muscle, but its spirit was shattered. I did not need to leave the airport to see, smell, hear, feel and taste the pain that would pave the streets to my destination.

Next

Above, I referenced 1947. It was on purpose. On Shabbat morning, our congregation was honored to host former Minister of Diaspora Affairs and Member of Knesset, Nachman Shai. We had a lengthy conversation with our community. At one point, I referenced this moment feeling like 1947. He corrected me and said, *"You mean 1948."*

While I am not above correction, I meant 1947.

On the 29th of November 1947, the United Nations voted to partition a piece of land which was governed under British rule, and before that under Turkish control during the Ottoman empire. The land was referred to as Palestine, though there was never a Palestinian country or Palestinian government in that place. There were Palestinian people living there, along with Jewish people and a myriad of other ethnicities, especially recent emigres from war-ravaged Europe.

The United Nations proposed taking this strip of land and divorcing it from the current British rule. It would then be split: 48% for a future Jewish State that had never to date existed in modern times. 48% for a future Palestinian State, that had never existed to date in modern times. The remaining 4% would be an international area near and around Jerusalem that would be governed by an international body.

This proposal was exuberantly accepted without any preconditions by the Jewish people. It was summarily rejected without any negotiations by the Palestinian people.

About six-months later, around 3:30 in the afternoon on May 14, 1948, upon Britain packing up their gear and leaving town, inside a small art gallery in Tel Aviv on the eve of the Sabbath, David Ben

Gurion declared the State of Israel. Minutes later, Lebanon, Syria, Jordan, Iraq, Saudi Arabia and Egypt all attacked the infantile country now known as Israel. The citizenry fought for over a year and lost 1% of the population only to ensure the Jewish people would indeed have a homeland. We won, but at a heavy cost.

When the cease fire was made, the Jewish people had a State. The armistice lines dotted a map with different borders than proposed, shaped by bloody and painful war with six neighbors. Jordan gained land, as did Egypt in the battle. The Palestinians were stateless, still.

I continue to refer to this time as 1947 with intention. The UN partition plan was rejected by the Palestinians and voted against by most of the Arab member states of the United Nations because they did not want ANY Jewish state to be present. Even if the territory were limited to Tel Aviv, or a strip the size of Gaza.

Today, on the mean streets of London and amongst the radical protestors shutting down Grand Central Station, none of these demonstrators are waving a flag begging for two-states for two-peoples. They are not questioning any more about borders or right of return or how to deal with Jerusalem. The rhetoric has taken a violent turn backwards in an attempt to turn Israel into a solely Palestinian State. It is a 76-year continuation of denying the right for a Jewish homeland and refusal to share any of the land with the Jewish people.

On October 7th, Hamas set our clocks back to 1947.

I volley between shock and resolve. I am shocked at the sheer audacity of continuing to deny Jewish sovereignty. I am dumbfounded that after turning the desert into a garden and sprouting skyscrapers, hi tech inventions and engineering baby eggplants to grow in sand, that we are supposed to walk away because Palestinians will settle at nothing less than the entirety of the land without any Jews present and will spill any amount of blood to achieve that goal.

I then lean towards resolve. I take mild relief at knowing what we are up against; a Palestinian mindset that explains the rejection of 1947, 1967, 2000, 2008 and more. It was never about their State. It was about ours. It was never about sharing land. It was about all of it for them and none for us.

After I brush off the shock, my spirit and determination become steely. We are not going anywhere. We are not budging. We are not moving. We will not clean up the mess the Palestinians make repeatedly by their poor choices and cries of victimhood. We will not fall prey to the crocodile tears of the Arab countries who care passionately about Gaza in a time of war and could care less about their poverty and self-inflicted squalor any other moment in time. Why? Because our enemies are fortified in demonizing Israel but have little desire to prop up Gaza and Palestinians.

It is 1947 again. The UN plan has been rejected again, so to speak. Until Guterres, the Secretary General of the United Nations, along with all the member countries can vote unanimously for the right of Israel to exist in peace, in sovereignty and self-determination in its ancestral homeland, well, then there is no conversation to be had and no negotiations to engage in.

If we must turn the calendar back to November 29, 1947, we can go it alone. The United States was then, and is now, our staunchest and most loyal ally. We will forever be indebted and appreciative for our shared values and deep, bipartisan friendship. But if Syria, Iran, Iraq and Yemen all choose to shoot rockets and throw hate our way, we know we triumphed once and we are confident we can do it again.

I am not cavalier about what that will take. Much blood and tears were spilled to build homes that sparkle as the sun rises against the Jerusalem stone. It will not be easy to rebuild our spirit and clean up the shattered glass. But we can and we will.

Jews have always been a people that carry lots of glue in our pockets. We take the broken and shattered pieces – of our Temple, of our exodus and persecutions in Spain, Russia, Eastern Europe, and of October 7th – and we put the broken pieces back together, even stronger than they were originally. It is a painstaking task that has constant reminders that we are not whole, perfect or pristine. But we are strong, even if we are so very fragile.

37

November 11, 2023

These streams have usually been a compilation of personal thoughts with a serving of history and a dash of opinion. For the next few days, while in Israel, I want to detail some experiences too.

It will take me months, if not years, to digest what we are seeing and experiencing.

I arrived from the airport, checked into the empty hotel and ran upstairs to my room to quickly shower. I grabbed the closest cab and we headed to Har Herzl, the Arlington Cemetery of Israel. A funeral for Yossi Hershkovitz was starting. While I did not know him personally, he once taught at the SAR school in Riverdale and was the principal of the Pelech Boys School in Jerusalem. We shared many friends in common. Yossi died in a tunnel that was booby-trapped by Hamas terrorists. He leaves both his parents, his wife, and six children.

The traffic crawled getting to the cemetery. Lining the streets were throngs of people standing at attention, waving blue and white flags, awaiting the funeral cortège for Yossi. Most of these people never knew him but they all loved him and wanted to pay homage for his sacrifice.

Upon entering the cemetery, makeshift tables with drinks, sandwiches and light snacks were available for anyone attending any funeral. I say *'any'* funeral because there have been dozens of funerals a day. There is a giant new section of freshly tilled soil that the dead of October 7th and most of the 45 – to date – soldiers who died in Gaza, are buried. It is haunting. A giant tent is set up over the graves. It will be there until they move to a new section. No *'if'* they move. We are all resigned to *'when'* they do.

Somehow or another I slithered my way towards the front of the masses waiting for the burial. My eyes scanned the crowd and I saw a familiar face. We were surprised to see each other. I asked if she knew Yossi and she pointed to her teenage son, fair haired and blue eyed with red rims, from tears.

"He was his principal," she said.

I put my hand on his shoulder and said how sorry I was. He just stared at me. What could he say?

Before the family walked in, about every fifteen minutes there were a set of announcements on the loudspeaker. They were not prerecorded. My Hebrew is pretty good, but I was not able to piece it together. They said something about the pain of the family and that we should all pray for the soldiers and wounded. Then they said we have 1 minute and 30 seconds. We need to get to the floor and hands on our head.

I had attended many a funeral in Israel but never a military funeral and never at Har Herzl. Was this a form of mourning for soldiers?

Was this a Sephardic custom? Do we greet mourners at the grave for this short time?

After the third round of announcements, I turned to that familiar face and sheepishly said, *"What is this custom about 1 minute and 30 seconds?"*

She said, *"That is how long we have if there are rockets overhead from Gaza. Get to the ground and cover your head."* She then went on to say that at a few of the funerals there were sirens in Jerusalem.

My God! I was fresh off the plane and totally oblivious to what was the reality and jargon of life here. Even at funerals, instructions for rockets and shrapnel overhead had to be given. My mind was on mourning. Everyone else's mind was on mourning *AND* on knowing how to protect themselves if rocket sirens are heard. This was their daily life, and I was walking right into it like a simpleton. Unaware. Naïve.

In the front of the open grave where the family was supposed to sit, were chairs for dignitaries. Yossi's commanding officer was there. A few others from his platoon. Noticeably present was the Mayor of Jerusalem, Moshe Lyon. He eulogized Yossi eloquently. Noticeably absent was Bibi.

When 9/11 happened, Mayor Rudy Giuliani attended EVERY fire-fighter's funeral. Every single one. All 343. Rudy might be a free-falling nutcase now, but at that horrible time for New York, he personified leadership and grace. Bibi's absence was noticed.

I looked back to the crowd, and while never very good at estimating crowds, there must have been 7-8 thousand people assembled. They joined in a soft chant of consoling songs. Have you ever heard 8,000 people sing softly? It is beyond description. It wasn't loud but the sounds were in stereo, from all directions.

This is the rain season in Israel, but it was unusually warm. Summer is hanging on and not letting go. I thought to myself, Israel doesn't need a rainy season. The collective tears will give all the water the country needs.

Yossi's father eulogized him. How strange that a father eulogizes a son?! Then, Yossi's oldest son spoke. In a painful poetry, his name is Be'eri, which is the same name as the Kibbutz near Gaza that was hit worst on the 7th of October. Now there is a second Be'eri that is shattered.

Please forgive me for what I am about to write. It hurt to hear those eulogies. It pained me to look in every direction and see grown, tall men, rifles slung over their shoulders, wallowing in tears. Whimpers were heard like a kennel full of puppies whose mother was taken from them. And at the very same time, right then and there, I felt whole again. For the first time in five-weeks my body was complete. My feet were exactly where my heart had been. They were united. I was home and exactly where I needed to be. That felt whole. It was incredibly painful, but right.

I went from the cemetery to my cousin's house where family from my side and my wife's side convened. We were in no mindset to go to a restaurant. We picked up dinner and ate at her kitchen table. This is not a 2PlateSolution.com trip.

I hugged each cousin tightly. They let go of me, but I would not let go of them. They were worried because I squeezed them so. They predicted that being in Israel would help me. I hope they are right.

Within two bites we began talking about the *Matzav*, Hebrew for the situation. Not the Jersey Shore situation. We danced from Hezbollah to Hamas to our kids to kids in the army to what Bibi should do and how Benny Gantz is handling the forced marriage of joint leadership and what we think of Biden and Blinken and more. It was a jagged conversation. We were all over the place and still, the conversation flowed. Six of us around the table and we were already disagreeing on little things like strategy and timing but united in resolve and purpose. We would pepper in some lighthearted moments to the meal and stopped every few minutes for check ins on each other's kids and family. Even as I exited, I realized I forgot to ask how one cousin's mom was feeling. I felt badly but also knew she understood.

After a very little sleep, I headed to a morning *Shiva* minyan for Rose Lubin. Rose was about the same age as my daughter. She made Aliyah and was a border patrol officer in the IDF. On October 7th, she happened to be at Kibbutz Sa'ad, which is near Gaza. The members of the Kibbutz heard there was a terrorist infiltration and six people, including Rose, stood at the gates of the kibbutz and fended off the terrorists for hours with handguns. In addition to shooting, Rose was instrumental in getting wounded kids from the Nova festival into Sa'ad for safety and medical triage. Rose was one of the many unsung heroes of that day.

A few weeks later, Rose was back in Jerusalem, working her beat in the Old City. A 15-year-old terrorist took a knife and stabbed her and her colleague. She succumbed to her wounds about 12 hours later.

Rose was a lone soldier. She was from Atlanta, and her dad's family was from Memphis. Like my wife and her family, she was a bonafide Southern Jewess. Her family all flew in to bury their daughter, grand-daughter, sister and niece. Rose was buried at Har Herzl. Her *Shiva* was set up outside the David Citadel hotel, in a large tent filled with plastic chairs and rows of soda bottles and lite bites. In that way it was like any other *Shiva*, though it wasn't.

I arrived a few minutes early and put on my Tefillin. I noticed a woman who seemed Western and bore an English accent. I found out it was Rose's aunt. We exchanged pleasantries and it was clear she would tell me who everyone is. She pointed out Rose's two brothers and sister. Then, she pointed to a finely dressed, sweet man who did not seem too old. Maybe early 70s. Svelte. Kind eyes. She said that is Rose's grandfather.

Her grandfather?! I had to see a grandfather say kaddish for a grandchild?

Sometimes, God is cruel.

The Minyan was full of people. Soldiers next to family, next to city officials, next to friends, next to other border patrol police, next to random rabbis visiting from the States.

Rose's little sister sat with an aunt and nestled herself into the crook of her shoulder. She lost her big sister. While I do not know any of the family dynamics, I am a little brother. I bet this little girl lost more than her sister. She lost her north star. Her idol. Her confidant. Her friend. She also lost her innocence and perhaps her faith.

My heart ached just looking her way.

When I connected with my bus driver for the week, Ovadiah, I told him that I went to the funeral yesterday at Mount Herzl. He asked, *"Which one?"* and listed the names of the dead who were interred yesterday like he was the foreman at the cemetery. When I said I visited the *Shiva*, he did the same thing.

Usually, *Shivas* are limited to family and social circles. In Israel that always expands a bit. In times of war, the social orbit has no borders. Everyone is mourning. Everyone brings support along with something they baked. It is one of the many beautiful colors about this place that shines brightest in the darkest hours.

257

One last reflection, and one last piece of data. Trigger warning. The reflection is about politics and the data point is hard to digest.

The cab driver who took me to the cemetery yesterday was from central casting. He was Mizrahi with a raspy voice from 3 packs of Marlboros a day. He did not wear a kippah, but he keeps kosher and prays thrice daily, in between his smoke breaks. You get the picture.

Before I even said hello, he murmured to me with shoulders shrugged, *"What's going to be?"*

I said to him, *"I have no idea. What do you think?"*

In Israel, every cab driver is a frustrated Prime Minister. They seem to have most of the answers to the world's problems if you bother to ask them and they are in the mood to share.

He says to me in his thick Hebrew, *"Every morning since October 7th, I put on Tefillin and I turn to pray to God. I say, 'God. How? Why? How in the hell did you allow me to vote for Bibi, God?'"*

That is **NOT** what I expected to hear from him.

He then held forth for the slow ride to the cemetery about how Bibi betrayed the entire nation. That the investigations and trials were child's play compared to this moment. He explained, *"There is no excuse for leaving the country vulnerable. For the army being MIA. For Bibi not owning this disaster, since at the least, he was in the pilot's seat when it happened. And for all the shenanigans that led to division and anger and protests which took our collective eyes off the ball."*

What makes his point even sharper for me, is this driver is cut from the cloth of someone who would usually lay down in traffic to protect Bibi. His sworn defender. Someone who thought Bibi could do no wrong. Ever. In his food chain there was God, then Bibi, then the Prophets and Angels and then his family.

Yet this wannabe Prime Minister who moonlights driving a cab agreed with Benny Gantz, which is the sentiment of most the country right now. First, we must decisively win this war. Decisively. Win it hard. Then, we deal with Bibi and elections. First things first.

How the mighty have fallen.

Data point. This is very sad and real.

I have been wondering why Israel, with all its technologies, still does not have a firm grasp on names and identities and whereabouts of all the dead and/or hostages. As painful a task as it is, it is five weeks later, and we still do not have clarity and finality on who is a hostage and who is dead and letting these poor families know their fate. It is unconscionable.

I found out why many believe it has taken so long.

The Israeli Air Force were the first to respond to the attack of the 7th. From two reliable sources, it appears they enacted the Hannibal directive.

When the pilots saw from the sky that terrorists taking Israelis civilians against their will into Gaza, they chose to kill them and the terrorists. This is the Hannibal directive. This was a difficult and very controversial choice the Israeli government chose to enact after the capture in 1986 of Israeli POWs. They were painfully and slowly tortured. Then, in 2006, this directive was re-instituted after the abductions of Gilad Shalit, Eldad Regev and Ehud Goldwasser. The Israeli government has wanted to stop kidnapping at all costs. Needless to say, this has been hotly debated and wildly painful before October 7th. All the mores so, today.

The potency of the bombs used by the air force has left little remnant of human life. Figuring out which fragment is human and which bone belongs to a terrorist versus a hostage is painstaking and slow. This is the reason we do not have all the names and data, yet.

Today, we believe there are 239 hostages being held against their will. We have no idea which of them are alive, injured or just lifeless bodies that will be leveraged for negotiations.

May they all come home safely and soon.

Important Addendum that I am sad I need to include. I will share it the only way I know how.

A car is a serious responsibility. If used properly, it can drive us to work, pick kids up at school, bring people to the doctor.

If used improperly, a car can be a weapon. It can hurt, maim and kill. So too, with words and information.

I wrote about the Hannibal directive in my Streams of Anxious Consciousness 37 post. I did so with a heavy heart and soft fingers. This situation and the ethical choices being made are impossible to answer.

The piece was not published by my blog host, The Times of Israel, for fair reason. The government has not shared any information about the Hannibal directive being applied on October 7th. While I have heard from several sources it was used, no statement from the government has been issued.

Further, and most painful, the propaganda of our enemies claim that Israel killed all the Israelis and there are no hostages in Gaza held by Hamas.

The last thing I EVER want to do is give fuel to our enemies. They have had enough victories with the pain and suffering they have inflicted on this country and its people.

At the same time, explaining some of what might have happened is of value to the concerned and moral reader.

I understand and appreciate why the blog host did not publish this piece. I also appreciate the need to know of a possible other narrative/side.

May those alive be brought home. May those dead, be buried with dignity and may their families have a sense of closure.

38

November 12, 2023

Not every hero wears a cape. This country is full of cape-less heroes. Scores of books will be written about them. Until then, I want to highlight a few special souls I have seen and met while in Israel.

There is a refugee humanitarian crisis in Israel. More than 200,000 souls have been evicted from their homes in the North and South of Israel. Hotels in resort towns of Eilat and surrounding the Dead Sea, which of course are empty because there are no tourists are here, have opened their doors to families and those without a place to plant themselves for the undetermined future. 200,000 people is more than can be satisfied in resort town hotels. Further, the Dead Sea and Eilat are very far from the rest of the country. These people need community now more than ever.

There are six five-star-hotels in Jerusalem. They are appointed with fine leather furnishings from Italy and specialize in customer service and breakfasts that will blow your socks off. Most of them are right near one another. Each has a name and a niche they cater towards. But only one of the five-star-hotels (I believe), the Inbal Hotel, under the leadership of General Manager Rony Timsit and Nahum Mazor, the VP of Inbal, opened their doors to refugees.

As we eat breakfast, there are families who were forced from their homes on the northern border of Lebanon, whose sweet little kids are innocently salivating over the pizza at the buffet, eating amongst us. Who knows how long they will be there. The parents look at these kids and are jealous of their innocence.

The hotel is not being paid by the government for these rooms. The refugees are not contributing a nickel, nor should they. The hotel is assuming a major financial loss, beyond wear and tear for this mitzvah. I applaud Rony and Nahum for leading by example and doing the right thing for these unlucky souls. They deserve capes!

Another cape worthy group

In Tel Aviv yesterday, we visited a narrow, almost communist architectural style building, smack in the center of town. The owner of the office space in the building started by donating an empty floor to the families of the hostages. Within a few days, he donated the entire building.

Each floor in the seven-story complex is dedicated to a different angle of the crisis: media relations, foreign press, negotiations, proof of life, psychological support and so on. It was there we met with two family members, each dealing with different realities. Every single person working the phones, typing on computers, liaising between families and the media, or even those bringing in catering is a volunteer. Every single one.

On the fifth floor of this building, we met with Meirav, the mother of 23-year-old Romy. Her daughter was doing what all 23-year-olds should have been doing on a holiday weekend, dancing at an outdoor music festival. She called her mom in a panic at 6:23 AM, when the barrage of rockets started to fly overhead. Romy was alarmed. Romy lives in the north. What did she know from sirens and rockets?

She was back and forth on the phone all morning with her mom. Calling in fright, tears and panic. At 10:12 AM she called her mom and said she was shot. Her best friend was shot too and wounded badly. The driver of the car they hoped to escape in was dead. Romy was in the backseat. She was in pain.

Her mother, intuitively understanding the severity of the moment, said to herself, *"If Romy is going to die from this gunshot, I want her to die knowing how loved she is."*

Meirav began telling Romy all the attributes and traits that made her so special. She told her all the places they were going to visit as soon as she gets back home. And she *WILL* get back home. She told her how loved she is.

Meirav heard her daughter moaning in pain. Then she heard Arabic and her daughter screamed. The line went dead.

About 24 hours later Romy's phone was pinged to Gaza, which is why her family is confident she is being held there. We have no idea how severe her wounds are. We do not know if she developed an infection. No one knows if Romy is getting medical aid.

Meirav is a pillar of strength.

Dvir is the uncle of 10-month-old twins. Dvir makes me look scrawny. He is strong, tough and steely at first glance. His eyes and voice were worthy of a different body. Dvir is spent, exhausted, worried and breathless. I got the idea his tear-tank was running on empty. Both babies' – his nephews – parents were killed early in the morning on October 7th. The babies are orphans.

Thankfully, they are too little to remember the trauma their family is carrying. I am sure that each simcha, family Shabbat dinner, *Siddur* or *Humash* ceremony will be loaded with pain and anguish for the surviving family that these children will never fully comprehend.

What Dvir told us about how the babies survived is even more horrific. He only recently learned from the IDF, Israel Police and Shaba'k what went down, since it has been proven that Hamas was not above brutalizing infants.

The terrorists took the babies out of the dead hands of their parents in the safe room and put them back in their cribs. There, they would lie hungry and in dirty diapers, and would cry. When neighbors and the IDF and first responders heard babies crying, instincts would compel them to run towards the sound.

The terrorists hid out on a roof and in bushes and assassinated every single responder who tried to rescue the babies. Hamas did not only kill 1400 people. They attempted to murder our ethos. They wanted us to second guess our intuitions of running towards helpless, crying babies.

Monsters.

Dvir and his family have the responsibility of mourning his sister and brother-in-law, looking after his parents who survived this tragedy and the loss of their children, and his family has the responsibility that is physical and equally emotional, to raise these children in as normal a fashion as humanly possible.

Meirav and Dvir need capes. The community supporting them right now needs capes. The person who donated the space for this group to convene deserves a cape.

A communal cape

The people of Tel Aviv have taken the square outside of the art museum and transformed it into *Kikar Hatufim* – Hostage Square. In the square, there are numerous art installations, countless pictures, signs and a national sit-in where families of the kidnapped are holding a 24/7 vigil. The vibe is like a hospital waiting room. People bracing for the worst and hoping for the best. This space has been a national catharsis center for near family members and the distantly connected civilian.

Everything in the square is donated, including the physical space. The food that is brought for people sitting, the songs sung, the raincoats and chairs are all an act of communal goodness.

The consolation and emotional triage this space has offered is incalculable. It has given comfort and support to the entire nation of Israel. All involved need capes.

Gloves but no capes

I just left Barzilay Hospital in the center of Ashkelon. We visited wounded soldiers. They are scattered amongst the patients of the hospital that are suffering illnesses which do not know about war. Cancer doesn't recede for war. Appendicitis doesn't skip a visit for war. COVID does not know from war. But war brings in trauma. Lots of it. Especially when you are close to the battlefield.

This hospital was command central for the first and worst injured of October 7th, because of its proximity to Gaza. As a result, soldiers, doctors, nurses, volunteers have set up homes near the hospital for the family of injured to stay. One family told us that strangers gave them the key to their home and said, you are staying at our home. We have stocked the fridge. We are staying with

STREAMS OF SHATTERED CONSCIOUSNESS

family in Tel Aviv, so you have this home to yourself while your son heals. Nurses and doctors and orderlies are working double and triple shifts with no overtime. Only because they need to. They want to. They must.

There are not enough capes.

I have been coming to Israel most of my life. I have never felt a sense of unity and cohesion like we are experiencing now. There is a slight sense of shame to think that so many small arguments and bickering and divisions dominated the narrative for many years. It tore at our fabric except, it seems to have been elastic. We are snapping back.

I saw a sign near the Knesset on my way into town Sunday night. In Hebrew it said, *Achdut Ad Nitzachon*. The slogan translates to *Unity until Victory*. It flows in Hebrew, but the literal translation can be critically parsed. What happens after victory? What then? Is the unity done? How long will the inertia of war and unity last? Can we milk it for all its worth? For all that we will need in the aftermath of this war.

I sure hope we do not revert to the bickering and debates. If so, we might have lost part of this war and its timeless lessons.

39

November 13, 2023

Nuance has been lost in the west. Ironically, in circles that boast of being more than binary, well-educated fools know either-or. One or the other. The proverbial shades of gray have been lost.

In Israel, nuance is baked into the air that is breathed.

A handful of years ago, Tamar Zandberg, the political head of Meretz (the ultra-left of Israel) was a guest speaker at the J Street conference in Washington. This would be a friendly crowd for her. They clapped and rah-rah-ed every syllable of her speech until she said, *"And of course, we can never allow Iran to gain nuclear capabilities. We will have to stop them at all costs."*

Crickets.

The left leaning, peace loving, tree hugging crowd did not know what to do when one of their darlings said something that wasn't so darling to them. Her words went against the grain of peace, the ethos of the left and didn't rhyme with Kumbaya.

The well-educated, well meaning, well purposed American Jews of J Street had no idea what *"yes, and"* looks like. They could not hold both truths.

To be totally transparent and fair, while not a J Street card carrying member, the same phenomenon happens in the other direction at AIPAC conferences. This is not a rant on J Street, rather one example of how right or left leaning organizations cannot hold two truths or negotiate nuance well.

At breakfast this morning, I sipped coffee with my dear friend who I will call, 'Ron.' This 40 something Sabra is a literal tree-hugger. Ron is the kind of guy who on any hike can tell you what flower is blooming, which variety of bird is circling overhead and is a dyed in the wool peacenik. He has led countless marches to end the occupation and is outspoken about peace. I do not agree with much of Ron's political views, but boy, do I love and respect him.

In between sips of espresso and nibbles of freshly picked cucumbers, Ron said to me, *"We (Israel) must engage with Hezbollah. Now. We must rid the country and the world of the threat they pose. A lot more soldiers and Israeli civilians will die, and innocent people in Lebanon too. Still, we must do it."*

Ron's approach made perfect sense to me. This left leaning, tree snuggling fellow who says we must go to war just clicked like a seat belt. Ron said it assuredly but with a grimace that resembled a heartburn face. He knows it comes at a cost. While Ron's non-binary approach made sense to me, I am not so sure it is something that will make sense to most of my Western friends who comfortably live in a binary world.

Maybe Ron knows that teenage kids living in the center of Israel in cities like Modi'in are peeing their pajamas in the middle of the night. Post B'nai Mitzvah aged adolescents are sleeping in their parents' bed. They wake up with night terrors and are sure they hear tunneling under the bed. They live in a high rise, so the concerns are suspect. But the fear is as real as it gets.

Refugees from the North staying in our hotel put the little ones to bed and go to the courtyard outside to puff a cigarette and drink Turkish coffee. I joined them last night, though I passed on the cigarette. They told me in no uncertain terms, they are not going back to their homes up North unless the threat of Hezbollah is eliminated. Not weakened. Not demoted. Eliminated. Their neighbors share their sentiments. After seeing the first act of Hamas in the play of terror, who can blame them?! Quiet borders are no longer the standard. Quiet borders with no enemies present and no stockpiled weapons is the new baseline. It must be. The strategy of the game changed dramatically overnight. Achieving that standard will be deadly and painful. Still, it is necessary.

The rabbis who stood with Rashida Tlaib yesterday in Washington DC, calling for a ceasefire repulse me. They never spoke to the people of the North or the parents changing wet sheets of an eleven-year-old. I have no interest cavorting with Tlaib. I can forgive those rabbis for their choice of friends. But, to call for a ceasefire today is living in that binary world, devoid from nuance, absent reality, missing context and political topography. It is stupid.

Calls for a ceasefire is nothing more than virtue-signaling on a world stage. Those who believe in peace and loathe the right wing and the bloodshed of war think the answer is to drop our weapons and run toward our enemy with outstretched arms, to a warm embrace. Cue the Enya music and roll credits. That is *not* how this movie ends.

What these *nudniks* do not realize is that our enemy will hug us tightly and then pull the pin on a grenade for us both to die. That is how this movie concludes. It is a horror show, not a feel-good drama.

In my second Stream, I quoted George W. Bush days after 9/11 who famously said, *"You are either with us or against us."* How do we call for a cease fire with an enemy who goes on EVERY media outlet and proudly proclaims that they will continue to kill and rape and pillage until every Jew is gone? And worse, they do not just say it. They have proven it!

Can these ceasefire rabbis not see that? Can they not appreciate that the value of peace is lost if there are no peace-loving people left alive?

Hamas is an equal opportunity terrorist organization. They do not differentiate between the left or right when killing Jews. Sadly, they do not even limit their killing to Jews. Christians are high on their targets too. Hamas and Hezbollah have no qualms about killing Muslims if they stand in the way of their stated agenda. Killers are killers.

Equally annoying to those calling for a ceasefire are the virtue signaling heads of state who have lamented the excessive women and children killed in Gaza. Justin Trudeau of Canada decried that the Israeli killing of women and children in Gaza must stop. Macron of France said almost the same sentiments. Both, and dozens of others put the onus on Israel for these *"unnecessary"* deaths.

Why can't Trudeau and Macron and others say, in a simple, non-binary way, *"We are heartsick over the death of innocent people in Gaza and Israel. We blame Hamas for instigating this war, causing this bloodshed and using these innocent women and children as shields and protectors for their evil purposes. Too many women and children have died. For shame on Hamas who are responsible for their death."*

In this proposed sentence, the sentiments are the same and the true culprit is exposed and clearly demarcated for the world to know.

Ironically, in this war, there is a binary choice. A good side and a bad side. To conflate the two in any way is dangerous. To cast any blame on Israel and its right to defend itself is criminal.

Of course, Israel is not above reproach. The people of Israel spent 10 months protesting about the wrongs of the government and its leadership, mistakes made, and images tarnished. In a post October 7th world, eradicating Hamas is not a tricky decision or one that should call into question our moral barometer. I am just not sure why so many outside of Israel struggle with nuance? For smart people, it is dumb!

40

November 14, 2023

When Steven Spielberg decided to film <u>Schindler's List</u> in black and white, he only highlighted half of his genius. The other half was displayed when he drew the viewers' attention in multiple scenes to the lone girl in a red coat. She was the only person that was in color throughout the movie. This unnamed girl's journey to the ghetto, then her wandering aimlessly during the chaos of the liquidation of the ghetto, and finally, her lifeless little body still wearing the red coat, being cremated, showed the short and painful arc of her tragic life in color amidst the dreary gray. Spielberg was reminding us that every person, every kid, every pair of shoes and each hat and coat is its own story. A unique history. A particular memoir, cut short.

(Shoah Foundation website, via Facebook)

On this mission to Israel, one of our very first meetings was with Dvir, the burly uncle of the 10-month-old twins I wrote about a few days ago. These babies' parents were murdered early on the 7th of October in their home. Dvir's nuclear and extended family live in K'far Azza, near the border of Gaza.

Yesterday, when writing about heroes without capes, we met with Hatzalah first responders who were the very ones who took custody of these orphaned infants early in the morning of the 8th of October when they could be saved, safely. The babies were crying ferociously and were dangerously dehydrated. The Hatzalah responders called their headquarters asking for counsel. Never had they encountered an experience with treating babies when no parents were present or accessible. On this same day, we met the medics who treated the dehydrated babies and visited the same hospital where they were examined and nourished and reunited with aunts, uncles and grandparents.

Today, we donned military grade helmets and bullet proof vests for a tour of K'far Azza. Three residents who used to live there, took us around and told us stories of people who lived in the Kibbutz. I intentionally used the past tense. They also shared the fate of each person as we passed their home. *"This one was killed. This one was kidnapped. This one was injured. This one was a miracle. This one was out of town that weekend,"* they shared matter-of-factly. Unreal.

A few minutes deep into the devastation and horror, tiptoeing over broken glass and charred walls and bullet holes in every direction, the guide pointed out the home where terrorists used the babies to draw people in and kill them. The very same twin babies whose uncle, Dvir we met, and who the responders from Hatzalah saved and brought to the hospital. We saw the remnants of their nursery and what must have been their stroller on the porch of their home. I could not believe how close we were to their story.

Then, we left K'far Azza and headed to a small village just a little North of Tel Aviv, called Shfayim, where my kids used to play in the water park during our summers in Israel. Most of the displaced residents of K'far Azza are making Shfayim their home for now. We went to meet these forced refugees and hear them recount their stories. Each was more frightening than the last. We saw the homes and destruction and their stories closed a loop of their nightmarish saga.

Upon walking in to Shfayim, I saw a woman whose face looked familiar, but I could not place her. She was on the floor playing with twin babies. I had a strange intuition.

Without permission, I plopped myself down on the floor where the babies were holding on to furniture, cruising. I turned to the woman and calmly asked in Hebrew, *"Are you Dvir's sister?"*

"Yes" she said with a look of some surprise – since I came out of nowhere and clearly knew her, but still, little is surprising her these days.

I then reached out my hands to the twins and one came to my embrace. I said, to her, *"These are the twins."* I did not ask the question. I was making a statement. She looked at me with eyes that said yes. No nod. No words. But we both knew.

I kissed one of the babies on his forehead like he was my own. He is all our babies. I played peekaboo with him. He flashed giant smiles my direction that showed me his baby teeth breaking through their gums. He kept a keen eye on his brother. Thank God for those smiles, or I would have been streaming tears. No one needed that. These kids will have a lifetime of people looking at them and crying. Let them smile and learn to walk.

On our first day of our mission, we met D'vir and heard his story and the story of his twin nephews. On our second day, we met the medics who rescued the twin babies and transported them to the hospital. We visited the hospital that treated them and reunited them with their aunts, uncles and grandparents. The next day, we saw the home where these twins lived and the place where life was ripped from their parents. Today, we walk into the relocated community of K'far Azza, now in Shfayim, and the first sight we encounter are these same twins. In the flesh. In diapers. Smiling. Drooling. Whining. Sucking a bottle.

It was like Spielberg's girl in the red coat. This coincidence was unrehearsed. Unscheduled. They were there in technicolor.

The twins' story has been woven into each day and is living in my heart and head. It will be forever. These babies. Our babies. Their pain. Our pain. Death and life. Smiles and tears. Despair and hope. One thread weaving through it all. Is the thread making a quilt to warm us or is the thread unraveling the blanket of security and comfort?

Time will tell.

41

November 15, 2023

Orange trees still grow on Kibbutz K'far Azza. They shouldn't. Anything alive that witnessed October 7th and its aftermath should die. It should rot quickly. But the orange trees are still blooming.

The Talmud teaches that when someone steals seeds and plants them, they will still bloom. That is the world's way, the rabbis explain.

I was tempted to pick an orange and taste it. I was sure it would be sour. Spoiled. Toxic. It had to be. Still, I couldn't pluck it from the tree. In some weird way, it felt like I was removing a witness from the atrocities that happened there. The fruit trees were connected to someone's property and taking it was stealing, even if the homeowners were no longer living there. Even if they were dead. Even if they were kidnapped and we know they would be fine sharing with an empathetic, fellow Jew. I couldn't touch the fruit. Those fruit trees haunted me.

K'far Azza (image courtesy of author)

For almost 30 years I have been leading groups of teens and adults to Poland to take testimony of the vibrancy of life that lived in Eastern Europe for almost half a millennium. We then pivot to the rise of Nazism and the unspeakable acts of degradation and murder that exterminated more than ⅓ of the Jewish population.

Walking in Birkenau, 78 years post liberation is walking in a museum. It is hallowed grounds and haunting, but the distance between the events of the Holocaust and our visit is two generations, sometimes even three. It is powerful and potent, but most is left to testimony and imagination that accompany the stacks of history books and research.

78 years later and Jews are still being killed for our mere existence.

K'far Azza is a mixed community of religious and secular Jews, Ashkenazim and Mizrahi. It is situated less than 1 kilometer from Gaza. The residents there had a slogan. *K'far Azza is 95% heaven and 5% hell.*

Until October 6th, life was a grand in the Kibbutz of about 1000 people. They farmed. They worked in high tech. They were doctors and lawyers and teachers and accountants and scientists and social workers. K'far Azza is full of moms and dads, sons and daughters, sisters and brothers, bubbies and zaydies, kids and adults. They are you and me.

5% of the time the residents of K'far Azza dealt with rockets. Usually because of Israeli policies or targeted assassinations or Iran's puppeteers pulling strings. They were relatively infrequent, and Iron Dome gave K'far Azza a sense of security from above. What happened here on the 7th came from the ground, just across the cabbage fields that was an international border. The residents of K'far Azza came face to face, eye to eye, tooth to tooth with Hamas terrorists living next door, who came to murder them.

K'far Azza (image courtesy of author)

Yesterday, I walked through the once bustling Kibbutz of K'far Azza. There were no generational divides. This was no museum or memorial. It was fresh. The sidewalks were lined with broken glass. The stench of burnt homes was pungent. Bullet holes the size of my knuckles freckled the façade of every building. Couches and beds were overturned, and computers broken into itty bitty pieces. Strollers with toys and pacifiers were strewn everywhere. Playgrounds were uprooted. Just a few weeks ago kids played carefree in those spaces. Now, spray paint by the IDF marks where bodies were found, and bullet casings were retrieved.

I came to K'far Azza for the very same reasons I visit Poland; to take testimony. To refute those who deny our painful history and now reality. To bring hope and hugs to the suffering survivors and to bring a proverbial hammer and nail for when it is a time to rebuild. And rebuild we will. But this pain is raw. In the Jewish timeline of mourning, we have just barely finished the *Shloshim* – 30-day period – post burial. Time has not begun to digest this atrocity. We are far from the process of healing.

A few homes in K'far Azza had a handful of spaces left intact. One office filled with smoke and some water damage had a row of organized folders listing all the Jewish holidays and books of receipts. I admired this person organization. With no DNA evidence, I was able to trace their family back to Germany. A *Yekke* Jew.

The Sukkot were still up in the yards. This nightmare happened on the official last hours of the holiday. One Sukkah had the texts for *Ushpizzin* still dangling on its walls. That is the hallowed ritual of inviting different guests into our Sukkot to break bread and enjoy the holiday. The sick irony was not lost on any of us.

K'far Azza (image courtesy of author)

In K'far Azza, each home has a Kibbutz issued address and name sign. They are uniform. On the house itself, people could hang their own nameplates that matched their spirit and vibe.

One sign was mangled, twisted, riddled with shrapnel and knocked to the ground. The apt family name on the address plate was Hebrew for "Lucky." Little luck would be found on these grounds on the 7th of October.

Terrorists infiltrated under the distraction of rocket fire at 6:33 AM. The Kibbutz of 950 souls was taken over, while most had not yet had their coffee, and all were still in pajamas. About 300 terrorists in all. Factoring who was away or on vacation that is almost 1 terrorist for every 2 people.

A survivor said to us it was like ants, they were everywhere. Arabic was heard all around and men in black ninja suits and green head bands rummaged carefree through people's belongings and shot women and babies, like they were paper targets. Murder did not move them. It didn't jar them. Affect them. They were nonchalant about raping a woman and killing her with a single shot to her head when they were done.

One woman was found naked, legs open and bloodied. She also had a pool of blood from a gunshot to her head. The monstrous animals finished raping her, killed her and then put a grenade in her hand so the responders who came to save and retrieve her would get killed.

In total 62 were murdered in K'far Azza. 18 people were kidnapped, including 7 children. We know nothing about their conditions or whereabouts. The Red Cross has still not visited ANY of the abducted.

Below is the most frightening data point.

THERE ARE DOZENS OF K'FAR AZZAS!

What happened in K'far Azza also happened in Be'eri. In Ofakim. In Netiv Ha'Asarah. In Nachal Oz. In Alumim. In Nir Am. In Magen. In Kissufim and countless more communities. More than 3,000 terrorists blew through gates and trampled walls and did unspeakable and unthinkable things. Their pulses did not even rise during this savagery. To call them animals is an insult to zoos and pets, worldwide.

The atrocities of K'far Azza were identical in these other places, but different. Each story is unique. Each family has been touched by *Mazal*, timing of being in the right place at the right time, or the curse of being in the wrong place in the worst time.

You might have witnessed physical destruction and devastation in your travels. I was in New Orleans post Katrina where death was abound and homes were leveled. I have never seen wreckage like this in my life. Most important to distinguish, K'far Azza was not a natural disaster. This was the most unnatural crimes carried out by subhuman monsters. This did not need to happen.

1200 were killed on the 7th 238 are held hostages. 5,000 are physically wounded. 9 million are emotionally traumatized. Each one is a story. A life. A fingerprint that is unlike any other in the world.

Our responsibility for today and tomorrow is to take testimony. We need to plant orange trees. We need to harvest fruits and to share the sweetness of its nectar and the bitterness of its rind for generations to come. That is the reason I came here. That is my motivation to keep coming back.

42

November 16, 2023

When I was sixteen years old, on a hot summer night in the suburbs of Detroit where I grew up, my parents let me use their new car to see a friend visiting from out of town. The plan was to pick him up at the hotel he and his family were staying, and to play a game of pick-up basketball, as we teenagers often did.

I parked the car in the lot outside the hotel, locked the door, hugged my friend and we headed back to the car except, it was not there. I was questioning my memory. I was sure I parked it in this spot. I did not see it. I walked up and down the lot and could not find the car. The keys were still in my hand.

I looked down and saw a large pile of broken glass where I remembered parking the car and it struck me. The car was stolen. Someone knocked out the window and took my parents' car.

Following police reports and my parents coming to pick me up, I got home to find officers parked outside our home.

My mother explained with the garage door opener was on the visor of the car. The police wanted to be extra careful and ensure we are safe, and no one comes to do further harm.

I did not sleep that night. I did nothing wrong. I drove safely and within the speed limit. I locked the doors. I used the car with permission. Still, I was violated. My sense of security that I had taken for granted was defiled. It inhibited me from sleeping soundly and feeling safe in my suburban, upper-middle-class neighborhood in Michigan. My sense of safety security was violently assaulted, and I felt it.

A speaker we shared breakfast with while in Israel this week, who allowed me to quote his remarks without attribution, explained that for the first time in its existence, Israel lost its sovereignty over the land. The country is coming to grips with the violation of its sense of security, safety and loss of autonomy.

For almost three full days, Hamas had control of the towns, Kibbutzim and villages in the Gaza envelope. Terrorists were walking freely and plucking food from people's refrigerators like they owned the property. They walked unreservedly throughout these villages as if they were taking a leisurely stroll. They ruled the area. Hamas' feet were on the coffee tables. One terrorist was found hiding in a home six days after the breach.

Israel most decidedly lost its sovereignty. Yes, we do control the area now and there is a strong and noticeable police and army presence blanketing the region. Still, I worry about how we gain our sense of security after losing our control – and in such a violent manner – ever again.

Was not Israel established in the smoke of the Holocaust so that sense of insecurity and vulnerability could never come to light? Was not the unspoken credo of Israel that if any Jew faces antisemitism, hatred or violence, they can come to Israel where they will be safe. That contract was broken. The sense of safety dissolved suddenly. Israel lost its credibility to speak or imply those sentiments again.

I do not remember when it was that I could sleep soundly again after my car was stolen. It took a while. The feeling of violation reverberated for years. I predict that the raping of our sovereignty and freedoms will take generations to rebuild. For those of us loving Israel from near and far, we are going to need kid gloves and to tread gingerly as this sense of security and trust is slowly reclaimed.

Next

My teenage son asked me today, in a hopeful tone, *"Dad, if all of the hostages are returned tomorrow, will that mean the war is over?"*

It is a good question. From his perspective, we are fighting the war to get the hostages back. I agree with him, kind of. But it is deeper than that.

The hostages complicate the strategy in this war. In fact, they make it counter-intuitive, and I am positive Hamas was not expecting our ferocious response.

When Gilad Shalit was held captive, we did not send in a force to rescue him. We negotiated. In the end, we traded over 1,000 prisoners for his safe return. At the time, I thought it was the greatest decision Israel could make. I celebrated Shalit's reunification with his family and nation. We have now learned the problem with negotiating with terrorists is it gives a road map to our weakest nerves and a license to do the same behaviors again.

Hamas must have surmised 250 hostages would yield EVERY Palestinian in Israeli prison would be set free in exchange for these civilians' lives. Hamas must have figured Israel would pay any price for their safe return. I think that is true. We would give them all the prisoners for the hostages, if we had faith that would happen. But Hamas did not think – to borrow a concept from Yitzchak Rabin, *of blessed memory*, – that we would wage war like there are no hostages and that we would negotiate for the hostages' release like there is no war.

I said to my son, that while I would dance and cry at the release of every hostage and the return of all bodies of Jews or those taken from Israel, it will *not* be the end of this war. We must keep going. We must eradicate Hamas.

It is true tactically; the war might change if we repatriated every hostage. Nonetheless, our goal must be to continue until Hamas and those connected to them are destroyed.

A few days ago, on our way to Barzilai hospital in Ashkelon, our phones went off with red alerts. Instantly, we heard the sirens blaring while aboard a chartered bus. Our driver quickly pulled to the side of the road, and we all ran for cover against a concrete wall. We saw the smoke trail of the Kassam fired from Gaza and then saw and heard the Iron Dome interceptors. The Dome shot down most of the rockets but two fell in Ashkelon. Thankfully, no one was injured.

In a crouched position next to that concrete wall, covering my head next to fourteen of my rabbinic colleagues, I yelled out, *"How in the **EXPLETIVE** do they still have rockets???!!"* I meant it.

More than 11,000 rockets have been fired from Gaza in the past five weeks. I know we said there would be no math in these Streams – so the average over 42 days of war is 261 rockets per day!

That is when I realized that this war will be over when no rocket is launched. Ever again.

If three months from now, or twelve months from now, or five years from now, one lone rocket is launched from Gaza into Israel, even if Iron Dome can intercept it, this war will be deemed a failure. We will have botched our role to make it safe for the people living in the South of Israel. Once *one* rocket can launch, regardless of its accuracy or potency, even if some sophisticated system can shoot it down, it brings the people living in Israel to a stark reminder of what was and what will be. That is unacceptable.

In the Jewish understanding of repentance, a person must do three things to fulfill the role of *Teshuva*. First, they recognize that which they did wrong. Second, they fix the wrong as best as possible. And third, they vow to never do it again. The entire time they continue to not do the act again, they are considered in the process of repentance, or *Teshuva* in Hebrew.

You can liken it to a person claiming to be a recovering alcoholic. She might say she has not touched alcohol in 34 years. From her vantage point though, she is still recovering and, in that process forever. There is no time limit for her to claim she is healed. The process is ongoing and never ending.

I am not applying this metaphor in some naïve attempt to offer Hamas a chance to amend their ways. They are a lost cause.

I am however sharing this idea that if Gaza remains rocket free, so to speak, and terrorist free, then we will be in the process of regaining our sovereignty and in the process of ending the war. We will not be done with this war until that happens. It will be ongoing and next to impossible to qualify, except in reverse.

The old idea of dealing with rockets sporadically and sleeping under the blanket of Iron Dome can no longer be our way of existence. We know where that leads. It is an appetizer in a terrorist's menu of horror and carnage.

We can also no longer to accept Israel *"mowing the lawn."* That was the phrase used by Knesset and IDF leadership that every few years, we would bomb Gaza and weaken Hamas and their abilities. The grass keeps growing back. This time, the weeds took over the yard.

How do I explain to my son that we will only know the war has ended and was successful if we can look back forty years from now and know there have been no rockets and no infiltrations. That is a backwards and unconventional standard to know of success.

In Judaism, we are used to backwards systems to determine progress.

When I ask people about their Jewish lineage, most can rattle off that their parents are Jewish and grandparents are Jewish, and trace back a few generations of history.

What I usually reply though, is to tell if someone did Jewish right, is for a grandparent to see if their grandchild is actively engaged in their Jewish identity. Then they know that they are Jewish, and they did *Jewish,* right. We do not look backwards; we look forward to know if we were behaving Jewishly.

So too, we are going to have to look backwards a long time from now, in a quiet and rocket free zone, to realize that we indeed were victorious in this war. I hope we are up for the wait.

43

November 17, 2023

Having just returned from Israel, everyone keeps anxiously asking, *"How was it? How was Israel? How are the people?"* As if they want an assessment from the family member who visited the wounded patient at her bedside.

It is hard to focus on one answer. Some things I saw made me feel low and sad as I have ever felt. Other moments I witnessed reminded me why Israel is strong, why we will prevail and overcome this moment and why I am so proud to be a Zionist.

My colleague, Rabbi Josh Ben Gideon remarked that the atmosphere in Israel reminded him of Dickens' Tale of Two Cities, *"It was the best of times, and it was the worst of times."* That is how Israel felt.

In a world of Twitter (X now), we do better with *'It was the best of times.'* Or *'It was the worst of times.'* Holding two truths makes our competing narrative hard to explain.

Perhaps you read last week about an Israeli coffee shop owner on the Upper East Side of Manhattan. Aaron Dahan owns and operates Caffe Aronne. He was unexpectedly knocked off his feet when his pro-Palestinian baristas quit in unison, leaving Dahan empty handed for the morning coffee rush.

Dahan, an Israeli born Jew, proudly hung a flag of Israel in his store and plastered the walls of his establishment with pictures of hostages who were taken from Israel on the 7th of October. The young, woke and naïve coffee makers working for Dahan decided to protest by donning Palestinian shirts and quitting. Apparently, they would rather be unemployed and stand on uninformed ceremony.

Dahan called his mother in panic and begged her to stop what she was doing and to get down to the store and help him make cappuccino. She did one better. She posted the story of what happened to Aaron online. Within minutes, it went viral. People lined up for hours just to order a macchiato or chai latte and support an establishment that is pro-Israel.

A few days before Café Aronne, Peter Tsadilas, the owner of the Golden Globe Diner in Huntington, Long Island began displaying Israeli flags and posters to support efforts to return the hostages taken in the Israel-Hamas war. Peter is Greek. The hostages have tugged at his heart strings. He thought he could raise awareness and do his small part from far away to make a difference.

Throngs of patrons to the diner complained. The pictures and advocacy made them uncomfortable. They wanted to enjoy his famous spanakopita without political interference. Tsadilas thought to himself, "These pictures make you uncomfortable? Goodness! What must these captives be dealing with? Or their families?" He held his ground, even though some patrons stop eating at his diner.

Tsadilas' story also went viral, quickly. Within a few hours, the Jewish community of Long Island channeled their inner New Jersey and started frequenting this diner. The Jewish community stood up and supported Peter in amazing ways with more customers than usual and better profits than the average month. Good for Peter and for us!

Some people tell me these stories saying, *"Rabbi. Did you hear about the coffee shop that was shut down because the pro-Palestinian workers quit en masse?"* or *"Rabbi, did you hear about the diner that was being boycotted for being pro-Israel?"*

A few other people tell me the other side of the story. *"Rabbi. Did you know the wait for a pro-Israel coffee shop in Manhattan is more than two hours?! That is incredible!"*

That is the conundrum of the Jewish story of today. It is either the worst of times or the best of times. In truth, it is both, at the *same* time.

The country and people of Israel were chock full of moments of despair, coupled with unprecedented moments of unity and strength. Naomi Shemer wrote in her song, *Al Kol Eleh,* *"We bless the honey, and the stinger of the bee."* That sums up the emotions at this moment.

This is not a novel concept. The mixture of emotions is something native to our Jewish cycle. Glass breaking under a Chuppah, pouring wine out from our cups at the Passover Seder feast, blasting the Shofar of hope to conclude Yom Kippur, fasting the day before Purim are all feelings that go against the grain of the prevailing emotion of the moment. We are a people without one absolute feeling at any given time. We are a mixture of bitter and sweet, honey and stinger, protesters and supporters.

In our reborn identity, we must do better at holding these polarities in the same hand and at the same time. We are capable of that and more.

Next

There is change afoot in Israel. It is awkward to describe, yet it is palpable on the streets and in the Israeli spirit. The people of Israel are about to be reinvented. Fortunately, on timing and not so fortunately for the reason, the Jews in the Diaspora are changing their identities too. In the long game, I am pretty sure this will be a good awakening for both.

Yossi Klein Halevi used a line with me this past week over breakfast in Jerusalem that resonated deeply. He said, *"David, how did we almost allow a divorce between Israeli and Diaspora Jewry?"*

That was the perfect metaphor. We had grown so distant, shared so few values, travelled in such different circles that our toes were no longer touching under the sheets. October 7th shocked us both into a shared rhythm with common identities and mutual enemies. We realized not only that we *do* have deep love for one another, but that we need our relationship to stay strong to survive. We are touching toes again. We are connecting again. It feels good and right.

My rabbinic office sees more than its share of marital couples on the brink of the abyss. For the many couples that have survived the darkest days, there are three key takeaways they have in common:

1) Hard work, serious sacrifice and dedication are needed to make changes.
2) Continually reminding the other of the past and the pain caused has a very short window of acceptability. Both parties need to look forward.
3) Lastly, and perhaps most importantly, all couples agreed that their relationship was stronger and better after going through their marital earthquake.

I predict that Israel and Diaspora Jewry will emerge from this moment stronger than ever. Pain and sadness are always the precursor for growth and development. We have both been seriously pierced and pained since the first week in October. I am convinced that this hard reset will result in the new and improved 2.0 version of our relationship.

Things will need to change, though. The nostalgia of Arik Einstein songs, falafel stands, silly t-shirts that read Guns n' Moses and buying trinkets in the Arab *Shuk* will need to be replaced with more serious, thoughtful, modern and mature connections. A new Israel and new gratefulness of our Jewish identity needs to emerge. We can have a reborn appreciation of Israeli music and musicians, and a renewed appreciation of the curious mind of the Israeli. The Start Up chutzpah spirit can be better understood by those living outside of Israel. At the same time, Israelis will need to ratchet up their understating and support of pluralistic Judaism and how our religious streams function and thrive. Israelis can better appreciate that American Jews are more than a blank check of support. And Israelis can be better educated on the cadence of Diaspora Jewish life.

In 50 years, I have never witnessed unity in Israel like today. When I said that line to my favorite cab driver, Shimon, he replied, *"That is because in 50 years we have never had unity like this. Ever!"* He continued, *"It is the only positive development to come out of this nightmare."*

The unspoken takeaway in Israel from this unity is that the status quo will not continue. Crooked politicians, religious streams bickering, negating non-Orthodox lifestyles, Jewish settler violence, systemic racism, threats of terrorism will no longer be tolerated. Extremism – on both sides – will no longer be stomached. It is about time! It is painful to appreciate what brought us here. Still, we are here, and we do not want to ever go back to what was. We will forge ahead with what can be. What must be. What can be. That will take both sides of the pond being in this together, in unity.

It would be tragic to let this moment of unity and harmony peter out in time. We cannot lose its momentum. It must be channeled for change and for good. That is up to all of us to have long memories of what was and the ability to let go of grudges and lingering resentments. We can hold those two incongruent certainties, simultaneously.

Ironically, a terror attack that reminds us of yesteryear will be the impetus that forges a new tomorrow. Let it be so.

44

November 18, 2023

On Saturday night, friends who are more like family joined us for dinner at a local restaurant. It was the first time I had interacted socially with another couple in five weeks. Dinner, a drink and some conversation about our kids was a noble attempt for all of us to take our minds away from reality. Sadly, it did not last long.

Before the waitress took drink orders, our friends, who I will call Jack and Diane, shared disturbing news about their sophomore son at a prestigious private school in New York. The 15-year-old student has been the subject of antisemitism from one of his teachers. Were this story not told to me first person, I would have a hard time believing it.

Their son's teacher made outlandish claims to Jack and Diane's son which included that Israel bombing Gaza increases the chances that terrorists will bomb the New York City subways, and thus Israel is endangering his (the teacher's) life.

He also claimed in class that the Nazis were really trying to acquire land, and in the process had to kill some Jews. Land procurement was Nazism's primary goal. Plus, the teacher refused to condemn Hamas.

Read those sentences again, slowly.

This teacher earned a PhD. He teaches impressionable high school students. He is on staff at a prestigious private school in New York City.

My wife and I were empathetic to their ordeal while incredulous to the reality of their situation. The school seems to be handling it as best as it can, for now. Jack and Diane are exemplary parents who have given a clinic on standing their ground and being supportive of their son, while taking the school and the teacher to task. Still, it is traumatic to be the victim of lies, mistruths and blame, and even harder when the victim is 15 years young.

The conversation detoured a bit after salad when Jack asked me how he "convinces" people on the margins that Israel is behaving morally.

We entered a long and respectful tête-à-tête about keys to enter conversation with anyone on the topic.

I firmly believe that each person needs to be asked two simple and foundational questions:

- Do you believe the Jewish people are entitled to live and exist in the Nation State of Israel?
- Do you believe Israel has the right, if not the obligation, to defend itself and its citizens from those who seek to harm her?

I said to Jack that if any person cannot answer 'yes' to both of those questions, no further conversation could be had. There is no 'convincing' to be done.

My point to Jack was that this is a moral war. When people pose questions that rank me less than other humans because of my religion or Zionism, I will not fight for my right to be seen equally and *THEN* argue why my country behaves morally. If human beings cannot see me as equal, we can have no conversation to move forward.

In essence, those two simple questions are the litmus test for entry to conversation and dialogue. But discourse cannot be had with anyone who cannot agree to those core, common criteria.

I pushed this point hard with Jack because we all must work on a level playing field. Sadly, the media, his kid's teacher and even much of society are not holding Israel and Jews to an equal standard.

Just today, international media is condemning Israel for a gunfight at the Indonesian hospital in Gaza. Have we not read this book already? The IDF claims that it was returning hostile gunfire from militants inside the hospital. I believe them. Here is why.

Sixty-three – and counting – soldiers have been killed to date in Gaza. These Hamas snipers and bombers and terrorists are devoid of scruples. They will hide behind children, shoot from ICU beds and ferry weapons in ambulances. This has been documented and proven. Still, Israel is expected to allow the terror to continue against them and not defend itself. The bleeding and leading story is still *"Israelis firing at a hospital"* when the story should be, *"Terrorists taking cover in a hospital and violating international law."*

Last week I was visiting a hospital in Ashkelon. I stood at the very spot where just a few days earlier a Qassam rocket from Gaza hit the hospital. It was near the pediatric ward. Thank God, no one was physically wounded. It did significant damage.

I am sure you all heard the United Nations condemn the bombing of the hospital. Or perhaps you tuned in when CNN, Fox, and the major three networks criticized Hamas for the attack on a building meant to provide medical treatment? Did you hear the outrage after the bombing of the Israeli hospital, a clear violation of international law? Perhaps you heard international leaders condemn the bombing by Hamas?

Of course, you did not. Neither did I. Do a google search of the rocket attack in Ashkelon and you will see all the Israeli news sites reporting on the missile landing and not one Western news source covering the story. That is the point. The playing field is not level.

Today, 29 babies in incubators were safely evacuated from Shifa hospital and transferred to medical facilities in Egypt. I pray for their health and well-being.
How ironic, that on World Children's Day, Israel helps coordinate and facilitate the rescue of these sick children while at the exact same time, fifty children have been held by Hamas for almost as many days (50), and no signs of life have been offered. We do not know if they are receiving medicine, nourishment or care. They cannot communicate with their parents or siblings. The International Red Cross (ICRC) has not been granted access to visit them.

If someone dares to denounce Israel for delaying the transfer or endangering the lives of these infants and is silent on the Jewish children ranging in age from ten-months to 18-years held against their will by Hamas, then they are frauds who traffic in double standards. They demonstrate another example of the uneven playing field plaguing the Jewish community.

Worse than that, when we are treated unevenly and unfairly, it begins to erode a sense of empathy for these premature children and the plight of the innocents. Compassion and care should be reciprocal. Why is the world seeing it as a one-way street?

A new form of asymmetrical warfare is being waged in Gaza and in the orbit of those who care about this war. One standard is set for Gazans, and another is set for Israel. It is shameful. These tactics are taken from the oldest playbooks of antisemitism, bigotry and hatred.

A colleague who has a high-ranking position in the Israeli government has spent the last four weeks in the Gaza envelope taking media personnel and political leadership around the destruction created by Hamas. He shares firsthand accounts of the terror that reigned in the Gaza envelope for almost 72 hours by terrorists in the very spot it occurred.

One major news network reporter, who was escorted through a kibbutz riddled with bullets and blood-stained walls, asked the Anglo-Israeli guide the following question:
"How do we know those are human remains in those body bags over there?"

The quick on his feet guide responded,
"Did you ask that question and look for proof of death after 9/11?"

How could any reporter think it is acceptable to imply that Israel staged this massacre? Is that any different than Holocaust denialism? Has the Western world all become David Irving?

Some come by it honestly. The Palestinian Authority, headed by Mahmoud Abbas, shared yesterday that Israel was responsible for the mass murder of the 340 kids at the Nova music festival on October 7th. They went on to claim that Israel had manufactured the entire ordeal and blamed the murders on Palestinians.

What a revolting blood libel. It is disgusting and shameful! Yet, we should not be surprised. Mahmoud Abbas, head of the Palestinian Authority for 18 years, wrote his dissertation denying the Holocaust. The title of his work is called, *The Secret Connection between Nazism and Zionism—1933-1945.* As recent as this past September of 2023, Abbas stated publicly that Adolf Hitler ordered the mass murder of Jews because of their "social role" as moneylenders, rather than out of animosity to Judaism.

Bear in mind, Abbas is the *"moderate"* Palestinian Israel should negotiate with. He is the address Israel should make peace with. He is the guy we should allow to govern Gaza after the war. Ridiculous!

During a press conference at the White house last week, reporters grilled the stand-in Press Secretary over the *"inconsequential"* number of rockets, guns and ammunition found at Shifa hospital since Israel has gained control of the medical enclave.

When surveillance video was produced by Israel showing Hamas bringing two hostages, abducted from Israel, bound and blindfolded to Shifa on October the 7[th,] reporters asked if those were all who were housed in the infirmary. As if to say, only two? Do those few hostages constitute invading the hospital? When extensive and elaborate tunnel systems were revealed under the hospital, the media asked for more proof of terrorist intentions and headquarters.

Seriously?

How many hostages warrant approval for the IDF to conquer the hospital? How many rockets or guns qualify as a guerrilla stronghold? How many tunnels under an emergency room comprise violence and terrorism?

I have been to hospitals in a few countries. I have never seen RPGs, AK47s, grenades, missiles and rocket launchers near an X-Ray machine. Have you? How many of those items constitute a terrorist headquarters or hideout? How many weapons form a non-lethal arsenal being housed near EKG and pacemakers? One rocket is too many. One gun is too many. One grenade is too many.

If we have different rules for entry and different guidelines for the same game, there is no evenness. We are not held to an equal standard. For a group that demands equality for the Palestinians, perhaps they should start with some equality for Jews and Israelis, too. We begin by leveling the playing field and demanding equal standards. When it fails to be equal, they better damn well call it out as loudly as they do towards us.

Perhaps we should begin all interviews and every conversation with the following simple questions:

- Do you believe the Jewish people are entitled to live and exist in our Nation State of Israel?
- Do you believe Israel has the right, if not the obligation to defend itself and its citizens from those who seek to harm her?

If anyone answers '*no*' to either of those questions, I am sad to say, they are an antisemite and hold Jews and Israel to a different set of standards. Those who answer '*no*' are not worthy of my time or energy, nor should they be of yours.

45

November 19, 2023

I never fully realized the gravity of Tal Becker's warning of a shared race for victimhood that is contested between Palestinians and Israelis. He would speak of it often at AIPAC summits or Hartman convenings, but the weight and pace of the contest was lost on me. Until this week.

I would disbelieve it were I not to see with my own eyes, grown and educated people tearing down signs of missing women, babies, elderly Holocaust survivors, octogenarian men, snatched form their beds in Israel and taken as hostage for God knows what price.

Four hostages have been released, to date. A few videos have been used to wage psychological warfare. Israel produced CCTV security footage of terrorists ferrying hostages into Shifa hospital. Some Israeli sovereign citizens were found murdered inside of Gaza. How else would they have gotten there? As I type, negotiations are happening to release fifty Israeli hostages for 150 prisoners. Still, a horde of people spend their free time strolling through parks and actively removing the signs of missing Jews and claim it is not real. That it is Jewish propaganda. How could it not be real, if there is a deal to release them?!

Mind you, these same people tearing down signs leave posters affixed to lamp posts in parks that are looking for lost dogs and cats from unknown entities. But signs of missing Jews come down.

I am satisfied with social media sites that shame these people. No tears have been shed for those terminated from employment or expelled from school because of amoral behaviors. Still, I contemplate what can make any person do such a heinous and cruel action as to deny our right of pain and victimhood.

Then it smacked me across the face with fury. I heard Tal Becker's words ringing in my ear about wanting to earn the victimhood grand-prize between Israelis and the Palestinians.

If Jewish children, women, the elderly and the innocent were taken during a day of rape, rampage and savage murder, and held against their will, all while blindfolded and bound and gagged, what could possibly be more traumatic and undeserved? What is more victim-like than that? Afterall, the definition of a victim is *a person harmed or killed because of a crime or accident or event or action.*

The kidnapping of close to 250 people - a broad sampling of all streams of Israeli society - is the ultimate victimhood prize Becker referenced. I assure you it is an award we would be happy to forego. Still, having signs posted on walls with pictures and stories and physical reminders, inherently negates the sense of victimhood and suffering of the Palestinian people. Apparently, two peoples cannot suffer at once.

Becker taught me countless times that the race to victimhood is futile. There is no winner. Both groups lose. Both the Israeli and Palestinian people and their nations are pained and traumatized. There are legitimate histories on both sides which evoke anger, resentment, frustration and sadness. There is a time to unpack those feelings. It is not now.

I came to realize recently that those who remove 'Missing' signs taped up around the world is a heartless attempt of refusing to cede the victimhood narrative or acknowledge the pain of one group over another.

It is reminiscent of a story in the Babylonian Talmud - tractate Yoma - about two kids who both want the honor of cleaning the altar after the sacrifices have been burned to God. The kids are running up the ramp of the altar. One kid, worried he would get to the alter second and lose the privilege of cleaning the ashes, kicks his friend from the ramp, where he falls and breaks his leg.

That ancient story is about doing something shameful, reprehensible and appalling so that an honor or rite can be bestowed. Is not a similar thing happening in parks around America and Europe today? Are the sign destroyers not kicking us from the proverbial ramp so they can deny our sense of pain and sacrifice, and they can retain the title of supreme victim?

Is that the medal either of us really pine for? Ultimate Victim?

Sadly, yes. It is.

Here is why.

The paradigm of support and allegiance in society is based on a simple equation: have versus have less. Power versus powerless. Oppressed versus oppressor. Since the time of Rocky Balboa (probably way before) the human condition inclines us to cheer for the ones who are 'less.' Power-less, have-less, help-less, use-less. The underdog. The little guy. The weaker party.

Rhetorically speaking, what is more powerless, helpless and useless than a ten-month-old baby taken from its parents? Or an 82-year-old woman suffering from dementia removed from her home and comforts? Or a 19-year-old boy whose arm was blown off held against his will with no medical treatment afforded him? Or a 68-year-old grandfather who needs medicines to stay alive?

For many who see Israel as big, powerful, strong, sovereign with a mighty army, yet at the same time in the role of suffering, is equivalent to saying that the wealthy, flashy, articulate Apollo Creed is the underdog in his boxing match against Rocky. To claim Israel is the suffering and weaker victim in this scenario is against the linear paradigm much of society has crafted. It makes them uncomfortable. It requires stutter steps. Nuance. Semicolons. They are ill equipped to work in a way where a strong, white, privileged people *can* be victims. It is just easier to tear down signs, deny a reality, and keep things neat and clean in columns simpletons can understand.

The ruthless act of tearing down missing signs is tantamount to Kanye ripping a trophy from Taylor's hands on the stage and declaring who the real victim, ahem…. I mean, victor, is.

This is a race to the bottom. No one wins. We are all losing. Stop tearing down the signs. Acknowledge our pain, hurt and suffering. We will and must do better acknowledging the pain and suffering of Palestinians too. Not Hamas. Palestinians. Denying pain of one is not the path to acknowledging the suffering of another.

Next – A quick and noteworthy observation.

Conversion to Judaism is a double leap of faith: the obvious leap of the candidate who irrevocably aligns themselves with the fate of the Jewish people. The second leap is by the sponsoring clergy, who even through study and training, have no crystal ball to unpack the real motives or future intentions of the Jewish person by choice.

My heart has been warmed by the dozens of people I have seen leading the charge at pro-Israel rallies, taking on their employers, challenging alma-maters, pushing their kid's schools and defending Zionism against keyboard-commandos, who are Jews-by-choice. Obviously, there is no Instagram badge for converts to Judaism. I can identify many because I personally served on the commission that approved their conversion. Others I know because they have shared their background.

Each time I meet with an individual who wants to become Jewish, I lovingly warn them that by affiliating with the Jewish people and linking their fate with ours, they might become the subject of bigotry, discrimination or antisemitism. Never during these warnings in my office did I imagine we would face a moment like we are now. The people who have carried forward with their journey have risen to the moment with grace and determination.

The alliance and advocacy of these precious humans have incontestably proven that they are as much a part of our history as they are our future. Each of these Jews-by-choice could have run for the hills or embraced an earlier heritage or previous identity when the going got tough. They didn't. They are all-in on Judaism and Israel. The Jewish tribe and the Zionist people are stronger and better with these souls amongst us. Kudos to my colleagues who have done a fantastic job teaching and bringing these individuals into our fold. And thank you to my brothers and sisters of choice. Our family is holier with you in it!

Last
As I submit this piece for daily publishing, my heart is fluttering with anxious anticipation of the release of fifty hostages, primarily children in an asymmetrical swap for 150 Hamas prisoners. One

Israeli friend phrased it best: *The entire nation is holding its breath. We can all sense it.*

Will it happen?

Who will be amongst the released?

Will Hamas pull a fast one?

Will Hamas take advantage of the pause to rearm, which will result in more dead soldiers?

What will the physical condition of the hostages be?

What will the mental condition of the hostages be?

What will be the reaction of those whose loved ones are not in the first batch of returned captives?

I cannot contain my nerves, excitement and worry. All of Israel feels the same. I have yet to digest these feelings. I just have intense ones. They are making me feel great and terrible, simultaneously.

May the hostages return to an embrace we can all witness and feel.

May the balance of hostages be soon behind them.

Amen.

46

November 20, 2023

The Gates of Heaven and Hell look the same. In fact, they are the same. I know this because I walked through them recently.

The iron, eight-foot-high openings are in a non-descript, non-combat positioned IDF base in Israel called Shura. Most army bases have young men and women scurrying about, all with guns slung over their shoulders and sleeping barracks that make any sleepaway camp bunk look like the Ritz Carlton. Not Shura.

Shura is broken up into two sections: One where the ritual and religious needs of soldiers are addressed. Torah scrolls, prayer books, *Tefillin* and *Talises* are housed and distributed on Shura and any religious matters that arise in the IDF or in times of war, the rabbis of the army, which is its own brigade, handle. Those rabbis are stationed at Shura.

The second area of Shura is focused on caring for and preparing dead soldiers. That is a 365 day a year job. A soldier who dies by enemy fire, a heart attack, or a car accident all come through Shura. It is the central morgue of Israel.

Except, Shura has become what New York City and other places were during Covid. Overloaded with death. In this case, by murder from the October 7th massacre. There are dozens of refrigerated trucks that house bodies and remnants of bodies on Shura. There is a loading dock where during times of peace, 1-2 stretchers are ready to take in cases that arise. Today, there are about 30-40 stretchers on the ready.

Hours after October 7th happened, scores of bodies began arriving at Shura. In the 75-year history of the country, nothing of this magnitude ever happened, nor was the country remotely prepared for an attack of this scale.

Teams of pathologists, rabbis and now, archeologists are painstakingly dealing with each body, and body part that used to house a sacred soul. They do so with care, grace, kindness and expediency.

The standard in Israel is to communicate an injury or death of a soldier to next of kin within fifteen-minutes. That is not a typo. Fifteen-minutes. That is the fastest in the civilized world. The United States, which boasts a strong time of communication aims for 24 hours. Israel races against WhatsApp, to be the first to tell family before they find out from any other source.

My dear friend, Rabbi Felipe Goodman told his congregation a detail that gives much needed perspective. Felipe said, *"When an American soldier in, let's say, Iraq dies, it takes a day to notify family and a few days for funeral arrangements to happen and burial to take place. That is because transporting a body back to America takes time. In Israel that all happens within 24 hours. Not only because of the Jewish imperative to bury as soon as possible. But because Gaza City to Tel Aviv is a 90-minute drive. The country is tiny. Fighting in Lebanon or terror in Jerusalem is not a significant divide of time or distance."* Rabbi Goodman is right.

When we think of the heroes of Israel, especially during times of war, our minds conjure up images of people like the strong and burly, Ariel Sharon, who was wounded three different times in battles protecting Israel. We think of Yoni Netanyahu, the hairy chested, muscular soldier who sacrificed his life saving hostages in Entebbe. We think of the eye-patched Dayan who was fearless and daring. I no longer think of those characters.

The image of mighty women and men, holding powerful machine guns, decorated in flak-jackets and adorned with ribbons of honor have been replaced in my mind's eye with simple, short, thick eyeglass wearing, nerdy looking men and women. They are mostly weaponless. They are manning the operations at Shura. These are some of the unsung heroes of this moment.

At Shura, I visited a room where families are given a last moment with their loved one. It is a solemn space draped with an Israeli flag, flowers and dim lighting. One Orthodox rabbi told me this room is as hallowed as the Holy of Holies in the Temple. He is right.

313

We saw from afar, the steel door that keeps the sacred rooms for ritual washing and identification of the dead. Behind the surgical masks covering faces of doctors and forensic specialists, were nameless folks doing the most holy tasks in a space as secure and private as the Mossad headquarters.

These same men and women, some religious and some secular, are the liaisons with bereaved families. They are handling with dignity, care, kindness and tenderness the remains of the fallen. These less brawny but equally heroic soldiers safeguard the respect due to those killed by terror or others fallen in battle. The solemnity with which they carry themselves along with the honor they afford families during their unbridled grief is unmatched.

I asked one of the rabbis that has been stationed in Shura since the night of the 7th when he was called up for reserve duty, how he is coping with the situation. It is a lot of trauma, blood and constant sadness.

He replied, *"I am usually an emotional fellow. I cry at movies. I am sensitive. Somehow, I have put up a wall when doing the agonizing yet necessary work that has been called upon me here. But once every ten days, before I go home and hug my wife and kids, the release valve is triggered, and the cries and screams come out. Then after a home visit, I steel up and prepare to walk back through the gates of hell."*

I replied to him, *"You mean the Gates of Heaven. What you are doing for these families is paving a pathway for their loved ones to feel respected and exit this world with dignity. It is holy work. You are guiding them towards heaven."*

The rabbi said back to me, *"We might be giving them heaven. We, the ones working here, are going through hell to give them the heaven they deserve."*

The rabbis and soldiers of Shura are heroes that deserve mention for their grace and heroism and leadership during this tragic time.

Next

All knew the Israel-Hamas war would have ripple effects on the Jewish community, worldwide. I did not know that we would feel those ripples so significantly in Bergen County, where I live.

The local Solomon Schechter School, where both of my kids graduated from the 8th grade has been at the epicenter of this war. Four families at the school had relatives who were killed on the 7th of October. Other families have loved ones being held captive. The hurt and grief is close.

Israelis in the North and South of Israel have been forced to evacuate their homes and relocate since the war began. Some who have family in America sent their kids on a plane to be with family and continue their education abroad. I have met 17-year-old high school seniors and 6-year-old first-graders who are in the same boat, in America. The younger ones came with at least one parent. As one congregant reflected yesterday, it is a modern-day Kinder transport, of sorts. A haunting yet beautiful image that evokes horror and hope.

The Solomon Schechter School of Bergen County has opened its doors to any student from Israel, free of cost. The language bridge offered coupled with many Israeli teachers, will be a welcome environment in an unwished-for time. To date, 44 Israeli students have enrolled at Schechter. That is an increase of 10% of their student body.

I could not be prouder of the school our family supports and our children attended. I am also lifted by the generosity of our community which has helped support the school during this unplanned financial challenge. It reminds me of the closing chapter of the book <u>Brighton Beach Memoirs</u>, where a Jewish family gets a visa out of Europe as the War is beginning. The large family will come and live in an already crammed Jerome house amongst cousins, in Brooklyn. No one cared. They were happy they got out and, as was written, people will share beds. What matters is they are safe.

A different kind of chapter is being written today where we are offering blessings and thanksgiving for those who are safe and able to find respite and a semblance of normalcy in schools and our community. We will figure out where they will fit in for class and how we will pay for it. What matters most is they are here, and they feel loved and welcome for as long as they choose to be with us.

47

November 21, 2023

Ecclesiastes teaches there is a season set for every experience. A time for every feeling. There is a time for war, and a time for peace. A time for dancing and a time for being still. A time for wishing and a time to be grateful.

The inference is that we can only experience one feeling at a time. How can we dance and be still simultaneously? It is impossible to wage war and experience peace concurrently.

At this sacred holiday of Thanksgiving in the middle of this trying time in history, I find myself wishing as much as I am feeling grateful. It feels sacrilege to wish on Thanksgiving. It is a day fashioned for gratitude. How could I want on this day?

It has always sickened my soul that we conclude Thanksgiving with a mad dash to consumerism and actualizing on our coveted desires during black Friday. We gather with appreciation and gratefulness and hours later, we wake early and trample strangers to get one of the televisions or toasters on sale. It doesn't conform with the spirit of the holiday.

That is why it feels foreign to gather around the table, with a bounty of food and surrounded by family and still be unsatisfied. Still, I am. I am salivating over Turkey and wanting more.

I am wishing for the quick resolution of the war in Israel.
I am wishing for the eradication of Hamas.
I am wanting every hostage to be reunited with their family.
I desire every Israeli to know how loved they are by Jews in the Diaspora.
I want antisemitism to be rebutted with pro-semitism.
I am wishing that our unity remains long past this conflict.

My list goes on of all I am hoping and wishing for.

At the same time, I have much to be grateful for today and every day.

I am buoyed by the imminent release of young Jewish children who are hostages and their future embrace with their family.

I am heartened by the level of unity I witnessed in Israel amongst all streams of the country.

I am appreciative of the United States government, Congress and the administration for their unwavering support of Israel during this time of need.
I am bowled-over by the level of engagement and support by our Temple Emanu-El Community for Israel and Israelis.
My hope has been restored seeing 300,000 strong for our solidarity march in Washington last week.
I am grateful for the IDF and the soldiers defending Israel and Jews worldwide.
The number of organizations and groups that have volunteered, donated and rushed to aid Israel has been incalculable and awe-inspiring and fills me with thankfulness.

My list of things I am grateful and appreciative for, runneth over.

When Moses received the Torah from God on Mount Sinai, they appeared in two tablets. Why two? Could not have God produced them on one tablet? Why separate them?

Perhaps God and Moses were teaching us that we can hold two truths at one time. During this unsteady time, we can wish while being grateful. We can dream and be thankful. We can laugh and cry. Like the tablets, we can hold both at once.

As we gather with family and friends, fully aware that the world and tumult around us can take no pause, let us exhale and take note of the many things we can catalogue that give our lives blessing and help us realize even amidst chaos, the multitude of blessings that rain from heavens. Thank God for those blessings. Make time to pray for more miracles and continue to fuel the fire of hope. It is what allows us to carry forward with our heads high and the energy to make the positive change our world so desperately needs.

48

November 22, 2023

Zhou Enlai, the first premiere of the Communist People's Republic of China was in conversation with Henry Kissinger in the early 70s, discussing the impact of revolutions on world order. Kissinger asked Enlai *"What effects did the French Revolution (1789-99) have on world perspectives of peace and capitalism?"*

Énlai replied, *"It is too early to tell."*

I do not think he was kidding.

Enlai, like other dictators not bound by democracy and term limits, take a deep long look at history. Democracies look at shorter spurts of time. Kings refer to America and Israel as fickle, because we elect new leaders on a set schedule of every two and four years, or in Israel, as soon as we are fed up with them. Enlai and monarchy like-folk look at history over 250 years at a time. Western democracies look at history over 25 years at a time. The divide is ten-fold.

Enlai and Kissinger – Getty Image

When Gilad Shalit was released in October of 2011, after five years of Hamas captivity in Gaza where he was deprived communication with his family or visits by the International Red Cross, I was ecstatic. This boy who was abducted at gun point from his tank in sovereign Israel was coming home. His parents, who had set up camp in a tent outside the Prime Minister's residence and sat vigil for years to advocate for his release, would finally get their wish. They could hold their son again in their arms. Gilad's siblings could hug him again. Joke with him again. Their family would be reunited. The country would be whole.

I remember crying when watching on the news, Gilad and his dad in each other's arms. I remember feeling the energy of the country, buoyed by his homecoming.

Israel paid a hefty price for Shalit. More than 1,000 prisoners, most with blood on their hands, were released from Israeli prison.

This included the driver who brought the suicide bomber to the Park Hotel in Netanya on Passover, who later killed 30 civilians and injured 140 people.

Also on the list of freed prisoners was Walid Abd al-Aziz Abd al-Hadi Anajas (36 life sentences) – who took part in the execution of the Café Moment bombing (2002), the Hebrew University bombing (2002) and the Rishon LeZion bombing (2002).

Tamimi Aref Ahmad Ahlam (16 life sentences) – Assisted in the execution of the Sbarro restaurant suicide bombing in the summer of 2001 was released as well.

Even with these names, and scores more just like them, I thought it was worth the exchange. Israel needed to prove to its citizens, all of whom conscribe to the army, we will bring you home, no matter what happens. Even if you are murdered in captivity, we will bring your body home for your family and for a final resting place in your home country. We will go any lengths to prove Israel will always have your back and never forsake your plight.

One person put a mathematical equation on the exchange: each Jewish life is priceless. 1000 people, as bad and dangerous as they might be, is a small price to pay to bring one Jewish boy home.

Arik Einstein, the Bruce Springsteen of Israel, composed a short song upon Shalit's release. The ballad melodized how great it is for us (the country of Israel collectively) to see him again. I watched the YouTube clip of Einstein's song and the reunification of Shalit about 500 times over the three days of euphoria Israel and Diaspora Jews enjoyed, following Gilad's homecoming.

Freed Israeli soldier Gilad Shalit (Photo by IDF viaGetty Images)

One terrorist who was released for Shalit was Yahya Sinwar (4 life sentences). Sinwar took part in the kidnapping of two Israeli soldiers in 1989 and was sentenced to life in prison. Sinwar is the founder of the Hamas security apparatus in Gaza. His brother organized the abduction of Gilad Shalit in 2006. Upon Sinwar's release, he was elevated in Hamas governance and made the second in command of Hamas' ground operations in Gaza. Sinwar was the mastermind of the October 7th massacre.

Enlai's words are ringing in my mind causing me a painful headache.

Was this a good idea to release 1000 terrorist prisoners in jail for crimes they were found guilty of in a respected court? Was it right for one Israeli soldier who was abducted from his post inside a tank within undisputed territory to yield so many criminals?

What I thought was a great moment in Zionist history was just the harbinger of something much worse. Something despicable. Something grotesque. An event so unspeakable, we could not have even dreamt of its depravity or crudeness.

Was our celebration in 2011 over Shalit's release premature?

What the Shalit deal proved is that Israel will make unbalanced, "disproportionate" trades for murderers. That is what made the value of 250 hostages stolen on October 7th, an astronomical price that could yield the emptying out of Israeli prisons throughout the country.

Knowing what I know now, would I still advocate for the Shalit exchange? Would you?

It feels sacrilegious to be cavalier or emotionless when talking about any Jewish, living soul. Shalit is a son, a brother and now, because of his release, a husband. He is not a number. To consider the strategic implications and not the human ones is equivalent to putting the case in a Petrie dish. It goes against the grain of the Jewish spirit. The Talmud teaches clearly, each hostage is worthy of redemption. There is no expense to be spared for the release of a Jew. Still, what if it costs more Jewish lives and hostages later?

Gilad Shalit's release evoked mixed opinions in Israel. While indeed, all were happy to see Gilad home, many thought the price was too high to pay.

One of the opponents of the Shalit deal was Miriam Wachsman. A Jew born in a German Displaced Persons Camp, who emigrated to Brooklyn and then Israel, Wachsman was a regular on the literal and figurative other side of the street across from the Shalit tent near the Prime Minister's residence, in Jerusalem.

In 1994, Wachsman's son Nachshon, was given a ride along the highway for his weekend break from the army. The group that picked him up were thought to be ultra-Orthodox Jews. In fact, they were terrorists from Ramallah dressed as observant Jews with the intention of abducting and torturing Israeli soldiers.

Within 24 hours after his kidnapping, intelligence lasered in on Wachsman location. Israel put together an elite team to retrieve Wachsman and eliminate the abductors. The intelligence did not know that the room where Nachshon was held was behind a wrought-iron door that needed breaching through heavy explosives. The ruckus outside the door alerted the terrorists. They shot Wachsman, after having ruthlessly tortured him, and one of the elite members of the IDF rescue team was killed in the operation too.

Miriam Wachsman would regularly say that she has deep empathy for the Shalit family. That if Israel could bring back their son, they should but, not by enabling more death of innocent people. Wachsman's worry was that the release of her son's murderer and other criminals would result in more bloodshed, anguish, pain and hurt for individuals and the country.

These bloody-handed terrorists set to be released were not rehabilitated in prison. They were emboldened. The bombers and killers would come home to a place free of scorn and full of festivity for the actions that led to their arrest and of course, their release. These fanatics hold a different ethical compass. Wachsman and her camp of followers held that the release of 1000 prisoners was too steep a price to pay.

While she did not know this at the time, Nachshon Wachsman's murderer, Jihad Muhammad Shaker Yaghmur, was released for Shalit in 2011.

Getty Image of Wachsman (z'l) and his mother, Miriam

International media is painting a sense of equivalency for the current release of the opening 13 hostages for 50 Hamas prisoners.

First, hostages and prisoners are not equal. Ever.

Second, 13 does not equal 50. Why Hamas, who are the bad guys here, always gets more is worthy of examination.

How would most Americans react were (fictious case, of course) Adam Walsh to be reunited to his parents after his abduction in a Florida mall in return for the release from prison of Jeffrey Dahmer, the Unabomber, John Wayne Gacy, Timothy McVeigh, Charles Manson and Ted Bundy? Now multiply that by 1000. Or in this case, 3 terrorists for every innocent person abducted. It hardly seems fair since Walsh committed no crime and these other convicts did.

The bombers, stabbers, saboteurs and criminals being released now for these hostages are in prison for attempted murder, detonating bombs and stabbings. These are not conscientious objectors. They are not people who are imprisoned for tax evasion or refusing to pay child support. They are bad people who did horrible things.

Juxtapose that to the four-year-old girl being released by Hamas, coming home to *her* country without parents – they were both murdered by Hamas on the 7th of October– committed the crime of being Jewish, and living in Israel. Unbalanced is not even the right word. Having to negotiate with demonic forces in such an uneven trade is a hard pill to swallow.

As I type this Stream, reports (no pictures yet) are flowing in about the release of these children and parents. Skepticism is keeping my hopes in check.

I was not alive in 1972, but I know the excitement my parents felt when Israeli Olympians were brought by bus and then helicopter to what they were hopeful was the end of a nightmare ordeal of their captivity by Palestinian terrorists in Munich, Germany. Sadly, it was just the first act of more brutality to follow.

Jim McKay from ABC Sports' words linger in the reel playing in every Jewish mind, *"They are all gone."*

Not until the hostages from Gaza are home, In Israel, reported as safe and healthy, will the light on that reel dim and the glow from smiles and embrace, prevail.

I wait impatiently.

I also have no trust in the devil we are dealing with. Israel has had countless ceasefires with Hamas. Every single one has been broken by Hamas. Even today, minutes after the agreed upon lull took effect, sirens blared, and rockets flew into Israel from Gaza. Like a bell ringing to end a round and the boxer takes some extra cheap shots against their opponent before heading to their corner, so too, Hamas launching rockets and firing shots after the cease fire takes place is flabbergasting. We cease and they fire. Sadly, the referee (read United Nations and civilized world) has come to expect this behavior and do absolutely nothing to reprimand the bad actor or actions. Instead, we negotiate the release of innocents with them. Why? Because we love life more than we believe in standing on ceremony.

The world is restless to see proofs of life of the balance of hostages. We are hopeful the ICRC will soon see the rest held in captivity and provide medicine and care. We must get word to the parents and children of loved ones about their family. Not many are expecting Hamas to meet the moment with honesty. Israelis are all excited 13 are home. We are anxiously ready and waiting for the other 235.

Does any group worry that Israel will not release the Palestinian prisoners and uphold their end of the deal? That Israel will welch? Of course not. Another example of the disproportion between these two parties.

The sun has set in Israel. Shabbat has begun. I am filled with hope and anxiety that these young, released hostages will celebrate the holy Sabbath with loved ones in Israel for the first time in seven long and dark weeks. I pray these kids will soon be savoring Challah bread and sips of sweet grape juice. I have faith that the overwhelming love and nation-wide embrace will quickly erase the nightmare of the past two-months for these innocent precious souls.

Please God, this Shabbat, may this dream be willed too.

49

November 23, 2023

In 1987, on a sunny autumn afternoon in Midland, Texas, 18-month-old baby Jessica McClure was playing in the backyard of her aunt's home, which was also a make-shift day care center. Suddenly, Jessica stepped in the wrong direction and fell down a tiny hole, 8 inches wide into an uncovered well. Her leg was pinned, and she was trapped in that well for 58 excruciating hours.

CNN, the only 24-hour news network at the time, covered the story non-stop. Riggers, ditch diggers, construction workers, psychologist and emergency first responders sent materials and staff to the small, non-descript home. The newly assembled team dug a parallel hole to the well and then drilled perpendicular to reach Jessica. It sounds simpler than it was. All the while, people sang nursery rhymes to the baby and pumped oxygen down the well to keep her alive and healthy.

The entire country prayed.

2 ½ days later, around 8:30 pm eastern time, a bandaged and dirty baby Jessica came up a mechanized pulley in the arms of Robert O'Donnell, the paramedic who treated and rescued her below the earth's surface.

It was a moment of God hearing the harmony of interfaith prayers. A modern-day miracle. She was alive and she would survive. I remember my mother crying watching the news, which was not novel. My mom cried all the time. But my dad choked back tears too. He was usually stoic. Seeing his emotions was extraordinary.

Moms and dads, sisters and brothers, grandparents and neighbors worldwide shed a shared tear that night, like our family did, as Jessica emerged into the bright spotlights.

Getty Images

The subsequent drama that surrounded Jessica's parents was more than the young couple could handle. Shortly after the incident, they filed for divorce. Robert O'Donnell, the EMT who cared for baby Jessica was troubled by the notoriety that came with his recognition. O'Donnell died by suicide a few days after the Oklahoma City bombing. He said to his mother watching the first responders, that those people are going to need years of emotional support following this tragedy.

Psychologists diagnosed O'Donnell with post-traumatic stress from the rescue. Jessica's parents, eternally grateful for the world's support and the actions of workers and first responders, are still wounded by those 58 hours, even 35 years later. Jessica was far too young to have lasting emotional suffering from the ordeal. She has a scar, a lasting reminder that extends from her hairline up to her nose. Jessica's family and rescuers were not able to evade the associated trauma and emotional wounds. Remember, baby Jessica had a good ending.

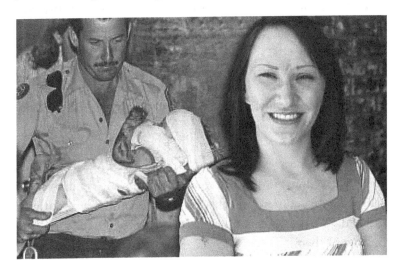

Yesterday, 13 Israeli women and children, ranging from 3 years young to 85 years old came out from their well. They were forced into that well. It was no accident. They were held there without nursery rhymes or songs and with tremendous apathy from onlookers, many who blamed them and their country for their plight. Some who even ripped down pictures, denying their darkness and captivity.

Upon their release, I was hoping for a baby Jessica response. I thought I would well up with tears, excitement and joy watching these long-awaited embraces. I thought my body would shake seeing these women and children back in Israel. I was sure that this reunion would have made me feel closer to God and full of thanksgiving on the appropriate weekend.

I did not have any of those emotions. I was numb. I am anesthetized from 49 days of trauma and emotionless from the drop in the bucket of those released versus those still held in captivity.

The Jewish world waited filled with tension, anxiety and fear yesterday. News trickled in and names of the released surfaced. Their freedom reminded me that 13 are home and 237 are still unaccounted for. Meanwhile, as we were biting fingernails and pacing, candy and gunfire were erupting in the West Bank as terrorists, three times as many, were released from Israeli prisons and their heinous convictions were expunged. It all felt so wickedly unfair and unjust.

My mind was heavy with projected thoughts of EMT O'Donnell and the McClure family. The emotional stress and trauma the 13 captives have endured, and their surviving families have suffered for 49 days is unthinkable. The hardest parts of rehabilitation are in front of them.

My heart was equally heavy thinking about the individual and communal toll this ordeal will have on nurses, doctors, soldiers, elected officials and negotiators, people driving the bus from Egypt to Israel, and countless others involved in bringing these captive Israelis back home. Each person addressing their physical and emotional health will have much on their plates. The imprisonment might be over for a few. The trauma is only beginning. That has me waking at night in a cold-sweated panic.

Trying to mitigate the trauma, Israel spent painstaking hours planning each moment of how best to greet these innocent Israeli civilians being released from Hamas captivity and to welcome them back to society. How would those tasked with gathering the hostages answer questions about their loved ones? Would the soldiers hold guns, even though they are in an active war zone? Can these liberated children feel hopeful, happy and loved coming from such a dark and scary place? What can they eat? Who can touch them? What will trigger their fears? Will they be malnourished? Physically sick? When is considered enough time for the Mossad and Shin Bet to interrogate the hostages to gather more data?

There are no chapters written about a scenario like the one unfolding now in any psycho-trauma books. You will not find a DSM that points to hostages being taken from their homes while asleep in pajamas, witnessing the murder of children and parents, and then being held for 49 days in dark, damp tunnels in enemy territory. Steven King novels do not address this kind of fright and horror. Even the most deviant minds could not anticipate such a situation. There are no examples of how to handle this scenario. Israel will have to write the chapter, again.

Hostages have been reunited with family and society before. John McCain, for example, was a prisoner of war. He knew as a Navy pilot that being shot down and enemy capture was a possibility. He was an adult when captive and then released.

But these are blameless and harmless children. Some are still in diapers and cannot count past ten. How could they know how to handle themselves in such harrowing conditions? Could any of us?!

Watching Israeli news today, I saw one man whose daughter is being held by Hamas in Gaza and has yet to be released. He was being interviewed about his feelings by a local broadcaster. The father explained to the interviewer the myriad of emotions he was experiencing. He said that he was very happy for these families whose loved ones were coming home, even though his family was not going to be reunited just yet with their girl. He was filled with tension, worry, excitement, concern and trepidation. He then said a line that released the tear valves.

"We are all Israelis. We are *one* family," he said. "When one person comes home, it makes our family a little more whole. For that, I am forever hopeful and appreciative. We just need to keep bringing them all home, as quickly and safely as possible, and complete that feeling. We can make our family and country whole again."

The baby Jessica moment I wanted of seeing people reunited did not feel as good as I hoped. Yet, hearing the resolve and watching the determination of the Israeli people, especially this father, was the medicine my aching heart needed. It was the balm to soothe my hurt.

The word Shalom (peace) comes from the Hebrew root, *Shin, Lamed, Mem*, which means complete or full. The Shalom in our world was shattered on October 7th. Today was another small step towards bonding those broken pieces back together again and making families and our country whole, while knowing we will forever be broken.

50

November 24, 2023

This will be my last Stream of Anxious Consciousness. At least for now. I am taking a pause after 50 days of chronicling the massacre against Israel on October the 7th and the aftermath of shock, trauma and anguish for the people and nation of Israel, along with the meteoric rise of antisemitism worldwide.

I am not pausing because I have run out of things to write about.

My friend, Ido Aharoni visited our synagogue this morning. Ido is a savvy diplomat and brilliant thinker. When I asked him what the outcomes of this war will look like and when we can expect to taste the fruits of our victory, Ido came back with a fantastic lesson I never synthesized until today.

After the murders of 11 Israeli athletes at the Munich Olympics, Golda Meir assembled a secretive group of Mossad agents and hitmen in a secretive operation called Wrath of God. Her directive was to spend unlimited resources to track down each person connected to the planning, implementation, siege and murder of the athletes in Munich, wherever they may be in the world. Once found, they would be eliminated. Golda, supported by Moshe Dayan, Generals Harari and Zamir, and her cabinet, wanted to send a clear message to any would be assassins and accomplices: Israel will find you and kill you.

It took 9 years for the initial list of masterminds and terrorists to be located, concluding with the assassination of Hassan Salameh. The operation transcended two Prime Ministers, Meir and Begin, and extended to not only those directly involved with Munich, but even people with ancillary connections. Locating and successfully removing Salameh happened almost a decade after Munich.

Ido was reminding all impatient Jews and any members of the instant-gratification society that we have been enlisted to run a marathon, not a sprint. While we are running fast now, we have a long distance to go.

When I wrote my first Stream on the night of October 7th, I intuitively knew that Israel and Diaspora Jewry would never be the same, and that was way before we learned the gruesome details, the tally of hostages and the count of the murdered.

The operation of eradicating Hamas will have many layers: removing the physical militants, destroying their arsenal and infrastructure and establishing a buffer for the future. Those goals will take a minimum of 3-4 more months to achieve. Eliminating the Hamas ideology will take a generation.

Hamas extends far past Gaza. They are in the West Bank of Israel and in Jordan and Egypt. Hezbollah, in Lebanon, is the same animal with different stripes. There is no way Israel can allow an enemy to camp on its border, and to amass hundreds of thousands of rockets. Hezbollah will need to be dealt with soon after this conflict winds down. Further, Israel cannot defeat Hezbollah alone. They will need American support. Most likely that will include rearming munitions, supplying loads of bunker busting bombs, Osprey aircraft and aerial support from the two battleship carriers in the region to keep the Houthis in Yemen and the remnants of Isis in Syria at bay. Make no mistake, the USS Gerald Ford and the USS Eisenhower and their extensive entourage is more than window dressing. Their presence is a clear signal to Iran and its nefarious proxies that should they act like a bully, our big brother is standing by to protect us and pounce on them. I doubt those ships or nuclear submarines in the Persian Gulf are going anywhere else soon.

Once Hezbollah is dealt with, Iran will need to be defanged for good. Iran can no longer bankroll terror and seek our destruction via stand-in. We will need to address the existential threats Iran poses. That operation will be lasting and ongoing.

When I visited K'far Azza last week, I realized that the best plan forward for the beleaguered Kibbutz is to bulldoze the entire space and rebuild from scratch. Of course, we will rebuild there. Memorials will be erected, and families will make the choice if they want to or can (emotionally) return. The process of rebuilding will take a minimum of 24 months.

The displaced people in the North will not go home until the Hezbollah problem is solved. Who can blame them? Do not expect that to conclude, even in the most miraculous diplomatic achievements before June 2024.

The infernos of antisemitism on college campus and main street might tamp down, but the heat and stench will last a while. The Jewish community has major work ahead on preparing our college students for being Jewish on campus. Activating Hillels, ADL and Chabad Houses to be more vigilant on security, and to better arm students with facts and tactics to put out these fires started by reckless and immature arsonists with truths, data, passion is mission critical. Enlisting support of allies to build bridges before the fires ignite or spread will be our first and second priorities.

University leadership will have a reckoning. Some presidents and chairs of the board need to step down. Others will need to be removed. All need to say in a full-throated manner that Jewish lives and Jewish security matters. If saying those words taste like vinegar for anyone, they need to take a long and deep look into their souls and ask why it is permitted to treat Jews differently. We will no longer tolerate being treated as 'other' while paying full tuition and gifting 7 to 9 figure donations from Jewish alumni.

The hordes of folk who spent their free time tearing down signs of souls kidnapped by Hamas claiming it was hoax, have been noticeably silent as the first tranche of hostages are released. Hmmm. The professors, airline pilots, physicians, social workers, police officers and babysitters who have spent the past 50 days denying Jewish hurt and advocating for Hamas and celebrating their despicable acts of October 7th, need to be fired and publicly shamed. As one diplomat told me, we cannot be satisfied they were dismissed. We must ensure they are never hired again. Their reputation for siding with Al Qaeda, Bin Laden and Hamas and negating Jewish torment must follow them for all the days of their lives. Or at least until they rescind and retract those abhorrent views.

The trauma Israelis endured on the 7th and the ensuing weeks will live with them forever. Fire fighters are still haunted by September 11th. So too are survivors of the Pentagon, gate agents of the doomed flights, and people who lost loved ones in all four places. Many who watched the towers get hit and collapse still suffer from PTSD. This trauma will not evaporate soon. Emotional and psychological support will be ongoing for all arteries of Israeli life. Our task is just beginning.

October 7th, 2023 was a special day in my life. I turned 50 years old. I was born as the Yom Kippur war began. It was October the 6th. My mother heard the news of a surprise attack on Israel while praying in America. Her water broke and a few hours later, officially early morning the 7th of October, I entered the world. 50 years after my birth, the biggest time marker of my life is indelibly stamped by war and Zionism, again.

The Black Sabbath Massacre happened on Simchat Torah. The festive holiday commemorates the conclusion of the cycle of reading the five books of the Torah. Interestingly, when we finish with the last words of the Torah, we do not pause and take a breather. We are not afforded a hiatus. We instantly roll the scroll back and begin the process of reading and interpreting the stories and teachings all over again.

The Torah is absolute yet never ending. What a fantastic paradox.

When I first was engaged to my now wife, Dori, we visited an amusement park. I was so excited to go on all the rides and roller coasters. The speed and thrill give me a high. Upon entering the park Dori finally broke the news to me she was dreading to share for fear of bursting the bubble of my excitement.

"I hate amusement parks," she solemnly confessed.

I was devastated. Would our marriage survive? Could this be the woman I would spend the balance of my life with? Is this the person I would create a family with? I felt dupped. Betrayed. I was shattered.

Then Dori said to me, "Hey. I will go on the Ferris Wheel with you."

Is there any ride more boring than the Ferris Wheel? Seriously! It just goes round and round so damn slowly. I hate the Ferris Wheel.

Getty Free Image

We were invited to board the bucket of the Ferris Wheel by the toothless, tattooed attendant. The door gingerly shut locking us in to our open cabin. No seat belts or warning were necessary. It was not a fright inducing or dangerous ride. Dori was smiling from ear to ear, so happy we could enjoy this moment together. I was faking – not too well – my enjoyment.

In simmering frustration, I declared how bored I was on the Ferris Wheel. "It just goes 'round and 'round. So damn slowly. Nothing changes. I hate this ride!"

Then Dori taught me one of the most profound lessons of my life.

"David," she said, "The ride might spin 'round and 'round, but the world around us changes every turn of the cog in this giant wheel. No one and no one thing stay the same as we circle in place."

Since that moment, I was positive I made the perfect choice in life partner.

This war has many echoes of yesteryear and yet, so much of our reality is different and new. Partners for peace were once adversaries while some we considered allies are ambivalent at best, foes at worst. We are circling another bout of what was, while we anticipate what might be. Much around us is the same and much is changing yearly, daily, hourly and by the minute.

Throughout these Streams, I have jogged our memory back to Egyptian bondage, expulsion in 1492, pogroms in Russia under the evil rule of the Czars, the rise of Nazism in Germany and throughout Europe, and the multitude of enemies Israel faced since the founding of the State. This has been half of the Jewish story. Victimhood, challenge, persecution, discrimination, weakness, belittling and denigration are synonymous with our identity.

The other half of the Jewish story is resilience, perseverance, hope, determination, grit, flexibility, strength, commitment, resolve, drive and tenacity.

These two competing narratives are the blend of circling in place while appreciating all that changes around us.

These chronicles comprise our remarkable history that is still being composed.

......

Epilogue

December 7, 2023

I am deeply appreciative to all the folks at Xlibris, who understood the urgency and timing of the contents and expedited the publication of this book. Obviously, the words and sentiments lose their potency the further we are from the start of the current conflict. Still, I believe this book holds an important and timely purpose for readers today and beyond.

Ten days have passed since I submitted my first manuscript for editing. We are now 60 days into this war; exactly two months since the morning, now known as the Black Sabbath, changed our world forever. The IDF continues to make amazing strides. They have arrested and eliminated countless Hamas leaders and terrorists. I believe we are closer to the end of the war then we were 10 days ago, but we still have a very long road ahead. 110 hostages have been returned, much of the Southern parts of Gaza, namely near and around Khan Younis have now been conquered by Israel. The strategic goals of the army have surpassed expectations.

I am back in Israel for the second time in as many weeks. The subsequent trips do not make painful sights easier to digest or the harsh realities easier to accept. It still hurts. A lot. Though, while back here in Israel, I have been doing more thinking about what the next days, weeks and months will look and feel like for this country and its inhabitants. The climb ahead is steep. All of this has conjured up a unique image in my head.

Since I was young, I loved to go fishing. It was one of the few activities my father and I enjoyed together and that he was always eager to participate in. I enjoy the same activity with my son. My favorite kind of fishing is deep-sea fishing. That is where you sail out to the depths of the ocean and drop a line anywhere from 60-180 feet, hoping to hook a "big one".

Inevitably, with people fishing next to one another along with the drift in current, fishing lines tangle. It is a huge mess when the lines cross, twist and knot. I typically find myself trying to detangle the line and weave the translucent string in and out of loops and holes to get them straight again. Most times, when I try and untangle the line, it makes an even larger tangle. Trying to see the source of the knot and the solution is frustrating, time-consuming, and tedious. Usually, my instincts are to cut the line, forget about the tangle, and let it fall to the bottom of the ocean. Then, I can re-spool the line and start fishing all over again. Except, that is a big 'no-no' in the fishing and environmental world. Cut fishing line pollutes the bottom of the ocean and is dangerous to sea life and coral health.

The image of a tangled fishing line is prominent in my mind's eye. I see many layers of tangles with loops and holes in Israeli society, here and now. Anytime one issue is solved, a new layer and tangle shows up. It feels never-ending.

While we have turned one corner with Hamas in Gaza, we still must figure out what our endgame will look like. Who will rule the Strip? How will we ensure a that repeat of October 7th can never happen again? And what corrections can be made to the educational system, so the cycle of hatred is arrested?

Israel also faces a serious threat at another border with Lebanon — Hezbollah. Citizens of the North will not feel safe to return home until the intimidation and dangers are removed. Hezbollah is a more sophisticated operation than Hamas with five times the arsenal and capabilities of our Southern enemies. They have amassed over 100,000 precision-guided missiles that could overwhelm the Israeli shield systems and hit sensitive targets throughout the country. Addressing the danger that Hezbollah poses is not an easy task. Surely, it will result in more bloodshed for Israelis and innocents in Lebanon.

At this time, approximately half of the hostages have been returned or, sadly, declared dead. There are still close to 140 souls that need to come home to their families and country. Finding them, negotiating for their release and, in some sad cases, the somber task of returning their bodies for burial in Israel, will be an ongoing nightmare until every missing person is accounted for and brought back home. We owe that to the families. We owe that to the country. Most of all, we owe that to these tortured souls who have been abducted. This is another complicated knot in the tangled mess that is life here.

Six unnamed leaders used the same phrase over the past month that captured my attention. *"The citizens of Israel deserve better than this government."* Or *"This government is not deserving of this citizenry."*

There is an immanent reckoning about to take place. It is bigger than ousting Bibi from power. It is about the masses removing the fringe elements of the Knesset and squelching the loud extremes that have owned the narrative for too long. Doing so will entail marginalizing those who would rather grandstand instead of being gracious. Those who are stubborn instead of subtle.

I predict a grassroots political revolution will soon happen. The new leaders will no longer tolerate noise and silliness and will instead focus on solutions, humanity, hope and possibility. This movement will be filled with Israelis of all stripes who will embrace the serious challenges and not look to demonize others in the process.

All elections are messy. This one will be especially so. It will also be a referendum on the factors that led to October 7th. That will be the first opening of a stinging wound for all Israeli society. It is just another twist in the snarl of life in Israel today.

The economic toll the last 60 days will have on Israel is incalculable. All tourism halted since the 8th of October. Palestinians living in the West Bank who usually relied on jobs within Israel have been denied access to work within Israel. We are talking about 200,000 people. Stores have been closed because workers are on reserve duty, or these places are not experiencing pedestrian traffic. Paying for the soldiers, their rations, the fuel, and the ammunition for this war in Gaza alone will cost billions of dollars.

All the displaced people in the North and South are unable to work which makes them unable to pay for mortgages and utilities. Hotels that are housing and feeding the displaced people are racking up enormous debt to take care of immediate needs for these displaced souls. Supply chain issues are countless. The crops in the North and South, especially in border communities, will not get harvested. That has created food security issues and significant loss of income. Even with financial aid packages from America, a recession will surely happen in Israel, and I am not sure when or how they can climb out of the challenge. All of this is only from the past 60 days. What will happen in the next 60? 120? 180? This is a huge knot in this ball of twine.

Antisemitism slept lightly in America. I have never seen or felt it wake so loudly and violently. The reverberations of Israel demonization and open Jewish hatred has never been more tolerated since World War II. The college campus is hot chaos with double standards for Jews abound. Even the heads of Harvard, MIT and Penn could not condemn hate speech and calls for genocide against Israel and its inhabitants under oath before the U.S Congress. Addressing the complicated nature of antisemitism in America today will take patient, creative and thoughtful minds to rebut and get in front of the narrative. It will be a tall order and just more line to twist and unravel.

All of this can make anyone feel like we should deal with the tangles by simply cutting the line. We cannot do that.

The truth is, we have 60 days behind us but far more than 60 days ahead.

We need to don our magnification glasses, shine a light on the rod and patiently begin the long and arduous task of detangling and extricating the line from the tangles that encumber us. More twists and knots will appear. We will not solve it all magically in days or weeks. It will take generations. If we take one twist and turn, pull and push at a time, we will make important progress. That is the only way we can earn a future worthy of our toil.

The task is great. The day is short. Let's get to work.

About The Author

Rabbi David-Seth Kirshner is the senior Rabbi of Temple Emanu-El in Closter, New Jersey. A natural leader, charismatic speaker and magnetic personality, Rabbi Kirshner embodies the best humanity and is an important figure in shaping the Jewish world.

In addition to leading and reinvigorating Temple Emanu-El and strengthening relationships one by one, Rabbi Kirshner is involved in the community at-large and holds many positions of leadership. Rabbi Kirshner is the Past President of the New York Board of Rabbis, was selected among 50 rabbis to participate in the inaugural class of the Kellogg School of Rabbinic Management at Northwestern University. In 2013, Rabbi Kirshner was appointed to the New Jersey-Israel Commission by Governor Chris Christie and was re-appointed in 2018, by Governor Phil Murphy. Additionally, Rabbi Kirshner is the Immediate Past President of the NJ Board of Rabbis, he holds a seat on the Executive Committee of the Jewish

Federations of North America (JFNA). He is a Rabbinic Adviser to the Shalom Hartman Institute. In 2009, Rabbi Kirshner was appointed to the National Council of the American Israel Public Affairs Committee (AIPAC) and in 2013, he graduated as a Senior Fellow at the Shalom Hartman Institute in Jerusalem, Israel. He is an adjunct Faculty Member of the Academy for Jewish Religion.

Rabbi Kirshner has written articles for many media sources and is regularly published in the Jewish Standard, the Bergen Record, Haaretz, The Times of Israel, The Huffington Post and the New York Times. He has been featured on national radio and television programs including Good Morning America, CBS, CNBC, WABC, WNBC, NPR, The Last Word, with Laurence O'Donnell, Nightline, MSNBC, Al Jazeera and Faith to Faith.

Rabbi Kirshner holds a BA degree from York University in Toronto, Canada and earned an MA in Hebrew Letters and rabbinic ordination from the Jewish Theological Seminary. Rabbi Kirshner is married to Dori Frumin Kirshner. They have two children. This is Rabbi Kirshner's first book.